THE
VAST
ENQUIRING
SOUL

This busy, vast, enquiring Soul
Brooks no Controul
No limits will endure,
Nor any Rest: It will all see,
Not Time alone, but ev'n Eternity.
What is it? Endless sure.

(Thomas Traherne, "Insatiableness")

Also by Ronald Russell:

Lost Canals of England and Wales
Waterside Pubs
Discovering Lost Canals
The Canals of Eastern England, with John Boyes
Rivers
Guide to British Topographical Prints
Lost Canals and Waterways of Britain
Discovering Antique Prints
Walking Canals, Editor
Cambridgeshire & Cambridge
Swimming for Life: the Therapy of Swimming
The Country Canal
Using the Whole Brain, Editor

THE VAST ENQUIRING SOUL

EXPLORATIONS INTO THE FURTHER REACHES OF CONSCIOUSNESS

RONALD RUSSELL

HAMPTON ROADS
PUBLISHING COMPANY, INC.

Cover design by Brickergraphics
Cover art by PhotoDisc

For information write:

Hampton Roads Publishing Company, Inc.
1125 Stoney Ridge Road
Charlottesville, VA 22902

Or call: 804-296-2772
FAX: 804-296-5096
e-mail: hrpc@hrpub.com
Web site: www.hrpub.com

If you are unable to order this book from your local
bookseller, you may order directly from the publisher.
Quantity discounts for organizations are available.
Call 1-800-766-8009, toll-free.

Library of Congress Catalog Card Number: 99-91427

ISBN 1-57174-153-4

10 9 8 7 6 5 4 3 2 1

Printed on acid-free paper in Canada

For Jill, and for the young explorers:
Dominic, Rachel, Susannah,
James, Hazel, and Matt.

And in memory of Suki
(who saw it through almost to the end).

CONTENTS

ACKNOWLEDGEMENTS

Many people helped me in various ways during the preparation of this book. I am grateful to them all, and I would like to mention especially Hilary Cox, Christina Damerell, Dr. John Evans, Linda Evans, Helene Guttmann, Angela Kelly, Crawford Knox, Joseph McMoneagle, Ian Morris, Louise Pembroke, John Pick, Tom Ross, Penny Sartori, Sharon and Michael DeValda, and the members of the Dumfries "Frontiers" lecture group. There are others whose personal experience I have made use of and I thank them sincerely. None of these are responsible for the opinions expressed, which, together with any failings or errors that may emerge, are my own.

I wish to thank the directors and trustees of the Religious Experience Research Centre and the Alister Hardy Trust for permission to quote from their publications, *Seeing the Invisible, Negative Spiritual Experiences*, and "De Numine," February 2000, article by John Franklin. I am grateful also to Colin Smythe, Ltd. for leave to quote from *The Meaning of Life, vol. 1—An Introduction to Scientific Mysticism*; to Pimlico for quotations from *The Passion of the Western Mind,* by Richard Tarnas; to Bloomsbury Publishing for material from *A Stranger in Paradise*, by Julie Chimes, and from *The Face of Glory*, by William Anderson; to Rupert Sheldrake for a quotation from *The Rebirth of Nature*, to Francis Thompson for extracts from *The Supernatural Highlands*; to New World Library for extracts from *Miracles of Mind* by Targ and Katra; to Broadway Books for extracts from *The Heart's Code*, by Paul Pearsall; and to

David Lorimer and the Scientific and Medical Network for several passages from *Wider Horizons* and *Network*.

I am happy to acknowledge the cooperation of Hampton Roads Publishing in allowing me to use extracts from *Body Mind Spirit;* and for the editorial help, well beyond the call of duty, of Richard Leviton.

The work and the personality of the late Robert Monroe provided the initial inspiration and I count myself fortunate in having enjoyed the privilege of his friendship in the last decades of his life. I am grateful to the trainers and staff of The Monroe Institute for the many experiences they helped to provide. The very existence of the *Journal of Consciousness Studies* is itself a gift to all those interested in this wide-ranging subject, and the same can be said of the Scientific and Medical Network and the Institute of Noetic Sciences. Credit is also due to the Academy of Religion and Psychical Research in the U.S., and the Churches' Fellowship for Psychical and Spiritual Studies in the U.K. for their enterprise in handling such stimulating topics in their respective publications.

Exploring the further reaches of consciousness tends at times to dissociate one from the domestic scene, and I am everlastingly grateful to Jill, who knows intuitively that which I have to plod away at, for giving me the freedom to write.

Preface

This is a journey of exploration into the further reaches of consciousness. It is not a venture into the unknown. Many of you will have already had experience in one or more of the areas we shall be exploring. Some will have journeyed out of body, once or twice or several times. Some will be used to telepathic communication or have had instances of precognition. Some will have attended channeling sessions or may themselves have channelled. A few may have known a near-death experience, while most, if not all, will at some time or other have experienced a moment or more of transcendence. What I now propose is that we should take time to explore these and other experiences with an object in view: to see what they can tell us about that great mystery, human consciousness.

We are neither zombies nor machines and we do not live in a mechanical universe. One quality that distinguishes us from zombies and machines is consciousness, our ability to know and understand, to be aware of ourselves and of the world around and beyond us. From time to time, for a variety of different reasons, our consciousness moves from its ordinary, everyday condition into an altered state, sometimes called a non-ordinary state, in which it seems to extend beyond the material world of our daily lives and reaches out into other realms. This exploration will take us into some of these realms accessible only when consciousness itself, whether we direct it or not, leads us there.

The question of whether consciousness, or any element of it, might survive physical death is especially intriguing. With this in mind, we shall look at claims of communication with the dead, at belief in past lives, and theories of reincarnation. We can consider whether the question of survival, and of what might survive, can be answered in some other way.

Since the early 1980s, I have been interested in the study of consciousness, especially consciousness operating in altered states. I have met and talked with people who, among them claimed to have had every one of the experiences detailed in the following chapters. Matching these claims against published examples, where they exist, helps to establish their veracity. While not all published examples can be authenticated, I think that it is possible to acquire a feeling for the truth.

This has brought me to understand that while consciousness is closely intertwined with the operation of the brain, the brain itself does not create consciousness. Consciousness is not simply a property of a closed system. To borrow a phrase from quantum physics, it is non-local; it is not located anywhere, either within the brain or without. In the following chapters I intend to show the reasons for this understanding, and the evidence on which it is based.

Throughout our explorations, whether we are in the area of distant healing, out-of-body or near-death experiences, extrasensory perception, remote viewing, channeling, or transcendence, we shall be searching for what the particular experience tells us about our consciousness. From this we may learn more about ourselves, about what and who we really are, and how we relate to the universe in which we live.

New Galloway
Scotland

CHAPTER 1

THE EXPLORATION BEGINS

The substance of the universe is in us; the one force, energy,
sustains that substance, and that substance of the universe is
our consciousness. (Antony Andreasen)

A man is sitting by himself in an isolated room on an American Army base. He has been asked to draw and describe the actual location of an unknown person for a specific time and date. He is told only that the person could be anywhere in the United States. No one except the government agency conducting the test knows where the person is. He draws a hilly landscape with several power poles. He notes "moving electricity in a form of grid work." He notes also "halo probably not visible to the eye." The person is standing on a hillside many miles away in the midst of a wind generation grid.

I am wandering around in a second-hand bookshop in a cathedral city. The owner asks me if she can help. I tell her that a friend has said there is something for me in the shop but I don't know what it is. The owner looks at me thoughtfully and suggests I have a cup of tea. While she is making it I start to think what the something—the book—might be. Recalling my friend's interests, I go to the sections on religion, psychology, and philosophy but I find nothing that feels as if it's for me. I drink the tea and continue to look around the shelves, pulling out books here and there and putting them back. I am becoming tired and confused and the owner is looking at me rather quizzically. I decide on a book and pay for it. I turn to leave the shop, pause as I approach the door, reach out and take a volume from an untidy pile of books waiting to be sorted. "This is it," I say to the owner, and without opening the book I buy it.

Outside I look at what I have chosen. The book's title is *Musrum*. It means nothing to me. I drive back to my friend's house, some twenty miles away, and hand her the book. She points towards a bookshelf. Lying on top of a row of books is a single volume. I pick it up. It is another copy of the book I am holding. Its title is *Musrum*.

∞

A woman is sitting in her office at a publisher's when the phone rings. A doctor is on the line. They have met before when she discussed with him a particular ability she seemed to have. The doctor tells her that he has a patient with him. He gives the patient's name and age and waits for her response. The woman has no medical training so she cannot respond in medical terminology. Instead she uses imagery. She tells the doctor she feels as if the patient has concrete running down his throat. She describes certain emotional issues that, she considers, preceded the physical condition. The patient, she says, is a drug addict and is so frightened to admit this that he cannot speak about it. The words freeze in his throat.

The doctor thanks her and rings off. Later he tells her that the patient has cancer of the esophagus.

∞

A man is in bed with his wife. She is asleep; he is awake, thinking of a glider trip he is to take next day. He feels certain physical sensations, like vibrations, beginning to affect him. Then he becomes aware of something pressing on his shoulder. He feels behind him but encounters only a smooth wall. He is lying against it and he thinks he must have fallen out of bed. But in the dim light he can make out no windows, no furniture, no door. There is only something like a fountain close by him—but it isn't a fountain. It is the bedroom light, sticking straight up. It is not a wall he is lying against—it is the ceiling. He is floating against the ceiling. Looking down, he is able to discern two figures in the bed. He must be dreaming—but who in a dream would be in bed with his wife? Then he realizes: it is himself. He is terrified. Perhaps he is going mad. He wonders if he is dying. With an enormous effort he manages to dive back into the bed. The next day he makes an appointment with his doctor. He is not dying, nor is he insane.

∞

In the year 1698, a woman servant in a household in the north of Scotland tells her mistress that her brother, who has the reputation of an honest man, will be hanged. The mistress is angry and dismisses the servant immediately. Soon afterwards the brother is caught stealing and is sentenced to be hanged, but his friends intercede for him and guarantee his future behavior. He is set free, upon which one of the friends finds the servant and tells her that she was mistaken. "He is not dead yet and will certainly be hanged," she replies. In the following year he is caught stealing again and this time he is duly hanged.

∞

A young man is coming to the end of a week's camping holiday in Scotland. Things have not gone well; he has not seen the birds of prey he was hoping to observe. He is tired, lonely, and disappointed. He feels his holiday has been a waste of time and everything seems pointless to him, including himself.

He is walking back to his campsite when he hears a sound he has never heard before. He looks up to see four buzzards directly overhead. He feels as if they had called to let him know they were there. All fatigue drops away from him, together with his pessimism and anxieties. He continues in his own words:

"The feeling of being narrow and cut off from something became a feeling of being vast and unbounded, as if I was connected with the whole universe. I understood William Blake's poem 'To see a world in a grain of sand.' Everything, including the stones on the path, seemed to be infinitely significant. As I watched the buzzards spiralling in the blue sky I felt identified with them and yet at the same time I was intensely aware of my own identity. I felt as though I were the center of the universe and at the same time the center was everywhere. I was conscious of a sustained power and the buzzards seemed to be a manifestation of it. . . . They were a reflection of everything I was feeling surging through me at that moment. . . .

"I felt as if a filter had been taken from my senses and I was seeing the concrete world as it really is and the purpose and meaning of it all. Time was suspended; I watched the buzzards until they were out of sight but I have no idea of how long it was. After I lost sight of the birds I literally skipped down the path on my way home. That one short experience gave significance to the week and to everything that had led up to it. There was harmony where there had been disharmony. I felt as if I had been given a gift from the gods." [1]

What do we make of experiences such as these? Do we mark them down as interesting but of no special significance, and leave it at that? Do we make judgements about the individuals who reported them, that they are deluded, suffering from hallucinations, or attention-seeking frauds? Or is there something we can learn here, something so important that it can lead us in to the great exploration of this time—the exploration of human consciousness?

---

[1] The opening quotation I found among the notes of Professor Antony Andreasen. Tony Andreasen was a distinguished surgeon who in the course of his life was surgeon to the Viceroy of India, doctor to Mahatma Gandhi, a researcher into open-heart surgery at the Mayo Clinic, and the organizer of medical services in several African countries. He was also a pioneer of various alternative therapies—and the wisest man I have known.

Sources of the examples at the head of this chapter are as follows:

1. McMoneagle, J. (1997), *Mind Trek*, Charlottesville, Va.: Hampton Roads Publishing.
2. This was a personal experience a few years ago.
3. Myss, C. (1996), *Anatomy of the Spirit*, New York: Harmony Books.
4. Monroe, R. (1971), *Journeys out of the Body*, Garden City: Anchor Books.
5. Thompson, F. (1976), *The Supernatural Highlands*, London: Hale.
6. Quoted in Maxwell, M. & Tschudin, V. (1990), *Seeing the Invisible*, London: Arkana.

In past centuries we have explored the world around us fairly thoroughly and we have explored ourselves, our physical bodies and, to some extent, our mental states. In the outside world we have begun to explore the further reaches of the universe; but in our inner world there still remains unknown territory into which only the first tentative steps have been made. Yet here it is, accessible to us all: the great domain of consciousness without which we would be no more than zombies, machines made of flesh and blood, functioning without awareness, alive yet lifeless, creation's final insult. As Peter Russell said in his pioneering study *The Awakening Earth* (1982): "It is possible that all of our development so far is simply paving the way for this inner exploration—the exploration not just of the mind but of consciousness itself."

Certainly the exploration has begun. The direction it is taking, however, is much more towards explaining than exploring. Now we see physicists, biologists, psychologists, philosophers, neuroscientists, theologians, and more—all equipped with the knowledge of their speciality—seeking to explain what has so far proved inexplicable. So there are as many attempted explanations as there are specialities—and more—to account for the variations in each branch of knowledge and each individual interpretation. But there is no agreement, except in general terms among the large number who maintain that consciousness is neither more nor less than a function of the brain and when the brain dies consciousness dies with it. That agreed, the interpretations diverge; the books mount up, the learned articles accumulate, the conferences multiply.

A selected bibliography, covering only studies of consciousness in cognitive science, philosophy, and neuroscience between 1970 and 1995, printed as an appendix in *Conscious Experience*, edited by Thomas Metzinger (1995), is 47 pages in length and contains nearly 1,200 items. And, although the battle-lines are not as firmly drawn, the in-fighting between the experts is the present-day equivalent of the conflicts over Darwinism in the later nineteenth century (and still echoed in the U.S. and several of its southern states).

So what has been discovered? Here are two positive statements:

Consciousness is a natural biological phenomenon. . . . It is caused by lower level micro-processes in the brain and it is a feature of the brain at the higher macro levels. (John Searle, *The Mystery of Consciousness,* 1997)

Consciousness is a function of an identifiable neural architecture, which we have termed the extended reticular-thalamic activation system. (James Newman, "Putting the Puzzle Together" pt 2, *JCS* 4, no. 2, 1997)

And here are some more:

Consciousness poses the most baffling problems in the science of the mind. There is nothing that we know more intimately than conscious experience, but there is nothing that is harder to explain. (D. J. Chalmers, "Facing up to the Problem of Consciousness," *JCS* 2, no. 3, 1995)

There is no scientific explanation for experience or consciousness. (Peter Russell, Albuquerque conference 1999)

While consciousness is in many ways the most familiar and accessible thing that each of us possesses, it remains one of the least understood phenomena in the world. (Danah Zohar, *The Quantum Self,* 1990)

Despite the great practical importance of consciousness, science has as yet made little headway in understanding the phenomenon or even in deciding what it is. (Brian Josephson & Beverly Rubik, *Life at the Edge of Science,* 1996)

I think I can safely say that no one understands human consciousness. (Richard Feynman, *The Character of Physical Law,* 1992)

Consciousness is a fascinating but elusive phenomenon; it is impossible to specify what it is, what it does, or why it evolved. Nothing worth reading has been written about it. (Stuart Sutherland, *The International Dictionary of Psychology,* 1995)

So, despite all the efforts to date, not much progress seems to have been made.

What has happened is that the scientists and the academic philosophers have taken over the field for themselves. The theologians have been pushed to the margins where there is no one except each other to talk to. As for the ordinary people—those who reported the experiences at the beginning of this chapter—they are no more than cannon fodder. Their experiences are dismissed as anecdotal; they cannot be used as evidence. Yet I would suggest that these experiences are of vital significance.

They are indeed evidence—evidence of the operation of human consciousness outside the normal commerce of everyday life. As Dr. Stanley Krippner, professor of psychology at the Saybrook Institute, San Francisco, says, "There are many legitimate experiences that are ignored by biomedicine. Examples are out-of-body, past-life, near-death, and peak experiences, as well as precognitive dreams and cosmic consciousness."[2] It is not only biomedicine that ignores these experiences. Scientists in other disciplines, and philosophers also, treat them similarly. If they cannot be subjected to laboratory testing, or replicated on demand, they fall outside the bounds of consideration.

These examples that Krippner gives, as well as others that are referred to in the following chapters, are usually subsumed under the heading "paranormal." This is defined as "abnormal, especially psychologically; not susceptible to normal explanations." A statistical study by George Gallup in 1982 indicated that about eight million Americans "have experienced some sort of mystical encounter"—a type of experience that comes within the paranormal brackets—during a close brush with death. Once people have heard out-of-body experiences described, it is surprising how many of them recall having such an experience that they had never previously disclosed. Instances of precognition, premonition, and telepathic communication are frequently recalled in conversation, and Cohen and Phipps, in their study of moments of enlightenment, often known as "peak experiences," gave their book the title of *The Common Experience*. So perhaps it is time to drop the word "paranormal" altogether. But before we do so, here is one more quotation:

"No theory of consciousness can be taken seriously that excludes the paranormal."

---

[2] Interview, "Medicine & the Inner Realities," *Alternative Therapies in Health and Medicine,* vol. 3.6. November 1997.

This was not said by a parapsychologist or a new age guru but by the physicist Amit Goswami.[3]

So what happens if instead of ignoring these experiences, treating them as abnormal, or at best pushing them to the sidelines of consciousness studies, we make them *central* to the discussion? What, if anything, do they tell us about our consciousness—where it resides and how it operates? I doubt if they will tell us what it is, although they may contribute to discovering an answer, one day, to this very difficult question. But they may help us on our exploration, leading us into areas that some of us may recognize from our own experiences, enabling us to evaluate them and appreciate them for what they teach us.

Before we go any further, it is only fair for me to make clear where I stand. My education in London several decades ago placed major emphasis on a sound knowledge of Latin and Greek. History and mathematics came next, followed by the sciences and modern languages. Other subjects were on the margin of respectability. The scientists were tucked away in a remote corner of the school buildings, surrounded by Bunsen burners, balances, and racks of test tubes; measuring, concocting, and dissecting; taught by a handful of lacklustre mentors, few of whom had even the familiarity of nicknames.

I specialized in history and with most of my fellow historians I proceeded to university. Many of the scientists came also but were seldom seen, spending almost all their time in the suburbs where the laboratories were situated. Then I spent some years in the Royal Air Force where, as I had little mathematical ability and a poor sense of direction, I was trained as a navigator. Following this episode I returned to university. The scientists were still laboring away. During the 1950s in the universities in the United Kingdom there were very few professors—perhaps no more than 350—and most of them were either eccentric or moribund. I recall meeting no more than two—one of whose fame rested solely on the obscene name

---

[3] Goswami, A. (1993), *The Self-Aware Universe*, New York: Putnam.

he called his dog. A mere handful of graduates studied for doctorate in philosophy, and for most of those few, 'philosophy' meant philosophy as the dictionary defines it.

Following my degree I embarked on a career in education. The labors of the scientists in the first half of the century were now bearing fruit. Men were rocketed into space and walked on the moon; barren women were enabled to bear children; nuclear power promised to solve all fuel problems; new medications proliferated; Francis Crick and James Watson claimed to have discovered the secret of life. The sciences grew, divided, and developed. All over the Western world new universities appeared. Where there were hundreds of professors there were now thousands, tens of thousands. Doctors of philosophy, once rare as orchids in November, now proliferated like dandelions in summer fields. Still more universities were needed to accommodate all these seekers after truth.

Science spread its tentacles across the world of knowledge. New disciplines, and some older ones, were entrapped and sought to achieve academic respectability as the social and economic sciences. Even such esoteric occupations as literary criticism could not escape this trend. Measurement, analysis, reduction, dissection, deconstruction—these were components of the new methodology. That very word with its pretentious suffix illustrates what was happening. Perhaps worst of all, language itself became corrupted. The heavily weighted multisyllabic vocabulary of scientific terminology found its way into all branches of knowledge and enquiry. So many enquiries, so much knowledge; then as the century drew towards its close the information age burst upon us. What more was there to know?

This is not to decry the enormous benefits that science and scientists have conferred upon mankind. Nor are scientists usually responsible for the misuse of their discoveries. It is a sad reflection on our history that the increase in knowledge has not been matched by any increase in wisdom as to how to use that knowledge. But we do need to consider whether science, or rather scientific method, has not, in some respects, outgrown its strength. Two definitions are relevant.

Science: knowledge ascertained by observation and experiment, critically tested, systematized, and brought under general principles.

Scientism: a belief that the methods used in studying natural sciences should be employed also in investigating all aspects of human behavior and condition. [4]

From these definitions it becomes clear that it is not science itself that has outgrown its strength. The problem is with scientism. Like a burrowing insect, it has insinuated itself into all sorts of areas where it has no place, into philosophy, literary criticism, and social studies among others. Fuelled by the arrogance of its adherents it steams on, leaving a trail of error, misapprehension and confusion in its wake. "It has intimidated an entire culture into disabling intellectual dependence upon a technique designed originally for the laboratory. The requirement to measure, quantify, and 'prove' has intruded into every area of social policy, belittling intuition and impeding reform," wrote David Nicholson-Lord, in *The Independent,* August 1991.

This may be illustrated by the "astonishing hypothesis" proposed by Francis Crick himself in his book *The Astonishing Hypothesis—the Scientific Search for the Soul* (1994). "You, your joys and sorrows, your memories and ambitions, your sense of personal identity and free will are, in fact, no more than the behavior of a vast assembly of neurones. As Lewis Carroll's Alice might have phrased it: 'You're nothing but a pack of neurones.'"

Crick is not the first scientist to think like this. To defend himself he suggests that the concept was first enunciated, though not in those exact words, by Hippocrates about 400 B.C. But two points in the way he expresses his argument are worth noting. One is the use of the words "in fact," which indicates that there is firm evidence for what he says. Such evidence does not exist. The second is his use of the second person instead of the first. If he believes this, why did he not say, "I, my joys and sorrows, my memories and ambitions ... " and so on? "I'm nothing but a pack of neurones." If he believes this, why not say so?

---

[4] *Chambers Concise English Dictionary.*

There is, of course, an answer: it is other people's consciousness that is studied by scientists, not one's own.

Arrogance sometimes leeches across from scientism to serious scientists. Richard Dawkins is professor of the Public Understanding of Science at Oxford University. His books have been described as "eminently readable" and he has won several awards and prizes. He writes persuasively and eloquently from the standpoint of Darwinism and it is a delight to find a scientist with such a gift for exposition.

In his recent book, *Unweaving the Rainbow*, Dawkins launches an attack on what he calls "paranormalism." This he interprets as newspaper astrology and performances on stage or television by self-described psychics and mediums. It is hard to see why such a distinguished heavyweight should spend his time and energy on such soft targets, but it is quite good fun and he clearly enjoys himself. He makes the point that the stage and television performances could be explained and replicated by a good conjurer and indeed the presence of a good conjurer or stage magician in the investigation of claimed psychic events is acknowledged by many researchers into the paranormal to be highly desirable.

Yet Dawkins is not aware of the research by Marcello Truzzi dealing with the use of conjurors in psychical research or of the efforts by Professor Robert Morris of Edinburgh University to bring conjuring into the parapsychology curriculum. [5] The one proviso is that the conjurers are experts with open minds, not professional debunkers such as James Randi whom Dawkins favors. Serious researchers in this field are aware of the problems presented by those who, as in other fields, are less than scrupulous in handling evidence.

Widening his attack, Dawkins declares: "If a paranormalist could really give a properly researched demonstration of telepathy (precognition, psychokinesis, reincarnation, perpetual motion, whatever it is) he would be the discoverer of a

---

[5] Truzzi, M., in *Advances in Parapsychological Research*, vol. 8, Jefferson NC: McFarland, p. 221 *et seq*.

11

totally new principle, unknown to physical science. The discoverer of the new energy field that links mind to mind in telepathy, or of the new fundamental force that moves objects without trickery around a tabletop, deserves a Nobel Prize.... If you are in possession of this revolutionary secret of science, why waste it on gimmicky television entertainment? Why not prove it properly and be hailed as the new Newton? Of course, we know the real answer. You can't do it. You are a fake."

This sounds like strong stuff. Yet there are many properly researched demonstrations of telepathy, precognition, and psychokinesis, some of them referred to and referenced in later chapters of this book. That physical science cannot provide an explanation does not invalidate the results of these experiments. Dawkins confuses stage and television entertainment with intensive laboratory research statistically evaluated. He is of course right to castigate broadcasting companies for misleading their audiences, but wrong in ignoring the outcomes of genuine research. With regard to reincarnation, research has yet to prove conclusively that the evidence stands up, but Dawkins' slapdash dismissal of a concept fundamental to the religious beliefs of millions does him no credit as scientist or human being. It is interesting also that he devotes several pages to a discussion of the meme, which he defines as "the unit of cultural inheritance . . . anything that replicates itself from brain to brain, via any available means of copying." He draws an analogy with genes, but there is "no properly researched demonstration," to use Dawkins' own words, that memes exist. [6]

So what has happened? A remark in *Unweaving the Rainbow* provides a clue. "The problems raised by subjective consciousness are perhaps the most baffling in all philosophy, and solving them is far beyond my ambition." To investigate the serious aspects of what Dawkins calls "paranormalism," some exploration

---

[6] See *Journal of Consciousness Studies,* vol. 6, May 1999, pp. 77-85 for a discussion on memes in two reviews of *The Meme Machine* by Susan Blackmore.

of subjective consciousness is essential, even if "solving the problems" is at this time beyond anyone's capacity. But if you are not going to get into the water you will never learn to swim.

"The feeling of awed wonder that science can give us is one of the highest experiences of which the human psyche is capable. It is a deep aesthetic passion to rank with the finest that music and poetry can deliver." So Dawkins writes in his preface. But science has its limitations, as expressed by Max Planck, Nobel Prize-winner and father of quantum theory: "Science cannot solve the ultimate mystery of nature. And that is because, in the last analysis, we ourselves are part of nature and, therefore, part of the mystery that we are trying to solve."

Another Nobel laureate, Erwin Schrodinger, eloquently expressed the limitations of science. "The scientific picture of the world around me is very deficient," he said. "It gives a lot of factual information ... but it is ghastly silent about all and sundry that is really near to our hearts, that really matters to us." Schrodinger pointed out that science knows nothing of beautiful and ugly, good or bad, God and eternity, and when it pretends to answer questions in those domains, the answers are usually very silly. The scientific view of the world is that of "a mechanical clockwork which, for all that science knows, could go on just the same as it does, without there being consciousness, will, endeavor pain and delight and responsibility connected with it, thought they actually are."

Schrodinger added that to construct this picture of the external world, science used "the greatly simplifying device of cutting our own personality out, removing it; hence it is gone, it has evaporated, it is ostensibly not needed."[7]

There is our word—consciousness. It is our human consciousness that gives meaning to everything about us. As a working definition of a difficult term, I suggest "the faculty of awareness and knowing, responding to the self, the world around us, and the realms beyond." Without consciousness

---

[7] See Wilber, K. (1984), *Quantum Questions*, Boston: Shambhala. pp.81-2.

there is no more than a display, a display with no one to admire it.

So, what about consciousness? How far back can we trace it? Did it precede the universe as we now have it? The biologist Gerald Edelman suggests in *Bright Air, Brilliant Fire* (1992), that primary consciousness, which he describes as "bound to a time around the measurable present, lacks concepts of self, past, and future, and lies beyond direct descriptive individual report from its own standpoint," developed about 300 million years ago. He considers that most mammals and some birds possess primary consciousness; snakes may be in, he says, but lobsters are out. From this rudimentary consciousness developed what he calls higher-order consciousness, which "is based on the occurrence of direct awareness in a human being who has language and a reportable subjective life."

According to the cosmologist Brian Swimme and the historian Thomas Berry, (*The Universe Story,* 1992) signs of consciousness began to emerge when primitive life, "the pioneering fish," moved from sea to land. Here conscious choice became the primary cause explaining this major evolutionary change. They continue:

"At the very least we can say that to understand the powers that shape life, we need to take into account the genetic mutations within such a species of pioneering fish, the selection pressures on that population of fish, and the consciousness of those pioneering fish. To ignore the fish's consciousness is to ignore a real and central cause in the life world. Any story of life's evolution must include mention of that consciousness occurring in the fish." Swimme and Berry suggest that human consciousness (Edelman's higher-order consciousness, which might also be described as subjective awareness) developed about 2.6 million years ago.

The earliest human societies seem to have been involved with the exploration of consciousness. Both in primitive animistic and shamanic cultures and in the developed civilizations of Babylon, ancient India, China, and Greece, this interest is evident. The ability to move into different states of consciousness, whether activated by drugs of some sort, fasting, incantations, the sound of drums or other instruments, was a vital component of worship, prophecy, and religious ritual and ceremony generally. The *Yoga Sutras* of Patanjali, the *Tao Te Ching* of Lao Tsu, and the *Dialogues* of Plato are among the monuments of these explorations. Distinctions between different states were significant, as exemplified in the Sanskrit language that contains a remarkably wide selection of terms to differentiate between such states. Many of these terms— karma, mantra, nirvana, samadhi, and, of course, yoga—have been adopted into our contemporary vocabulary.

The scientific exploration of consciousness is of very recent origin. Jeffrey Mishlove in *The Roots of Consciousness* (1993) suggests that "for most of the late nineteenth and twentieth century the scientific and philosophical investigation of consciousness occurred within the tradition that started with psychical research." This research was largely involved with mediumship and attempts to communicate with the physically dead. The major contribution to the philosophic investigation of consciousness came from the American philosopher and psychologist William James, an influential and original thinker. James founded the American Society for Psychical Research in 1885, and was deeply interested in the well-known medium Mrs. Piper on whom he wrote a report for the Society for Psychical Research in England. In his later writings James saw the necessity for metaphysics and science to work together "hand-in-hand" and his paper "Does Consciousness Exist?"[8] is a landmark in consciousness studies, even though he comes extremely close to denying the existence of consciousness altogether.

1973 was a significant year in the revival of interest in the study of consciousness. In that year two pioneering organizations appeared, one in the U. S. and one in England. The Institute of Noetic Sciences was founded by the astronaut

---

[8] James, W. (1912), *Essays in Radical Empiricism*, reprinted in *Selected Writings,* London: Dent, Everyman Library.

Edgar Mitchell, Noetic Sciences being defined as "those that study the mind and its diverse ways of knowing in a truly inter-disciplinary fashion." The Scientific and Medical Network, an informal international group consisting of scientists, doctors, and other professionals who were prepared to challenge the prevailing materialism and to explore a reality based on a spir-itually inspired approach, was founded by a small group head-ed by George Blaker. As both these organizations flourished, the study of human consciousness became a major part of their concerns. In subsequent years the study of consciousness has returned, in the words of the editors of the first issue in 1994 of the *Journal of Consciousness Studies*, "to the academic agenda after nearly a century in exile," where it had been ban-ished by the well-drilled adherents of behaviorism and logical positivism. Science immediately made what almost amounted to a take-over bid. Of the twenty-one members of the *Journal's* original editorial advisory board, all except three were scien-tists. By 1999, with twenty-seven board members, there was a degree of leavening with the inclusion of five philosophers and two representatives of religion; the rest were scientists, includ-ing psychologists and psychiatrists (although some orthodox scientists might blanch at their inclusion). There were no rep-resentatives from music, literature, or the visual arts. Despite this imbalance, the *Journal* as a forum for the ongoing debates is proving to be extremely valuable. In the same year as the *Journal* was founded, the first annual conference, "Toward a Scientific Basis for Consciousness," was held in Tucson, Arizona. Many other conferences involving science and con-sciousness, most of them international, took place in the 1990s.

This association of science with consciousness was quite controversial at first. Talking with the psychiatrist R. D. Laing in the late 1970s, the physicist Fritjof Capra, later recalling the conversation in *Uncommon Wisdom* (1988), mentioned that he had become very interested in the nature of mind and con-sciousness. Suddenly Laing opened an attack. "How dare you, as a scientist, even ask about the nature of consciousness," he began. "You have absolutely no right to ask that question, to even use words like 'consciousness' or 'mystical experience.'"

The main point of Laing's attack, Capra comments, was that science "has no way of dealing with consciousness, or with experience, values, ethics, or anything referring to quality." Yet it was Capra, especially in *The Tao of Physics*, who was one of the first to show that it was possible for a scientist, as opposed to a philosopher, to make a thoughtful contribution to the study of consciousness.

In 1997, in an article entitled "An Integral Theory of Consciousness," the philosopher and psychologist Ken Wilber, a pioneer of the study of consciousness, listed twelve of what he described as "the most influential schools of consciousness studies." They comprised the following: 1. cognitive science; 2. introspectionism; 3. neuropsychology; 4. individual psychotherapy; 5. social psychology; 6. clinical psychiatry; 7. developmental psychology; 8. psychosomatic medicine; 9. nonordinary states of consciousness; 10. Eastern and contemplative traditions; 11. quantum consciousness; 12. subtle energies research. Wilber indicates that there is no suggestion of a rank order here, but the ground softens towards the end of the list.

Searching for an integral approach to consciousness, making use of all of the above, Wilber proposes three agendas:

Continue research on the various particular approaches.

Confront the simple fact that, in some cases, a change in consciousness on the part of researchers themselves is mandatory for the investigation of consciousness itself.

Continue to grope our way toward a genuinely integral theory of consciousness itself. [9]

It is as if he is saying, "Here is a jigsaw puzzle, but there is as yet no way of telling how the pieces fit together. They have no firm edges; they are more like Jell-O than plywood. If you can see them as Jell-O rather than plywood, you may find a way to complete the puzzle—if such a way exists."

---

[9] Scientific Medical Network (1999) *Wider Horizons*, Fife: Scientific & Medical Network. See also Wilber (1997), "An Integral Theory of Consciousness," *Journal of Consciousness Studies*, vol. 4. no. 1.

In one version of this essay, however, Wilber concludes with the following eloquent paragraph:

> And when we pause from all this research, and put theory temporarily to rest, and when we relax into the primordial ground of our own intrinsic awareness, what will we find therein? When the joy of the robin sings on a clear morning dawn, where is our consciousness then? When the sunlight beams from the glory of a snow-capped mountain, where is consciousness then? In the place that time forgot, in this eternal moment without date or duration, in the secret cave of the heart where time touches eternity and space cries out for infinity, when the raindrop pulses on the temple roof and announces the beauty of the divine with every single beat, when the moonlight reflects in a simple dewdrop to remind us who and what we are, and when in the entire universe there is nothing but the sound of a lonely waterfall somewhere in the mists, gently calling your name—where is consciousness then?[10]

That comes from the heart, not the head. It's the poor old heart that often gets kicked into the corner when scientific research is in progress. However, in the following chapters you may find an answer to the question that Wilber asks: Where is consciousness? Somewhere on the way to searching for this answer we may come across that other essential to our being—the soul.

My own interest in investigating human consciousness—or at least some of its manifestations—dates from 1986 when I made my first visit to The Monroe Institute in Virginia. The Institute, a research and educational organization, is dedicated to the exploration of human consciousness. For four decades the Institute was led by its founder, Robert Monroe, who developed

---

[10] Scientific & Medical Network (1999) op. cit.

and refined a technology called Hemisphere Synchronization based on multiplexed audio binaural beats that enabled listeners to experience different states of consciousness. The unique combinations of sound frequencies produced an EEG frequency-following response in the brain and this it seems facilitated consciousness shifts. [11] For my part, the experience wasn't a road-to-Damascus type revelation, but rather as if I had been living most of my life in a room without realising that the curtains were closed. Gradually they were drawn back and I was able to get a glimpse of what I had been missing.

Monroe himself preferred to speak of "phases" of consciousness rather than "states." He avoided terms such as "higher" and "lower" and for the sake of being understood used numbers to refer to the different phases. Each number has a verbal equivalent; for example, "Focus 12" is a condition of expanded awareness and "Focus 15" is where one is oblivious to time. During the day you shift continually from phase to phase. Monroe's audio technology enabled you to control this phasing and, if you so wished, to remain in one phase for the duration of an exercise. Once you became used to the process, you no longer needed the audio guidance to be able to change your state or phase of consciousness as desired. [12]

Coming into consciousness studies from this angle means that while you lack the theoretical background, you do have a useful range of experience. You are an explorer rather than a would-be explainer. You lack much of the technical vocabulary and have to learn it, at an age when such learning does not come easily, in order to understand what others are saying. You lack the discipline of a training and career in, say, neuropsychology or cognitive science. You have problems with concepts

---

[11] See Atwater, F. H. (1997), "Accessing Anomalous States of Consciousness with a Binaural Beat Technology," in *Journal of Scientific Exploration*, vol. 11, no. 3.

[12] Russell, R. (ed.) (1993), *Using the Whole Brain*, Charlottesville, Va.: Hampton Roads.

such as "qualia." [13] You are not a reductionist and you lack the rigidity, the narrowed vision, which academic disciplines tend to impose. Put it this way: you can sometimes see round corners when others may see only straight ahead. You are not an authority; you are by no means an expert. But at least you don't say daft things such as "You're nothing but a pack of neurones." [14] My experience with the Monroe materials inspired a special interest in one of Wilber's twelve "major schools of consciousness studies"; non-ordinary states. I am also a "day visitor" to some of the others, especially introspectionism, and psychosomatic medicine. From time to time I might call in at Eastern and contemplative traditions, and subtle energies research; quantum consciousness has some attraction also. But for me the remaining doors are, except for an occasional peep, closed.

Non-ordinary states (or phases) of consciousness are the principal material of the chapters that follow. Of the other schools that are relevant to this study, introspectionism is largely to do with intentionality and subjective experience, and psychosomatic medicine is concerned with mind-body interaction and various healing processes. Eastern and contemplative traditions—or most of them—draw distinctions between "ordinary" consciousness and "higher" states that are reached through pursuing certain practices that are part of those traditions. Subtle energies research investigates types of energies that affect mind-

---

[13] See Metzinger, Thomas. ed. (1995), *Conscious Experience,* Schoningh, Imprint Academic. In *Consciousness Reconsidered* (1992), O. Flanagan defines a quale as "a mental state or event that has, among its properties, the property that there is something it is like to be in it." I hope that helps.

[14] See Watts, Fraser (1994), "You're Nothing but a Pack of Neurones!", in *Journal of Consciousness Studies,* vol. 1. no. 2. Commenting on Crick's philosophy, which he describes as "beset with imprecise and overly broad-brush positions," Watts adds, "It is not uncommon for scientists to write sober science for most of a book, but to go rather wild at the beginning and the end, or even just in the last chapter." That is what Crick seems to have done with his "astonishing hypothesis."

body links and are said to be essential to consciousness. The theory of quantum consciousness mainly derives from the recent developments in physics, including such discoveries as Bell's theorem and the experiments of Alain Aspect.[15] Behind the closed doors are the theories that fix consciousness firmly in the brain as a product solely of biological development, that relate consciousness entirely to neural systems or computer science, that seek to explain it mathematically, socially, or culturally.

Wilber observes that "researchers tend to choose one or two of those approaches very early in their careers, usually under the influence of a significant mentor, organization, or academic department. And, human nature being what it is, it then becomes extremely difficult for them to embrace, or sometimes even acknowledge, the existence of other approaches. Evidence that supports their position is avidly accumulated; evidence that does not is ignored, devalued, or explained away." Wilber continues by maintaining that "nobody is smart enough to be wrong all the time," and that "each of them has something extremely important and valuable to say." Hence, to arrive at an integral science of consciousness we need "to include, synthesize, and integrate all twelve of those important

---

[15] The clearest and most succinct explanation of Bell's theorem that I have found is in Dean Radin's *The Conscious Universe.* "In the 1960s, physicist John Bell mathematically demonstrated that according to quantum theory a pair of particles that were once in contact, but have since moved too far apart to interact, should nevertheless instantaneously behave in ways that are too strongly correlated to be explained by classical statistics. As Bell wrote in 1964, 'there must be a mechanism whereby the setting of one measuring device can influence the reading of another instrument, however remote.'" Radin adds: "What this means is that apparently separate particles would not really be separate after all but remain connected regardless of how far apart they were." The experiment by Alain Aspect and his collaborators demonstrated that when two quantum objects are correlated—he used photons in the experiment—what affects one also affects the other no matter how far apart they are. (NB. This is very much a layman's description and grossly over-simplified.)

approaches." Bearing in mind that there may be more than twelve approaches and that some of them may prove to be, as the pigs of *Animal Farm* put it,"more equal than others," we can be excused for wondering just how long this might take.

There are also questions to be asked about Wilber's thesis. First, none of these approaches provides an answer to Wilber's own question:"Where is consciousness then?"What is the answer to that? Where are the polymaths who could handle with expertise and confidence these twelve, and maybe more, approaches? Unless, which seems unlikely, there are radical changes afoot, the conventional academic education required for most of these topics is not designed to enable its products to deal with such an unconventional subject. Consciousness is too ungainly to fit into a well-tailored suit; how much less likely is it that it can fit into a suit made up of elements from twelve others?

Then there is the question of language. The more one reads in this area, the more it becomes clear that we need a language of consciousness at least as much as a science of consciousness. It is easy—fatally easy—to drop into the jargon of science or philosophy so that meaning disappears in a forest of polysyllables. Let me quote a single sentence taken (almost) at random from a recent issue of the *Journal of Consciousness Studies*.

"The 'fundamental regional specificity' of the self requires a phenomenological-empirical methodology, for only such a methodology can provide insights into both foundations and development, that is, into both the origin and history of the sense of self; 'universal structures of the province in question,' i. e. , the province of the self, require a phenomenological methodology for only such a methodology can provide ever-deepening elucidations of invariants of the sense of self, invariants Husserl delineated prelusively in his discovery of 'fields of sensations,' an 'I govern,' and so on." [16]

This is the final sentence of a fifty-line paragraph that runs for just over a page. The discipline of the author is philosophy.

---

[16] *Journal of Consciousness Studies,* vol. 6, April 1999, pp. 61-62.

One of the sadder features of the age is that so many philosophers seem able to communicate only with other philosophers, but it may be unkind to suggest that they have to justify their existence, or their university stipends, by developing a language that no one else understands. Their predecessors, at least their English-speaking predecessors—Hooker, Hobbes, Locke, Berkely, Burke, Russell—managed to keep the lines of communication open to anyone interested enough to read their works. One of the blessings of Professor Daniel Dennett, author of *Consciousness Explained*, is that, whatever we think of his interpretations and conclusions, we can always understand what he is saying. All we can hope for is that whoever in the future reveals a comprehensive philosophy of consciousness (if such a thing is possible) can convey it in language that communicates rather than obscures.

Consciousness Explained is Dennett's major work, referred to in the bibliographies of just about every study of the subject since its publication in 1991. The title highlights the question raised earlier: How can you hope to explain consciousness until you have explored it? The only way you can explore it is through experience. Near-death, out-of-body and peak, or transcendent, experiences are relevant to this exploration. So are the different kinds of extrasensory perception. Even though such phenomena as remote perception and precognition have been tested and studied in close detail the findings are almost always sidelined or overlooked, when they are not derided or regarded as fraudulent, by the heavyweight consciousness buffs. Music, painting, and poetry have enormous influence on human consciousness, but as conventional scientific methodology cannot deal with their effects, they are left outside consideration. As Schrödinger says, "Science cannot tell us a word about why music delights us, of why and how an old song can move us to tears." However, there may be no reason why it should try. There are times and circumstances when silence is preferable to speech.

But there may be another way of looking at it. Perhaps a science of consciousness—using science simply as "an organized body of knowledge"—needs to develop as a separate entity rather than by taking bits and pieces from existing sciences, branches of sciences, philosophical and psychological theories and ideas. It needs to make more use of experience, to spend less time in the laboratory and library, or in front of the computer, and to listen to what people say. It needs to relax its obsession with examining only the brain, to pay attention to the rest of the human being, especially the emotions, and to study the relationship of individuals to each other and to the world at large. It needs to simplify its language, open its heart, talk to—and listen to—more women. Also, by its very nature, in the study of consciousness the student is an essential part of the study. He cannot separate his own consciousness from the consciousness he is studying. He needs to be detached and involved simultaneously for he is part of the puzzle and part of the solution.

That is by no means all. When working on the first draft of his book *The Self-Aware Universe*, published in 1993, the physicist Amit Goswami realized that there were "deep inconsistencies in the material." Attached as he was to the belief instilled from his scientific training that everything, including consciousness, is made up of matter, he could not see how something material could act causally upon matter itself. He rejected the Descartian theory of a dualistic consciousness as presenting insuperable difficulties, but he did not know how to proceed from there.

One evening Goswami was discussing with a friend his ideas about consciousness, which he had arrived at from his knowledge of quantum theory. Eventually the friend, Joel Morwood, stopped him. "You're wearing scientific blinkers that keep you from understanding," he said. "Underneath you have a belief that consciousness can be understood by science, that consciousness emerges in the brain, that it is an epiphenomenon. Comprehend what the mystics are saying. Consciousness is prior and unconditioned. It is all there is. There is nothing but God."

Retelling this exchange in the published version of the book, Goswami continues:

"That last sentence did something to me that is impossible to describe in language. The best I can say is that it caused an abrupt flip of perspective—a veil lifted. Here was the answer I had been looking for and yet had known all along."

When everybody else had gone to bed, Goswami went outside. The sky was so hazy that he could see only a few stars. Then in his imagination the sky became the radiant one of his childhood and suddenly he could see the Milky Way. He recalled an Indian poet who fancied that the Milky Way marked the boundary between heaven and earth. Goswami, the physicist, remembered that in quantum locality heaven, the kingdom of God, is everywhere. The words of Jesus came to him: "But man sees it not."

"We do not see it," Goswami continued, "because we are so enamoured of experience, of our melodramas, of our attempts to predict and control, to understand and manipulate everything rationally. In our efforts we miss the simple thing—the simple truth that it is all God, which is the mystic's way of saying that it is all consciousness. Physics explains phenomena, but consciousness is not a phenomenon; instead all else are phenomena *in* consciousness. I had vainly been seeking a description of consciousness within science; instead, what I and others have to look for is a description of science within consciousness. We must develop a science compatible with consciousness, our primary experience."

This is not a novel discovery. Aristotle and Spinoza are among those who, through the ages, have maintained something similar. Buddhists also may identify with the statement by Goswami's friend. As we work our way through some of the various manifestations of consciousness in the following chapters, we may see how far this accords with our own understanding.

Perhaps in time a science compatible with consciousness will be developed. Even now the child who will become the Einstein of consciousness studies may be growing up. He or she is unlikely to be taught anything about it at school but his or her interest may be sparked by one or more of the experiences similar to those I shall be describing later.

Now that the subject has become topical, and that we are in a new millennium, there is much talk about a shift in consciousness, a sort of upward movement that will lead to a kinder, better world. Much of this talk is unspecific and vague, expressions of hope unsupported by action. But there is a more serious element also, indicated by such an association as, for example, the Club of Budapest, in the words of its president, Ervin Laszlo, "dedicated to promoting and facilitating the evolution of a new consciousness."[17]

I am not sure, however, that there is or can be such a thing as a "new" consciousness. Swimme and Berry suggest in *The Universe Story* that perhaps the most momentous change in human consciousness in the European world since its emergence in the Paleolithic period began in the sixteenth century. This is how they explain it:

"The change was from a dominant spatial mode of consciousness, where time is perceived as moving in ever-renewing seasonal cycles, to a mode of consciousness whereby the universe is perceived as an irreversible sequence of transformations. This change in perception from an abiding cosmos to an ever-transforming cosmogenesis has had enormous consequences not only in every phase of the human but throughout the entire range of Earth functioning, since this intimate understanding of the universe brought with it almost magical powers of human intrusion in the process through scientific technologies. The failure of humans to understand this change in consciousness, and their corresponding failure to integrate human technologies with the technologies of the natural world, are perhaps the most profound causes for the disturbed condition of the planet in the late twentieth century."

If we accept this explanation, it is not so much a new consciousness that is required but a rectifying of the failures mentioned above. We have not yet come fully to terms with this transformation, which is still in progress. But it is vital that we do come to terms with it before we succeed in irrevocably damaging our sustaining Earth.

What is needed for the sort of world our deeper thinkers envisage, a happier, kinder world, more ecologically sensitive,

---

[17] See interview in *Kindred Spirit* magazine, no. 42, Spring (1998).

less aggressive, more humane, is an increase in awareness, in sensitivity, in compassion, in individual responsibility—an intensification of those qualities we already have in our consciousness. It is not that we need anything new; what we do need is to make better use of what we've got. Change of this kind cannot be imposed from the top down; it has to move the other way, from those who select, elect, and support our politicians, if it is to have any effect.

Does this mean anything at all? For the sake of the future, we must hope that it does. If that child is to become the Einstein of consciousness studies it is through a more thoughtful and determined education that its abilities must be fostered and encouraged, its perceptions sharpened and extended, and its sympathies broadened. As the child grows both physically and mentally it needs to become aware of what others have discovered through their experience of altered states: that we are much more than our physical bodies, that time and space do not have to be our masters, that we are aware of our interconnectedness with all humanity, with all creatures and plants, with the Earth that supports us and with the cosmos that surrounds us.

In the chapters that follow, I shall be concerned with some of the experiences that are relevant to the exploration of consciousness but are frequently omitted or pushed to the sidelines. These include types of extrasensory perception and anomalous cognition (remote viewing), distant healing, claims of communication with discarnates, theories of reincarnation, near-death and out-of-body experiences, and personal experiences that are described as mystical or transcendent. In considering this material we are not concerned with what you or I believe, but in what the evidence, the theories, and the accounts suggest. At the end we have to ask what we understand by the seventeenth-century poet Thomas Traherne's concept of "the vast enquiring soul," as quoted in the opening pages of this book. In what sense does it exist? And where is it to be found?

CHAPTER 2

MIND, MATTER, SPACE, AND TIME

Do you remember how electrical currents and 'unseen waves' were laughed at? The knowledge about man is still in its infancy. (Albert Einstein)

Many years ago I was on a troopship heading for South Africa via the Mediterranean and the Suez Canal. A popular (and illegal) pastime was a game called Crown & Anchor. This was a gambling game involving a board with six squares (crown, anchor, heart, spade, club, diamond) and two dice with the same six symbols. You placed your money on your chosen square and if that square turned up on one or both of the dice you were a winner. Within a few hours I lost everything.

As we approached Alexandria, Egypt, where some of the troops were due to disembark, I happened to notice that the rogue who had been running the Crown & Anchor board was collecting his gear. I asked him what he was going to do. "I'm off," he said. "I've made enough from you lads to keep me happy for a couple of months. Then I'll sign on as a steward on a ship heading for Liverpool and make enough for a couple of months there. That's all there is to it." He smiled—he could afford to.

"So how do you do it?" I asked. "You might as well tell me—I've no more to lose."

He took a pair of dice and a small cup from his pocket. "Shake 'em and roll," he said. "Keep 'em covered." I did so.

"Crown and Diamond," he said. "Look."

He was right. Time and again I threw; each time he called correctly. He took the dice from me and threw them himself.

"I'll throw Heart and Spade," he said.

He did. So it went on with him calling exactly what he would throw—before he actually did so.

I examined the dice. They seemed to be quite normal.

"Keep them if you like," he said. "They're just ordinary dice. I've got plenty more."

And off he went. That was my introduction to psychokinesis, the ability of mind to affect matter. Of course, he might have been an exceptional conjurer—I don't know. [18]

Gertrude Schmeidler, a major figure in the study of parapsychology, defines psychokinesis (often referred to as PK) as "a physical change that corresponds to a mental intention—one that cannot be explained by intervening physical processes." She adds that the term has two other uses. "It can mean the ability to produce a PK change, and it can designate a large, bizarre physical change when no corresponding mental intention is known (as in poltergeist cases)." [19] PK lends itself to laboratory research as small changes, invisible to the naked eye, can be measured by instruments and the experimenter can interact with a machine such as the random number (or event) generator, thus excluding variables or problems when other minds are closely involved in the trials.

The mundane exercise of throwing dice and attempting to influence the fall by mental intention was for many years an oft-used test for the existence of psychokinesis. Between 1935 and 1987, according to a search of the studies by Dean Radin and

---

[18] The ship was the *Monarch of Bermuda*, the date 1944. The episode could be described as a learning experience.

[19] Schmeidler, G. "Recent Research Reports," in *Advances in Parapsychological Research*, vol. 7, p. 198 *et seq.*

Diane Ferrari,"a total of 2,569 people had attempted to mentally influence 2.6 million dice throws in 148 different experiments, and just over 150,000 dice throws in 31 control studies where no mental influence was applied to the dice. The total number of dice tossed per study ranged from 60 to 240,000; the number of participants per study ranged from 1 to 393." Radin and Ferrari found that the overall accuracy rate for the control studies was 50.02 percent, this being odds against chance of two to one. For the experimental studies the rate was 51.2 percent. They comment: "This does not look like much, but statistically it results in odds against chance of more than a billion to one."[20] You can do your own research on this when playing board games such as Ludo, Snakes and Ladders, or Monopoly, if the fancy takes you.

The favored laboratory method that came to supplant the dice-throwing studies made use of the either the random number generator (RNG), an electronic device that produces a random series of "bits"—the numbers 1 and 0—or the random event generator (REG), which operates in a similar way. The experimenter seeks to influence the RNG so that it produces more of one number than the other. Examination of 832 studies, many of which were conducted by the Princeton Engineering Anomalies Research (PEAR) laboratory, in Princeton, New Jersey, produced similar control and experimental results to the dice studies. In the Princeton and other studies in recent years some experimenters were situated remotely from the RNG—up to thousands of miles away. This made no difference to the results; nor did experiments where the participant created the intention before the RNG data was generated.

When all the findings of these and similar experiments, using targets including a geiger counter, a gas discharge device, and a mechanical cascade, have been taken into account, the criticisms dealt with and the accusations of fraud

---

[20] Radin, D. (1997), *The Conscious Universe,* San Francisco: Harper Edge, p. 133. Subtitled "The Scientific Truth of Psychic Phenomena," this book is essential reading for anyone with a serious interest in this subject.

and collusion convincingly rebutted, it seems to be established that mental intention can have an effect on small material objects and the behavior of electronic circuits. Physics professor William Tiller, lecturing at the Science and Consciousness Conference in Albuquerque in 1999, is assured from his own extensive experimental evidence that "you can embed an intention into a simple device."

This gives rise to the question as to whether there are any ways to improve performance. In a recent review of "Methods of Enhancing PK Task Performance," the Icelandic researcher Loftur Gissurarson examines six possible methods: hypnosis, yoga and meditation, relaxation, feedback, negative reinforcement and punishment, and visual imagery. [21] What emerged from the best constructed experiments was the indication that mental relaxation, described as a frame or mode of mind that is "non-competitive, non-striving, non-analytical, passive and effortless," encouraged positive results. Gissurarson concluded that yoga and meditation techniques merited further research, and goal-oriented imagery, practice, and a high level of interest were all significant. One effective experimenter mentioned "a state of immersion in the process that leads to a loss of awareness of myself and the immediate surroundings," and another said "I don't feel any direct control over the device, more like a marginal influence when I'm in resonance with the machine. It's like being in a canoe: when it goes where I want, I flow with it. When it doesn't, I try to break the flow and give it a chance to get back in resonance with me." [22]

The phrase "in resonance with the machine" is interesting. It expresses a condition that a racing driver, an aircraft pilot—anyone working with a machine in a state of mutual dependence—is likely to recognize and accept as an essential contribution towards top performance. To find it used in a

---

[21] *Advances, op. cit.* vol. 8.
[22] Jahn, G. J. & Dunne, B. (1987), *Margins of Reality,* Florida: Harcourt Brace, p. 133. This pioneering study made a valuable contribution to attempts to formulate a science of consciousness.

"hands off" interaction may have significance in attempting to come to some understanding of human consciousness and might provide an opening for further research.

The existence of psychokinesis does not depend on the results of laboratory experiments. In the world outside the laboratory many of us have come across people who appear to have psychokinetic ability. This sometimes occurs when electronic devices are involved; stopping a lift at a chosen floor without pressing the button, interfering with lighting systems or radio reception are examples. Intention may or may not be involved. There is also the so-called "Pauli effect," named after the physicist Wolfgang Pauli whose mere presence in a laboratory was sufficient to cause glass to break or equipment to malfunction. There are suggestions that electromagnetic force or geomagnetic activity may affect PK but so far no substantial evidence has emerged to justify them.

Certain individuals have achieved fame through their apparent psychokinetic ability. These include the nineteenth-century medium D. D. Hume, the Icelander Indridi Indridason, the Russian Nina Kulagina, Uri Geller, Matthew Manning, and several Indian holy men including Swami Rama, Swami Premananda and, perhaps the best known today, Sathyi Sai Baba.[23] Making objects move, appear, and disappear are the feats most often reported; others include affecting the weather and creating images on unexposed film. Kulagina, Geller, Manning, and Swami Rama have all been subjected to testing under what have been described as controlled conditions. Sai Baba's feats have been witnessed by many thousands who are convinced of his psychic abilities. Commenting on reports of this kind of PK, Gertrude Schmeidler simply says, "Each case is

---

[23] Sai Baba, born 1926, is a highly regarded Indian guru with a strong European and American following. He has a reputation as a miracle-worker. A study of the psychic phenomena associated with him, *Miracles are my Visiting Cards,* by Dr. Erelendur Haraldsson, professor of psychology at the University of Iceland, was published in 1987. Some devotees regard Sai Baba as God.

unique. We can expect continued controversy about these unusual individuals." It might be that what is really needed when investigating these feats is the presence of an experienced—and unprejudiced—stage magician. But whatever conclusions are eventually arrived at, the arguments between believers and skeptics will still continue.

Leaving my Crown & Anchor PK operator (and any others like him) out of account, unless means are found whereby psychokinetic ability can be developed under controlled conditions this ability may not seem to have much practical use. This cannot be said about extrasensory perception (ESP), which can be defined as the ability to acquire information through apparently inexplicable means. ESP is customarily divided into four categories: telepathy—where the information is transmitted to or appears to come from another person; clairvoyance—where the information appears to come in real time but not from another person; premonition—where the information is a warning that something is going to happen; precognition—where the information could have been obtained only by knowledge of the future.

Of the different kinds of ESP, the one that most people are familiar with is telepathy—the transfer of information from mind to mind. Just when you are thinking of someone the phone rings and that person is on the line. A husband is shopping; his wife recalls something she omitted from the list; the thought enters his mind and he buys it. Coincidence? If it happens only occasionally that may well be the explanation. But if it happens frequently then coincidence must be ruled out. Telepathic experiences may shade into what are called telesomatic experiences, as when someone close to you suddenly falls ill or is involved in an accident and you sense that something serious has happened. Similar communication also seems to happen between certain individuals and their pets; for instance, dogs appear to know when their owner is approaching home. [24]

---

[24] See Sheldrake, R. (1999), *Dogs That Know When Their Owners Are Coming Home*, London: Hutchinson.

Studies on telepathy have been conducted since the 1880s. Many of the more recent studies have involved the Ganzfeld method, which means "whole field." Ganzfeld depends on placing the receiver in the experiment, the person to whom the information is being sent, in a state of sensory deprivation so that everyday input is shut off and the system becomes more sensitive to subtle messages. More than two and a half thousand Ganzfeld experiments took place between 1974 and 1997. Dean Radin, reviewing experiments in telepathy in *The Conscious Universe*, comments as follows:

"We are fully justified in having very high confidence that people sometimes get small amounts of specific information from a distance without the use of the ordinary senses. . . . From the beginning, each new series of telepathy experiments was met with its share of skeptical attacks. These criticisms reduced mainstream scientific interest in the reported effects, but ironically they also refined the methods used in future experiments to the point that today's Ganzfeld experiments stump the experts."

While some experts still remain skeptical and others are stumped, the non-expert seems to find telepathy more acceptable than other manifestations of extrasensory perception. It is a phenomenon that occurs so frequently in daily life—or seems to do so—that the word has passed into common usage. The involuntary reception of thoughts generated by another person often merits no more than a passing comment. Episodes of this kind cannot by their nature be scientifically verified outside the laboratory, and inside, where the conditions are artificial and spontaneity is almost impossible, they are far less likely to occur. Hence in three fairly recent books dealing with the brain (*The Human Brain*, by Susan Greenfield), the mind (*How the Mind Works*, by Steven Pinker), and consciousness (*Consciousness Explained*, by Daniel Dennett), there are no references to telepathy at all.

This brings us back to the limitations of scientific method which says: if you can't observe it, measure it, or replicate it, it does not exist. If mind is confined to the brain and consciousness is located in the brain-mind, then telepathy, which transcends space and time, not only does not but cannot exist.

Only through instruments—telephone, fax, radio, e-mail—or by pigeon-post, smoke-signals, drumming, alpenhorn, or shouting very loudly, could we communicate at a distance. But our *experience* tells us that telepathy is real. When the affinity between communicators is strong—for example with twins, lovers, spouses, parents and children, or close friends—the more frequently telepathic communication is likely to occur, almost always happening spontaneously, in the split second. The impact of the communication is such that the receiver is usually impelled to act upon it without giving it a second thought.

In response to those who deny the possibility of telepathy, the psychologist Lawrence Le Shan points out their fundamental error. "It is simply not legitimate to say that because the *bodies* of two subjects in an experiment are 300 miles apart, that their *consciousnesses* are also 300 miles apart. In the geometric space that their bodies exist in, the 300 miles makes a difference. Their consciousnesses do not exist in geometric space; the term 300 miles makes as little sense in the realm of consciousness, the realm in which their thoughts and feelings exist, as to say they are 300 foot pounds or 300 volts apart."[25]

There is no warrant for refusing to accept the existence of ESP simply because it appears to contradict the ground rules of orthodox science. Such refusal is a fallacy of scientism. Yet in one particular area an impressive body of scientifically acceptable evidence has been accumulating over the past three decades. That area is known as remote viewing.

The phrase 'remote viewing' dates from the early 1970s, although the phenomenon itself is nothing new. In their study of psychic abilities, *The Mind Race* (1984), Russell Targ and Keith Harary refer to the first well-controlled remote viewing experiment as being recorded by Herodotus.[26] Various cultures and tribes appear to make use of this ability. To take just one example, an anthropologist friend of mine was living with

---

[25] Le Shan, L. (1987) *The Science of the Paranormal*, Wellingborough: Aquarian Press, p. 97.
[26] Targ, R. & Harary, K. (1984) *The Mind Race,* New York: Villard Books.

a tribe on the Upper Amazon some years ago and was missing her family at Christmas. Seeing her miserable expression, one of the elders asked her the reason. Would she like to see her family? he enquired. And, somehow—she never understood how—he enabled her to do so. There they were, opening their presents around the Christmas tree.

In his book *Mind Trek*, Joe McMoneagle, one of the most outstanding of present-day remote viewers, seeks to isolate and define the term. "Throughout this book, the term 'remote viewing' will be mixed quite frequently with the taboo word 'psychic'. They will mean approximately the same thing....The most important difference you should know is that remote viewing, or RV as it is called, is always done within scientific or approved research protocols. Psychic, on the other hand, usually implies that the information came to someone paranormally, without any specific controls applied. . . . In brief, RV represents the scientific or research side and psychic stands for the experiential, subjective, or that which has been observed through application."

The word "psychic," strictly an adjective but nowadays often used as a noun, is certainly taboo in scientific circles and in many religious circles also. The noun "psyche," from which it derives, is defined as "the soul, spirit, mind: the principle of mental and emotional life, conscious and unconscious." One of the definitions of "psychic" is "beyond, or apparently beyond, the physical; sensitive to or in touch with that which has not yet been explained physically." What has happened is that the term has become associated with stage performers, mediums, and new age weirdness generally, and is often applied to anyone with sharpened intuition or more than average perception. Recent investigators have tended to talk of "psi research" to escape from the connotations of "psychic," but essentially what is being researched is human consciousness and there may be no need to look for other terminology.

Remote viewing is a special technique in which a viewer seeks to draw or describe a target—a building or location, a person, photograph, event, or object of some kind. The target is either at a distance or is totally concealed. It may be a feature on the surface of a planet or an item in an envelope or box. For testing purposes a strict protocol is followed. All known means of receiving any information are blocked and the viewer may be shut into an isolation chamber or Faraday cage (an electromagnetic energy-free zone). No one in contact with the remote viewer knows what the target is. In some tests a monitor, ignorant of the nature of the target, is at hand to ask questions to prompt the viewer. A person known as an outbounder may be sent out to observe the target during the session and the viewer would be asked to draw or describe what the outbounder is observing.

For practical purposes a viewer may be called in to help the police search for a missing person—a runaway, a criminal, or a victim of kidnapping. A viewer may be commissioned by an oil company to serve as a prospector to remote view and report on various possible sites around the globe. In both testing and practical processes, the viewer usually receives feedback after completing his report to confirm the accuracy, or otherwise, of his attempt.

In the past, prophets and oracles were used by kings and governments to find and reveal information about their enemies. More recently, in 1919, the Czechs had a two-man "psychic spying" unit who were hypnotized and then asked to report on Hungarian army dispositions. During the Cold War, reports that the Russians were experimenting with similar techniques began to disturb U.S. intelligence. Then in the early 1970s, Dr. Hal Puthoff, a scientist specializing in laser physics and engineering, began work at the Stanford Research Institute. He obtained a grant to conduct experiments into psi effects and before long was joined by an artist, Ingo Swann, who had been taking part in similar experiments in New York with Gertrude Schmeidler.

They began a series of tests in which Puthoff placed an object in a wooden box and Swann was brought in to divine what was in the box. Hearing of what was going on, the intelligence community became interested. One day two men from Washington arrived with their own target, which they placed in the box. Swann said "I see something small, brown, and irregular, sort of like a leaf, except it seems alive, like it's moving." The object was a large, live, brown moth that the visitors had caught on their way in. The men were from the CIA, concerned by the reports from Russia and looking for a laboratory in which a classified investigation could be carried out.

Another scientist, Russell Targ, joined Puthoff, and a large number of experiments took place over the next few years. Targets were no longer objects in boxes but, to begin with, were sites in the San Francisco Bay Area chosen under strict control. Later the distances were extended to take in sites elsewhere in the United States and then around the world. Swann suggested using geographical coordinates, down to minutes and seconds, and under test conditions he showed that it was possible to identify and describe places and objects at those particular locations. Swann also remote viewed the planet Jupiter shortly before the NASA *Pioneer 10* flight. He found a ring around the planet and thought he might have viewed Saturn by mistake. However, *Pioneer 10* revealed that a hitherto undiscovered ring did in fact exist. [27]

Soon the research team was augmented by several other viewers, including Pat Price, a former police commissioner, Hella Hammid, a freelance photographer, and a Vietnam veteran, Joe McMoneagle. Summarizing the early years of the operation, in the words of Dr. Puthoff, "the back-and-forth criticism of protocols, refinement of methods, and successful replication of this type of remote viewing in independent laboratories has yielded considerable scientific evidence for the reality of the phenomenon. Adding to the strength of these results was the discovery that a growing number of individuals could be found to demonstrate high-quality remote viewing, often to their own surprise." [28]

---

[27] Targ and Puthoff describe some of the feats of Swann in *Mind Reach*, New York: Dell Publishing (1977).

[28] *Journal of Scientific Exploration*, vol. 10, no. 1, contains several reports on the U.S. government-sponsored remote viewing programs. They include evaluations of the programs by Professors Jessica Utts and Ray Hyman along with reports by Edwin May (who directed the program for some years), Hal Puthoff, and Russell Targ. This issue is essential reading for anyone with an interest in remote viewing.

To begin with, the project came under the auspices of U.S. Army Intelligence. In 1987, the Defense Intelligence Agency took over leadership of what by this time was a joint-services program. Most of the information about projects and targets over the next twenty years has yet to be released, but Dr. Puthoff has commented in general terms about the ways in which the programs developed. Much of the effort, he says, "was directed not so much toward developing an operational U. S. capability, but rather toward assessing the threat potential of its use against the U.S. by others. . . . As a result much of the remote-viewing activity was carried out under conditions where ground-truth reality was *a priori* known or could be determined, such as the description of U. S. facilities and technological developments, the timing of rocket test firings and underground nuclear tests, and the location of individuals and mobile units. And, of course, we were responsive to requests to provide assistance during such events as the loss of an airplane or the taking of hostages, relying on the talents of an increasing cadre of remote-viewer consultants."

Dr. Puthoff also notes that problems with analysis of data sometimes arose through the belief systems of certain individuals who declined to be involved, either because the concept was judged to be "unscientific nonsense" or because "even though it might be real, it was possibly demonic." His own conclusion, based on his experience as research manager of the program for several years, is that, despite certain ambiguities, "the integrated results appear to provide unequivocal evidence of a human capacity to access events remote in space and time, however falteringly, by some cognitive process not yet understood."

Russell Targ, who worked with Puthoff until 1984, stated his belief that "the remote-viewing data has made a significant contribution to our knowledge of our relationship to a non-local universe in which we are interconnected and increasingly interdependent," adding that he hoped "our awareness of this interconnectedness derived from research into our psychic abilities will also promote greater compassion among all people."[29]

---

[29] Ibid.

While about 95 percent of the results of the remote-viewing program are still classified, enough has been released to give a good idea of the accuracy of which viewers were capable. In 1974, the CIA asked for a report on "a Soviet site of great interest" for which the coordinates were provided. These were given to Pat Price. He began to describe what he saw. "I am lying on my back on the roof of a two- or three-story building. It's a sunny day. The sun feels good. There's the most amazing thing. There's a giant gantry crane moving back and forth over my head.... As I drift up into the air and look down, it seems to be riding on a track with one rail on each side of the building. I've never seen anything like that."

Price sketched the layout of the buildings and the detail of the crane as he saw it. He was also able to see inside the building he was lying on top of and described "a large interior room where people were assembling a giant, sixty-foot diameter metal sphere. He said that it was being assembled from thick metal 'gores' like sections of an orange peel, but they were having trouble welding it all together because the pieces were warping." Price's information was later confirmed in much detail by high resolution photographic reconnaissance satellites, including the construction of the spheres, supposedly needed to "capture and store energy from nuclear-driven explosives or pulse power generators." The site that he was asked to view was the Soviet atomic bomb laboratory at Semipalatinsk in the U.S.S.R.[30]

A viewing by Joe McMoneagle in 1979 provides another example of remote-viewing spying activity. An officer from the National Security Council brought in to the unit a number of photographs taken by a spy satellite. They showed a large industrial facility by the sea, somewhere in northern Russia. The particular target was a building with sides estimated at over a quarter of a mile long.

---

[30] Targ, R. & Katra, J. (1998), *Miracles of Mind,* California: New World Library, pp. 46-48. Also *Journal of Scientific Exploration*, vol. 13. no. 1, spring 1999, article by Russell Targ.

McMoneagle was handed a segment of one of the photographs showing no more than a section of roofing and was asked to look inside the building. He saw a submarine under repair, a heap of construction materials and, in another area of the building, a very large submarine under construction. He gave several details about its appearance including the number of missile tubes. Asked to discover when the submarine would be launched, McMoneagle saw a channel being constructed from the factory to the sea. Four months after the initial viewing the submarine was floated down to begin trials. Satellite photographs at a later date confirmed the accuracy of the viewing.

In 1995, the CIA was required to evaluate the remote-viewing program, now known as Stargate, and contracted the American Institutes for Research to conduct the review. As a result of this review, the program, then administered by SAIC (Science Applications International Corporation), was closed down. Dr. Edwin May, who had worked with the program since 1975 and had been its director for the past nine years, during which most of the research took place, firmly believed that the CIA had determined on closure for political reasons even before the review was completed. The two academic evaluators disagreed on their interpretations and Dr. May maintained that much of the available evidence had been ignored. He admitted that in the final two years, the period covered by the evaluation, morale in the unit was low and "the emotional environment had deteriorated to the point that the viewers wanted to leave the unit and some of the staff had already left in disgust." But he deplored the fact that the positive results of the previous eighteen years were unconsidered. Interestingly, the conclusion reached by the CIA that the results obtained by remote viewing "are not practical in the real world of intelligence collection" are contradicted by the wording of the citation for the Legion of Merit awarded in 1984 to Joe McMoneagle "for excellence in intelligence service."

The citation stated: "He served most recently as a Special Project Intelligence Officer . . . [and] as one of the original planners and movers of a unique intelligence project that is revolutionizing the intelligence community. While with SSPD he used his talents and expertise in the execution of more than 200 missions, addressing over 150 essential elements of information [EEI]. These EEI contained critical intelligence reported at the highest echelons of our military and government ... producing crucial and vital intelligence unavailable from any other source. ..."

It is possible that the publication of sensational accounts of, for example, the claimed discovery by remote viewing of the presence of pregnant Martians beneath the New Mexico desert by an individual briefly associated with the remote viewing program, may have affected the government attitude towards the project. This, however, cannot be proved. But regardless of this sort of nonsense there was no doubt in the mind of Professor Jessica Utts, a statistician from the University of California at Davis, one of the two academics appointed to report on the project, that anomalous cognition, as remote viewing was often referred to, was "possible and has been demonstrated. This conclusion is not based on belief, but rather on commonly accepted scientific criteria." She continued as follows:

"I believe that it would be wasteful of valuable resources to continue to look for proof. No one who has examined all of the data across laboratories, taken as a collective whole, has been able to suggest methodological or statistical problems to explain the ever-increasing and consistent results to date. Resources should be directed to the pertinent questions about how this ability works. I am confident that the questions are no more elusive than any other questions in science dealing with small- to medium-sized effects, and that if appropriate resources are targeted to appropriate questions, we can have answers within the next decade." [31]

That decade ends in the year 2005; so far the resources have not been targeted.

In the military context, remote viewing, to be taken seriously, has to operate within protocols similar to those applied

---

[31] *Journal of Scientific Exploration*, vol. 10. no. 1. spring 1996.

when viewers themselves are being tested. It must also be shown that the results can be replicated. For much of the time when the SRI/SAIC project was functioning the Princeton Engineering Anomalies Research Laboratory was also conducting experiments in what they preferred to call "precognitive remote perception."[32] The first recorded example of this precognitive perception had actually occurred spontaneously at SRI with Pat Price as the viewer.

For this trial the laboratory director, Bart Cox, drove away from the laboratory and turned whichever way he felt like at intersections and road junctions. Price said that there was no need to wait until he arrived at whatever destination he decided, as he could simply look "down the time line" and see where the car and driver would be in half an hour's time. He described a harbor with small sailboats and a building with Oriental features. This was an accurate description of the Redwood City Marina with a nearby restaurant with a curved roof similar to the roof of a pagoda. The Marina car park was where Cox's car drew up. [33] Hella Hammid also succeeded with four precognitive trials, and the Princeton Laboratory later organized 227 experiments in precognitive perception, finding that it made no difference whether the viewer looked hours or weeks into the future. Now that he is working for his own company, Joe McMoneagle occasionally demonstrates remote viewing on television. When asked whether he found the lights, cameras, and audience distracting, he replied that

---

[32] Radin (1997), p. 103. Radin gives an example of a trial where the percipient and agent were separated by 2,200 miles. Some forty-five minutes before the agent randomly selected a site, the percipient described the following impressions: "Rather strange yet persistent image of [agent] inside a large bowl—a hemispheric indentation in the ground of some smooth man-made materials like concrete or cement. No color. Possibly covered with a glass dome. Unusual sense of inside/outside simultaneity. That's all. It's a large bowl (If it was full of soup [the agent] would be the size of a large dumpling)."
The agent was visiting a large radio telescope at Kitt Peak, Arizona.
[33] Targ & Katra (1998), p. 126.

he does the viewing the night before in his hotel room before the target has been selected and simply repeats his perceptions in front of the cameras next day. He says that one possible explanation (amongst many) is that he is in some way sending himself information from the future. [34]

Time, then, appears to be no obstacle to the proficient remote viewer. Nor is space. McMoneagle has viewed the surface of Mars, has explored the origins of mankind and has published a wide variety of predictions for the next hundred years, several of which, since their publication in *The Ultimate Time Machine* (1998) have been realized.

One area, however, in which remote viewing does not seem to be successful is in predicting lottery results. This has nothing to do with ethics. Rather, the history of remote viewing experiments shows that it has so far not been possible to guarantee accuracy in reading letters and numbers wherever they might appear. In fact, accuracy can never be guaranteed, whatever the target. According to McMoneagle there is no such thing as a one hundred percent success rate, and finding lost persons or objects is the most difficult target to hit. He considers remote viewing as a tool like many other tools, most effective when used in conjunction with other tools. He describes it as "a small but finite crack in the door to how we may interface with reality." [35]

There are certain similarities between the out-of-body (OB) state (see chapter 5) and remote viewing although there are significant differences with regard to the operation of human consciousness. In both modalities it is possible to "travel" to a specific target, to observe and, if required, to report back. McMoneagle notes the differences precisely.

In the out-of-body state:

1. You arrive at the target just as if you had gone there physically.

---

[34] McMoneagle (1997).
[35] Ibid. p. 235.

2. You know that your consciousness is totally ₴
   target location and where you left your phy₋.
   body is somewhere else.
3. You see objects and people at the target location just
   as if you were seeing them with physical eyes. Both
   animate and inanimate elements are seen with such
   pristine clarity that you can actually discriminate
   molecular movement within them.
4. Seeing into the next room requires having to pass
   through a wall, which feels something akin to pushing your body through a veil of Jell-0.

In the remote viewing state:

1. You access the target location with your mind only.
2. Consciousness is still located with the physical body
   and you are always aware of this.
3. In remote viewing you can communicate and
   respond instantly to questions, while in the out-of-
   body state you cannot report until you return to your
   physical body and if you need to know more you
   have to replicate the OB state quickly, which is usually impossible. [36]

Collection of data in the remote viewing state is very
quick—almost instantaneous. Processing it, understanding it
and putting it into a context that makes sense, however, takes
a great deal of time and energy. It is in the processing that the
skills of the viewer become apparent. In remote viewing the
amount of data available seems to be far greater. It's hard to
see if someone is East European or West European in the out-
of-body state. In remote viewing, the information seems to be
more readily available.

The remote viewer, then, always remains firmly focused
within this reality—the reality of everyday life. Perhaps the

---

[36] Ibid. p. 127.

nearest comparison is with dowsing, not dowsing to find water or metal beneath your feet, which may depend on your sensitivity to electromagnetic fields, but dowsing "at a distance," using geographical coordinates.

The PEAR precognitive remote perception trials were carried out in a similar way to the work at SRI and SAIC. They used a "percipient." who was required "to generate a written description of an unknown geographical target where the "agent" is, was, or will be stationed at some prescribed time, and then to fill out a checklist of questions on which subsequent analytical judging schemes are based." The agent (the "outbounder" in SRI parlance) spent up to fifteen minutes at the target and was also required to fill in a checklist. This last sometimes presented problems as the forced choice involved tended to dilute the results. The target was either selected at random from a number chosen by someone not otherwise involved or was selected by the agent when working in an area where there was no pool of targets available.

In these trials professor Robert Lahn, in charge of the PEAR operation, reports that most of the perceptions were performed precognitively before the agent arrived at the site, and even before a site was selected. Obviously no communication was permitted between the percipient and the agent until both had completed their tasks. Some trials also resembled the SRI trials where the perceptions were recorded once the agent was in place. Between 1978 and 1987, 334 trials were published using 40 percipients. [37]

Here is an extract from one percipient's report: "I have the feeling that [the agent] is somewhere near water. I seem to have the sensation of a very large expanse of water. There might be boats. Several vertical lines, sort of like poles. They're narrow, not heavy. Maybe lamp-posts or flagpoles. Some kind of circular shape. Almost like a merry-go-round or a gazebo. A large round thing. It's round on its side, like a disc ... it's like a round thing flat on the ground but it seems to have height as

---

[37] See Radin (1997), ch. 6.

well. Maybe with poles. Could possibly come to a point on top. Seeing vertical lines again. Seems to be a strong impression, these vertical lines. No idea what they could be. . . . A definite sensation of being outside rather than in. Water again . . . to one side of where [the agent] is, I get the feeling there's a kind of small building. Could be a shed. . . . Predominant colors seem to be blue and green. . . . water again. Some very quick impression of a fence, a low fence . . . steps. I don't know where they're leading to. . . . The steps sort of lead up to like a path or walkway. Like a boardwalk. And there's a fence along it. There's people walking along it, and there's vertical lines along that walkway. . . . "

The distance between the percipient and the target was approximately 5,600 miles. The viewing took place almost 24 hours before the agent arrived at the location. The target, described with remarkable accuracy was the Danube Bridge at Bratislava, Slovakia.

Detailed analysis of the PEAR trials may be found in *Margins of Reality*, by Robert Jahn and Brenda Dunne. They point out the "essential dilemma" of their research: "By its nature, the remote perception process is inherently impressionistic in character, yet to render it scientifically credible and pragmatically dependable, it must be reduced to analytical and quantitative terms. Thus we find ourselves fishing in a metaphysical sea with a scientific net far better matched to other purposes." So far the resources to manufacture the right sort of net are not available. Yet there are some rare and splendid fish to be caught.

It is interesting to note that, faced with evidence of successful remote viewing experiments, a standard response is "Oh, that's just telepathy!" It is possible that, in some instances, telepathic communication between the minds of the viewer and the agent who is observing the target may occur. If this could be proved to be so then it would be remarkable confirmation of telepathic ability. But where there is no agent or outbounder, or when no one else knows what the target is, or the viewer is working with geographical coordinates or a photograph selected blind from a large number, then the explanation that "just telepathy" is at work must collapse.

There has been some debate as to whether remote viewing can be taught. Research over twenty-five years has shown that this is unlikely. It seems to be a natural talent, possibly even an additional sense. While many people may have this talent, to a greater or lesser degree, what training systems probably do is to demonstrate or reveal the talent that the individual possesses. Training may polish this talent but it is doubtful if any significant improvement can be effected. Those who present themselves for training will have some reason to believe that they have this ability so they are largely self-selected. Hence some of them may turn out to be capable of a degree of remote viewing although very few are likely to be consistently effective.

Precognition, a variant of extrasensory perception, is often involved in remote viewing. It has a long-recorded history. Many examples of precognition may be found in old narratives of second sight from the Highlands and Islands of Scotland. Here is a sample from Aubrey's *Miscellanies*, compiled in the seventeenth century:

"Those that have this faculty of the Second-Sight see only things to come, which are to happen shortly thereafter, and sometimes foretell things which fall out three or four years after. For instance, one told his master that he saw an arrow in such a man through his body, and yet no blood came out, and that if it came not to pass he would be deemed an imposter. But about five or six years after, the man died and being brought to his burial-place, there arose a debate anent his grave, and it came to such a height that they drew arms and bended their bows, and one letting off an arrow shot through the dead body on the bier-trees, and so no blood could issue out of a dead man's wound. Thus his sight could not inform him whether the arrow should be shot in him alive or dead, neither could he condescend whether near or far off."

Several of the recorded accounts of second sight concern forecasts of death or disaster. "They see these things visibly but none sees them but themselves," replied a correspondent to a question of Aubrey's. "For instance, if a man's fatal end be hanging, they'll see a gibbet, or a rope about his neck; if beheaded, they'll see the man without a head; if drowned, they'll see water up to his throat; if unexpected death, they'll see a winding-sheet about his head; all of which are presented to their view." Despite the occasional occurrence of happier visions, such as forthcoming marriages, the gift of second sight was seldom welcomed.

John Morrison, the minister in Petty, near Inverness, Scotland, was a reputed seer in the Highlands in the eighteenth century. At the end of one sermon in 1773, he suddenly launched forth as follows: "Ye sinful and stiff-necked people, God will, unless ye turn from your evil ways, sweep you ere long into the place of torment; and as a sign of the truth of what I say, Clach Dubh an Abhainn, large though it be, will be carried soon without human agency a considerable distance seawards." An extract from Anderson's *Guide to the Highlands* reads:"On the south side of the bay of Petty an immense stone, weighing at least eight tons, which marked the boundaries between the estates of Lord Moray and Culloden, was, on the night of Saturday, February 20, 1799, removed and carried forward into the sea about 260 yards. Some believe that nothing short of an earthquake could have removed such a mass, but more probable opinion is that a large sheet of ice, which had collected to the thickness of 18 inches round the stone, had been raised by the tide, lifting the stone with it, and that their motion forward was aided and increased by a tremendous hurricane which blew from the land."

Morrison predicted the evictions that took place later in his parish, the deaths of individual parishioners, and accurately foretold his successor as minister "a stammering Lowland minister who will neither have English nor Gaelic."

The best-known of Highland predictions is credited to the so-called Brahan Seer, Coinneach Odhar. He foresaw the doom of the House of Seaforth, with the last chief being deaf and dumb whose four fine sons all predeceased him. "Lamenting the last of his sons, he shall sink in sorrow to the tomb and the last of his possessions shall be inherited by a widow from the east who will kill her own sister. As a sign that these things are coming to pass, there will be four great lairds in the days of the last Seaforth. Gairloch shall be hare-lipped;

Chisholm shall be buck-toothed; Grant shall be a stammerer; and Raasey an idiot. These four lairds shall be allies and neighbors of the last Seaforth and when he looks around him and sees them he will know that his sons are doomed to die and that his broad lands shall pass to strangers and his race come to an end."

All this happened exactly as foretold. In 1815, the line ended with the death of the last Lord Seaforth and in the following years the estates were sold.

There have been many reported examples of second sight in recent years. One in particular concerns the local postman in Newtonferry on the island of North Uist, also in Scotland. He arrived exhausted at the house of the local veterinarian, unable to continue his round. "After he had regained some of his sense, he explained that in rounding a dangerous corner beneath a rock bluff he had 'seen' lying at the roadside the remains of a smashed motorcycle and the badly mutilated bodies of a young man and woman. About a year later one of the worst road accidents in the island's history occurred at that same spot when, on a black night, a young honeymooning couple were killed outright when their motorcycle skidded."[38]

Francis Thompson, in *The Supernatural Highlands* (1976), explains that the Gaelic word for second sight is *da-shealladh*, which means "two sights," perhaps conveying the idea that a vision of the world of sense is one sight, but a vision of another world, populated by people living, but not within actual sight of the seer, or living but in another time, is another, rarer, sight. He adds that there seem to be two categories of visions: "those which involve living people, contemporary with the seer and often his or her own friends or relations, who appear as wraiths and might be taken as 'precognition'—the ability to foretell events about to happen, and which do occur within a short time of the forecast; the other category contains visions

---

[38] Much of this material comes from Francis Thompson's *The Supernatural Highlands,* London: Hale, (1976).

of events which often involve those not yet born and which are more difficult to explain.... The latter sights are contained in the visions of the true seer, the person able to project far into the future, and though he or she has no means of knowing whether the vision will come to pass they are sufficiently convinced of their gift that the details of it are set down and recorded."

Research into second sight is hampered by the fact that so many of the incidences are in Gaelic. There is also a floating boundary between fact and folklore. Nevertheless there can be no doubt that the gift exists. It may be that genetic inheritance is involved; in the isolated communities where second sight was reported there would have been a complex web of interrelationships.

In contrast to Highland second-sight experiences there are the precognitive abilities of the Dutch psychic Gerard Croiset. Over a period of twenty-five years, Croiset participated in a number of experiments known as the "chair tests." These tests followed a similar pattern. The experimenter would take a seating plan for a future public event in a large hall anywhere in the world and would select a seat at random. The only provision was that there was to be no reserved seating for the event. Croiset would simply be asked to describe the person who would be occupying the chosen seat. Nearly every time he was able to give a full description of the person, including dress and occupation and sometimes even details from their past. In *The Holographic Universe*, Michael Talbot gives the following account adapted from the *Journal of the American Society of Psychological Research*.

"On January 6, 1969, in a study conducted by Dr. Jule Eisenbud, a clinical professor of psychiatry at the University of Colorado Medical School, Croiset was told that a chair had been chosen for an event that would take place on January 23, 1969. Croiset, who was in Utrecht, Holland, at that time, told Eisenbud that the person who would sit in the chair would be a man five feet nine inches in height who brushed his hair straight back, had a gold tooth in his lower jaw, a scar on his big toe, who worked in both science and industry, and sometimes got his lab coat stained by a greenish chemical. On January 23, 1969, the man who sat down in the chair, which was in an auditorium in Denver, Colorado, fit Croiset's description in every way but one. He was not five feet nine, but five feet nine and three-quarters."

Croiset's ability parallels the ability of those remote viewers who are able to transcend time as well as space. In more than three hundred trials, Jahn and Dunne found that precognitive information was produced in well over half of the experiments. The dream state may also be fruitful. Many people who can recall their dreams are likely to have experienced in them future events that later come to pass. A number of trials at the Dream Laboratory at Maimonides Medical Center, Brooklyn, New York, produced convincing evidence that most of the volunteers who took part could produce precognitive information in dreams. [39] Countless numbers have had this experience outside the laboratory and need no convincing that this precognitive ability exists.

Premonition, or forewarning, is a variant of precognition. It is similar to presentiment, defined by Dean Radin as "a vague sense or feeling of something about to occur but without any conscious awareness of a particular event." While presentiment can, to some extent, be tested in the laboratory, premonition is an "in the moment" personal experience with implications usually affecting the individual. It is a warning, often of some impending disaster or tragedy. It may come in a dream, as in the following recollection:

"I dreamed that I saw a corpse on a bed, and the details of the face which included an open mouth were imprinted on my mind with extraordinary clarity. I awoke feeling troubled and felt that the dream was in some way connected with my mother. Usually I forget dreams but the impression of this one haunted my waking hours at intervals during the next few days. [A week later the dreamer received a message that an aunt she was close to was mortally ill.] When I entered the room I

---

[39] Ullman, Krippner & Vaughan (1977), *Dream Telepathy*, New York: McMillan.

received a great shock. I was astounded to see the corpse exactly as in my dream ... with the mouth wide open and all the details of the face just as I had seen them a week previously." [40]

Another instance appears to have foretold a wartime disaster: "At the beginning of the war I had a waking experience of a city on fire. I saw the appalling holocaust, buildings falling, and people dying on an uncountable scale. All through the war I waited for this fearful thing to happen to me and it never did. Not until long afterwards did I recognize my experience in the fate of Dresden, a city I dearly loved and in which I had spent the last year before the war broke out." [41]

A further example shows the enormous personal problems that the gift—or curse—of premonition can present. I met Pat, a lady in her mid-thirties, after a talk I gave at a U.S. air base in East Aglia a few years ago. She told me that about a year previously she had been walking in the town where she lives with a child about six years old, the daughter of a neighbor. She stopped on the edge of the pavement waiting for a gap in the traffic so she could cross the road. In the moment she knew what was about to happen. The child would catch sight of a friend on the other side of the road, would run out into the traffic, be knocked down, and killed immediately. She reached out a hand but it was too late. The child had already stepped out onto the road. A second or so later she was dead.

This was not Pat's first premonition, although none previously had been followed by such a tragedy. Although she was in no way to blame, she went into a deep depression for many months. The questions kept recurring. Knowing what was to happen, could she have prevented it? Why didn't she call out? Could she have moved more quickly? Nothing could lighten the weight of guilt. Yet she was guilty of nothing.

Since then, Pat has had several premonitions. Generally they have been of a comparatively mundane nature, such as breaking

---

[40] Jakobsen, M. (1999), *Negative Spiritual Experiences*, p. 45. Religious Experience Research Center, Oxford, Occasional Paper.
[41] Ibid.

a valuable object or receiving news of a friend's illness. Even so, they terrify her. As long as they continue, she lives with the fear that again she will have a premonition of another fatal accident and will be unable to do anything about it. At times she wonders if it is ever possible to take action to change the future. Years after the event, she still goes back in her mind to that moment at the roadside. If she knew there was going to be an accident, why did she not step into the road herself and save the life of the child?[42]

Many scientists do not accept that precognition or premonition can exist, because, as Dean Radin says, "it raises the perplexing possibility that causation sometimes 'flows backwards.' This is deeply troubling because most scientific models assume that cause and effect 'flow' in only one direction." An orthodox explanation of Pat's roadside experience would ascribe it to perception interpreted by her intelligence; she perceives the child standing close to the road, the traffic moving along, the other child on the far side. The picture, as it were, coalesces. She is not seeing into the future but interpreting the present. She stretches out her hand but it is too late.

Yet the evidence from hundreds of trials and laboratory testing of precognition cannot simply be set aside. Michael Talbot, who studied the evidence for precognition for his book *The Holographic Universe*, concluded: "The literature is filled with examples of people who were able to use their precognitive glimpses of the future to avoid disasters, instances in which individuals correctly foresaw the crash of a plane and avoided death by not getting on, or had a vision of their children being drowned in a flood and moved them out of harm's way just in the nick of time." He mentions also Ian Stevenson's research that revealed "nineteen documented cases of people who had precognitive glimpses of the sinking of the *Titanic*."[43]

Precognition in its various forms can be regarded as evidence of consciousness operating outside the bounds of

---

[42] A personal communication.

[43] Talbot, M. (1991), *The Holographic Universe,* New York: Harper Collins, p. 211 and notes.

space and time. It shows us that it is possible to glimpse future and bring back instantaneously to the present the knowledge or perception we have gained. It may not be necessary to change our view of reality, to propose, for example, the universe as a giant hologram to account for the ability of the mind to contact or perceive the future. Our perceptions may not always be accurate but that may be because there are other forces at work that we are ignorant of. But when they do prove to be accurate, even when a disaster or tragedy we have foreseen comes to pass, they demonstrate to us how much more we are than our physical bodies, how much more freedom our consciousness has than if it were no more than a prisoner of the brain.

There is one more phenomenon that needs mention. Charles Dickens described it in a chapter of *David Copperfield*. "We all have some experience of a feeling, that comes over us occasionally, of what we are saying and doing having been said and done before, in a remote time—of our having been surrounded, dim ages ago, by the same faces, objects and circumstances—of our knowing perfectly well what will be said next, as if we suddenly remember it."[44]

This experience is generally known as déjà vu although, as Dr. Arthur Funkhouser points out, that is not strictly accurate. The experience is not simply "already seen" but "already lived through." Funkhouser mentions two variants; one is a recollection of something previously felt and the other the experience of visiting a place for the first time and finding it wholly familiar.[45]

Various explanations have been proposed, such as that one may have read about the place or situation earlier and have forgotten that one has done so, or that an out-of-body excursion or a precognitive dream might be responsible, or even that the experience is a symptom of temporal lobe epilepsy. However if we can accept the validity of these experiences—and they occur so

---

[44] From Chapter 39. Quoted by Arthur Funkhausen, Scientific & Medical Network *Network* 57, spring 1995.
[45] Ibid.

frequently that it is difficult not to—we can see that they fit neatly into the concept of the non-locality of consciousness, along with the other types of experience that we have described in this chapter. If we grant that consciousness, while being largely affected by the operations of our brain, is ultimately not constrained by time and space, then the déjà vu experience and its variants can be accepted as manifestations of its non-locality. There is then no need to complicate the issue with theories of time or neuropsychology or to use déjà vu as evidence of reincarnation.

Most of the topics discussed in this chapter deal with the acquisition of information by means of extrasensory perception. Research into aspects of ESP, and also into psychokinesis, has sought to establish validity by using the nearest possible approximation to orthodox scientific method. By this time, it seems from the statistical evaluations to be clear to all except the prejudiced that this research has achieved what it set out to do. These abilities have been demonstrated to exist.

In the world outside the laboratory, however, most of us knew this all along. It is good to know that our experience can be scientifically validated, but it is hard to see how this can help us improve our performance, should we wish to, or add to the sum of human happiness or to the meaning or purpose of life. We need to learn how to improve the ability of mind/consciousness to affect matter, for example, how to obtain information through remote perception, how to communicate mind-to-mind. The more we can discover about our consciousness, the more of our potential as human beings we are likely to realize.

Is it worthwhile, then, to seek to make parapsychology acceptable as a science? By trying to do so, there is a danger of moving into the fallacy of scientism, of attempting to use scientific method in areas where it is simply not appropriate. Once we can agree that these various abilities exist we can see what they add to our understanding of consciousness: that it is not confined to the individual brain but can operate independently of time and space.

Now we shall go further into our exploration, probing into those areas where neither science nor scientism will help us find our way.

CHAPTER 3

DISTANT HEALING

"The imagination of man can act not only on his own body but even others and very distant bodies. It can fascinate and modify them; make them ill, or restore them to health."

(Avicenna, [980-1037A.D.])

Two women, Jane and Marina, are together in a quiet room in the suburbs of a northern city. Marina is lying on a massage table while Jane is working on the muscles of her right arm. In the bedroom of a house some three hundred miles away a third woman, Lisa, some years younger than the others, is lying on her bed. As Jane continues to work, Lisa feels the muscles in her right arm contracting and relaxing. In response to a word from Jane, Marina begins to breathe deeply. Lisa also breathes deeply. The treatment continues, with Marina's movements and responses being echoed by Lisa. As Jane steps back, indicating that she has finished, Marina sits up and removes a photograph from beneath her blouse. The photograph is of Lisa.

Jane is employing a therapy known as kinesiology. Her patient, Lisa, injured her arm in a motor accident. Marina, a friend of Jane, is being used as a surrogate for Lisa in this instance of distant healing.

Distant healing may be defined as affecting for the better the health of another person but without any physical contact being involved. In some instances the recipient may not even be aware that any process is taking place. Distant healing is usually considered a type of spiritual healing.

Now we have two words whose meaning we should establish. "Spiritual" presents an immediate difficulty as not only does the dictionary give several definitions (nine in the copy I have), but for many people the word brings along with it "airy-fairy" connotations, while for others the term is synonymous with "religious." Yet the dictionary puts "religious" as the last of its definitions. Dr. Rachel Remen, medical director of the Commonwealth Cancer Help Program, has a useful comment on this in a frequently reprinted piece from the *Noetic Science Review:*

"The spiritual is not the religious. A religion is a dogma, a set of beliefs about the spiritual and a set of practices that arise out of those beliefs. There are many religions and they tend to be mutually exclusive. . . . Yet the spiritual is inclusive. It is the deepest sense of belonging and participation. We all participate in the spiritual at all times, whether we know it or not. . . . Perhaps one might say that the spiritual is that realm of human experience with which religion attempts to connect us through dogma and practice. . . . Religion is a bridge to the spiritual—but the spiritual lies beyond religion." Dr. Remen adds, "The most important thing in defining spirit is the recognition that spirit is an essential need of human nature."

Healing means, literally, to make whole. While medical doctors may sometimes speak of "healing," Dr. Larry Dossey, author of *Healing Words* and *Prayer is Good Medicine,* says that he cannot recall the term "healer" ever being used in his medical training. "If my medical colleagues and I had been called healers, we would not have known whether we were being praised or damned. We were training to become surgeons, internists, and pathologists, not healers." He adds that there has been little change in the past three decades. "The concept of the healer remains virtually absent in medical training, and 'healing' continues to be used in a narrow physiologic sense." Dossey quotes a notice displayed in a hospital where spiritual healers had been treating patients contrary to accepted practice: "There will be no healing in this hospital!"[46]

It is the practitioners of complementary, or alternative, medicine who have adopted the term "healing" to describe what they do. In the United Kingdom the Confederation of Healing Organizations is the name of the overall body for the general oversight of complementary medicine. With six thousand members, the National Federation of Spiritual Healers is its largest contributory body. There are thousands more individuals who practice different kinds of healing work but belong to no regulatory organization. There is no comparable organization in the United States although there is an Office of Alternative Medicine as a constituent of the National Institutes of Health. Gradually orthodox medicine is becoming less dismissive of the efficacy of the various forms of "healing," although general acceptance is still far away. It is understandable that, in a profession where training and qualifications are vital, suspicion of those apparently lacking in these respects is widespread. Moreover, finding one's way amongst the various modalities—faith healing, reiki, seichem (a development from reiki), therapeutic touch, shiatsu, crystal healing, kinesiology are just a few—can be confusing, and where claims for their effectiveness are made it can be difficult to verify them. Papers published in authoritative peer-reviewed journals discussing trials and results using one or more of these methods do not as yet exist. Here and there, however, healers who belong to a recognized organization are permitted to work in hospitals and this concession is slowly being extended.

Dr. Daniel Benor, founder of the Doctor-Healer Network, would group most of the healing modalities together under the general term "spiritual healing." This kind of healing, he says, is given in two different ways: 1. With a laying-on of hands,

---

[46] Dr. Larry Dossey is a leading proponent of the art of healing. His ideas and experience are contained in five books: *Recovering the Soul* (1989), *Meaning & Medicine* (1991), *Healing Words* (1993), *Prayer is Good Medicine* (1996), *Be Careful What You Pray For* (1997).

with the hands lightly touching or held near the body (but not touching it) for about five to thirty minutes; and 2. As absent (distant) healing, by wish, meditation or prayer, which may be sent from any distance, even from many miles away.[47]

However, using the term "spiritual healing" presents a problem. There are those who aver that all healing is essentially spiritual, and others who, suspecting something esoteric, cavil at the term and would run a mile to avoid using it. Also, while saying "I am a doctor" is always acceptable—and is a recognizable statement of fact—saying "I am a healer" can sound presumptuous. It depends on the tone of voice. (Many healers are too diffident to make such a statement. "I am not comfortable with being called a healer," wrote one respondent. "I tend to say I am more like a plumber, if anything." And, despite the use of the word by healers who write books, I have never heard anyone treated by a healer refer to him or herself as a "healee.")

Those healers who seek to explain what they do— although many make no attempt at explanation—have several different ways of expressing it. They may talk of channeling energy from some source, often divine; of relying on intuition or using visualization; of seeing auras and working on them; of sending energy; or simply of sharing space. Daniel Wirth, director of Healing Sciences Research International, an organization based in Orinda, California, specializing in the study of alternative and complementary medicine, proposes four models, all of which would apply to distant as well as contact healing: 1. a transfer of electrical, electromagnetic, or other type of energy from practitioner to patient; 2. a specific state of consciousness within the practitioner or patient, or both; 3. an information exchange or communication by direct or intuitive processes between practitioner and patient; 4. a process which, according to those theorists with religious affiliations, is effective due solely to the Grace of God.[48]

---

[47] Scientific & Medical Network, *Wider Horizons, op cit,* p. 133
[48] *Advances, The Journal of Mind-Body Health,* vol. 9. No. 4 fall 1993.

Most healers would find one or more of these models with which they could agree. Some might add a fifth:"I don't know what I do. I just do it."

Jane Katra holds a doctorate in public health and has taught classes in nutrition and health at the University of Oregon. She has been a spiritual healer for over twenty years, and has sought to clarify what happens when she is working:

"I believe the kind of healing I do—spiritual healing— entails the belief in a unifying force in the universe that transcends the healer's (or any other individual's) separate identity. For me, spiritual healing involves a belief in a non-local primary consciousness, and this consciousness expresses itself or unfolds through a channel created when a healer shifts his or her attention from self-consciousness to helping another, and from separateness to joining together. I participate by surrendering my own will and entering a non-ordinary state of consciousness, so that a transpersonal mind may express itself through the opening provided by my willingness to be its vehicle. This merging of consciousness for the purpose of healing entails trust by both patient and healer. In my practice, it also embodies the concept that giving is receiving. I believe that my participation in a healing interaction lifts my consciousness as well as the consciousness of the patient. We make contact with a universal consciousness together, and I believe that connection permits a spiritual power to affect human activity."[49]

This explanation implies that distance between the two people involved makes no difference as it takes for granted that consciousness is not bound by space or time. The explanation is also based on Katra's belief about the way that consciousness operates. There is a growing body of evidence about what she calls the "merging of consciousness," which appears to cause the merging or synchronization of brainwave patterns, as can be seen by studying the EEG traces of pairs or groups of meditators. In laboratory testing this synchronization can also be observed with pairs of individuals

[49] Targ & Katra (1998), pp. 223-4.

using sensory stimulation, or through intentional attempts to communicate one with the other. Larry Dossey maintains that most healers work in what he calls "the state of non-local reality," which "involves participating in an altered state of consciousness that is very similar to meditation or prayer. In this state they see themselves and the patient as one, as the subject-object bridge is completely overcome."[50] One experienced healer points out that there is no need for a period of intense concentration; the connection or identification with the patient may take only a moment's thought.

With reference to brain-wave patterns, there was a pioneering experiment in 1991 by Dr. Edgar Wilson, who was director of the Colorado Association for Psychophysiologic Research. He was studying the way that healers worked, and came across a seventy-seven-year-old New Zealander, Rod Campbell, who had discovered twenty-five years previously that "he had something about his hands that could transmit healing energy to others." In a lecture delivered in 1992, Dr. Wilson described the way Rod worked:

"Rod would hold his hands over someone, who would feel warmth, vibration, energy moving. . . . We had brain-wave measuring apparatus on both subjects, and we would switch back and forth between the two, and I had a magnetometer above Rod's head. He made beautiful spikes of ascending frequency and power as he went into his healing mode. I'd say, 'Rod, you can heal him now,' and he would do it; I'd say, 'Rod, you can stop,' and he would. He said it just came through him. When he was working on someone, the subject's frequency would change, and change back when he'd finished."

Although the brain-wave frequencies of Rod and his subject were not consistently identical they changed at precisely the same moments. Wilson commented: "It seems that suddenly there's a shift from the center of the head out to the temporal areas as you go from loss of time/space awareness to an awareness of deep empathy, those moments in our lives

---

[50] Dossey, L. (1989), *Recovering the Soul*, New York: Bantam, p. 59.

when we lose the sense of separateness from each other and from our world. Those are the moments when we are able to strip away that last little vestige of fear, to know that we are part and parcel of the same stuff, transcendent stuff."[51]

Replicating Wilson's experiment would not be difficult, although it is already established that at moments of focused concentration the brain's electrical activity increases sharply. However this type of research has so far had little attention paid to it. Yet as a means of investigating what actually happens in the brain-wave frequencies of participants in distant healing it would be comparatively simple to activate, using a protocol modelled on that which has proved applicable to remote viewing. It would at least provide a clue to what is still largely a mystery.

Of all the distant healing modalities, prayer is probably the oldest and the most frequently applied. Most of us at one time or another have found ourselves praying for the recovery of someone we love who is seriously ill, whether we think of ourselves as "religious" or not. Indeed, orthodox religion may have little to do with it. Religion organizes prayer, but there is no evidence that the kings and queens of the United Kingdom, members of governments, or the clergy, who are prayed for regularly in church services, live longer, have happier lives, or suffer less from sickness as a result. Within a conventional religious framework the way that prayer is worded necessitates the intervention of an external god to whom is given the responsibility of responding to our requests. This, however, is not the only way of praying. Daniel Wirth suggests that "by concentrating on a source of healing that is outside of ourselves and accessible to only a chosen few, we are directing responsibility for healing to someone or something outside ourselves. To take such an approach would be to miss completely the most important point which true spiritual healers and the forefathers of medicine have propounded in reference to the healing process— that all healing, whether spiritual, psychological, or physical,

---

[51] Russell (1993).

originates from within the individual and is activated by true love and compassion."[52] The words of the Dominican theologian and mystic Meister Eckhart (c. 1260-1327) are relevant here:"You may call God love; you may call God goodness. But the best name for God is compassion." With this in mind, the simplest and perhaps the most appropriate healing prayer consists of the four words "Thy will be done," uttered with all the love and compassion in one's heart.

But can prayer heal, and if so, how? In *The Conscious Universe,* Dr. Dean Radin looks at the case against:

"The orthodox opinion that praying for a distant person cannot heal, or that any form of distant mental healing is impossible, is based on the conventional belief that the mind is simply an emergent property of the physical brain," says Dr. Radin. As a result, the mind gets "localized" in the brain, and is seen to be dependent on this organ's physical functions. If we grant this premise, it means that a healer located at A cannot affect the physiology of a patient at location B (at a considerable distance) because there is no apparent mechanism by which the patient at location B can possibly be affected. This is why distant mental healing is impossible and why praying for others is only wishful thinking, according to this physical model of consciousness."This logic is unassailable if the standard scientific assumptions are correct," says Radin."But are they?"

In the 1960s, the idea of mind-body connections—that changes in the mind can affect the physical body—was regarded for the most part as dangerous nonsense. Yet anyone who has been aware of the turmoil in the stomach and intestines before a dreaded interview will know that this is not nonsense. Moreover, recent studies have shown that medical staff may speed death in a patient after a terminal illness has been diagnosed by giving the patient that information. Today the idea that the mind can affect the condition of the physical body is widely accepted even though the mechanisms that underlie the link are not fully understood. Evidence that the

---

[52] *Advances, op cit.*

mind can affect not only its own body but also distant physical systems—other bodies—is beginning to accumulate, although we still don't know how it does so. Until very recently medical science has ignored or rejected this evidence. Now, however, controlled, double-blind studies in distant healing are in progress in a number of medical schools and hospitals and nearly sixty medical schools in the U. S. have developed courses in religious and spiritual issues. [53]

One often-quoted study using prayer from a distance took place in the early 1980s in the coronary care unit of San Francisco General Hospital under the auspices of Dr. Randolph Byrd. It involved 393 patients who had, or were suspected of having had, a heart attack. They were divided into two groups, each receiving the same good quality medical care. One group was prayed for by prayer groups throughout the U. S., whose members were "born again" Christians, both Protestant and Roman Catholic, and who were active members of a local church. Each patient was prayed for daily by several of these 'intercessors' who knew only their first names, their diagnosis and the outline of their condition. This was a controlled double-blind study with neither the medical staff nor the patients knowing who was being prayed for. The severity of illness in both groups was statistically equal. At the end of the study, it was found that the prayed-for group did better in several ways, with, as examples, fewer patients developing congestive heart failure or requiring antibiotics or the use of breathing tubes. [54]

This study, however, does not seem to have aroused much enthusiasm in orthodox medical circles. One can understand that with the training they receive and the limited resources at their disposal very few doctors would even consider entering what they fear might prove to be a professional minefield. Also the study itself raises certain questions.

---

[53] See Scientific & Medical Network *Network*, no. 70, Aug 1999, p. 19.
[54] The study is reported in full in the *Southern Medical Journal*, 1988, 81[7], pp. 826-829.

Dr. Byrd himself and the members of the prayer groups were all devout Christians; by not praying for one group of patients were they therefore deliberately denying them the possibility of divine help? It would be helpful to know what the members of the prayer groups believed they were doing. Were they leaving it to God? Or did they think their own minds or intentions were important participants? Dr. Byrd indicates that it was the Judeo-Christian God who was prayed to and admits that how God acted in the situation was unknown, questioning whether the prayer groups were treated by God as a whole or if only the prayers of individuals were answered. Also it was not known if any patients prayed themselves or which of them held any religious convictions. It is interesting to note that when it was suggested to one close-knit group of AIDS patients that a small-scale experiment on similar lines be enacted, they rejected the idea on the grounds that if prayer was to be part of their therapy it was to be applied to all or to none.[55]

The Byrd study brings into focus some of the problems associated with assessing spiritual healing. First, it is to date the study that is most often referred to in detail in the popular literature. This indicates how difficult it is to set up a study involving a large enough number of patients and keeping within a tightly designed protocol. Then while it appears to indicate the efficacy of prayer it provides no scientifically acceptable evidence as to how prayer works. The patients in this study were aware that the experiment was taking place and had signed consent forms but they did not know which group they were in and therefore did not know if they were being prayed for. It would help to know which group they believed they were in, but, as it is, there is no way of knowing if patient expectation played any part in the results. In two other smaller trials, in which the patients were ignorant that they were involved in an experiment, the differences in improvement between the prayed-for and not-prayed-for groups were not statistically

---

[55] Personal communication.

significant, although in both trials the prayed-for group, to quote the findings, "did slightly better."[56]

While the Byrd study specifically involved Christian prayer, a more recent project at the California Pacific Medical Center in San Francisco made use of a number of experienced professional healers who had already undertaken healing at a distance, including medical professionals as well as a wide variety of lay people. This project involved AIDS patients with a comparable degree of illness; it incorporated two studies, a pilot with twenty patients and a larger follow-up study with forty patients, each group divided into a control and treatment group of equal size. Described as "a methodologically airtight collaborative research project" neither the patients nor the researchers knew to which group individual patients belonged.

The procedure was described in a summary of the project published in *Noetic Sciences Review*. "The healing intervention consisted of each patient in the treatment group receiving healing efforts from one healer at a time, one hour per day, six days per week, for ten weeks. The healers worked on a rotating schedule so that every week each patient was treated by a new healer. Thus, by the end of the study, each patient had received 'healing effort' from a total of ten different healers." The healers used their own techniques, which might include energetic or spiritual healing, working with chakras, using prayer or visualization, utilizing crystals, or shamanic practices.

Six months after the treatment ended, the patients were assessed by a variety of accepted methods. "Patients in the treatment group had acquired significantly fewer new AIDS-defining diseases than people in the control group, their overall illness severity scores were significantly lower, they had significantly fewer hospitalizations, and those hospitalizations were significantly shorter. In addition, treatment patients showed significant improvement on psychological status, including decreased depression, decreased anxiety, decreased anger, and increased

---

[56] *Advances in Parapsychological Research*, vol. 8, pp. 143-145.

vigor, compared to controls." Interestingly, nearly half of the control group guessed they were being treated and about the same proportion in the treatment group guessed they were not being treated, which seems to discount for this trial any suggestion that patient expectation was a factor. [57]

Following on from the Byrd study in the use of prayer, but with many refinements, a major experiment on prayer and healing was launched in 1997. At the time of this writing, the experiment is still in progress. It is under the direction of Dr. Herbert Benson of the Mind/Body Medical Institute in Boston, Massachusetts, and is funded by the John Templeton Foundation. This study involved 1,800 patients at three major American hospitals, all of whom were due to undergo coronary artery bypass graft surgery. These patients were divided into three equal groups: one group to be prayed for by members of various religious organizations and one group not to be prayed for. These patients were told they *might* or *might not* be prayed for but did not know which group they were in. The third group were told they *would* be prayed for. (There was no fourth group told that it would *not* be prayed for!) A two-year follow-up period is planned.

Commenting on this study, Professor Russell Stannard, a physicist and a trustee of the Templeton Foundation, points out that it aims at testing just one aspect of prayer. "Prayer in its totality is multi-faceted, consisting as it does of worship, thanksgiving, contrition, self-dedication, contemplation, meditation, etc. Intercession is but one component. Not only that, the experiment is concerned solely with those intercessory prayers offered up on behalf of strangers. Like many others, I suspect that the central core of intercessory prayer has more to do with the agonising, involved prayers of loved ones and intimate friends than with those of distant strangers." [58]

A ray of light—a very small one, by no means a searchlight—on distant healing is thrown by the results of a very

---

[57] *Noetic Sciences Review*, no. 49, Aug-Nov 1999. Full report was published in the *Western Journal of Medicine*, December 1998.
[58] *The Christian Parapsychologist*, vol. 12, no. 7, September 1997.

small study involving only three patients, by Dr. H. Rehder, a hospital doctor in Hamburg, in 1955. These patients were confined to bed and had been "medically abandoned." Rehder, who seemed to care deeply about his patients, contacted a famous healer in Munich who agreed to heal these patients from a distance, sending healing at specific times in the mornings. Rehder told no one about this and no effects on the patients were observed. Then, without telling his patients what had already happened, Rehder informed them about this healer, gave them a book by him to read, and did his best to convince them that distant healing would work. He further told them what time of day the healing would be sent—a time when he knew the healer would *not* be working. He told the healer nothing of this.

Reviewing this study, the researcher Sybo Schouten of the University of Utecht commented: "The results were quite astonishing. In all three cases, in addition to strong feelings of increased well-being, various objective improvements in the conditions of the patients were observed. Within a few months all three were well enough to leave the hospital. According to Rehder these results were not unexpected. It is the belief that counts, not the method that the healer adopts. If nothing works any more, then often belief still does. Belief can become very strong, especially in the case of patients who are desperate and have already suffered for a long period of time, and partly because, due to illness, patients tend to become less critical." [59]

Such assessments as are possible indicate that the healing effects may be more noticeable when the receiver is either aware of what is happening or believes that something is happening, although the California study does not seem to bear this out. One of the unknowns in the Byrd study is what the patients themselves believed. It would be important to know how many of the patients actually believed (a) that distant healing through prayer could work and (b) that they

---

[59] *Advances in Parapsychological Research,* vol. 8, p. 138.

themselves were actually in the prayed-for group. This also applies in part to the Benson study.

Much of the argument about healing by prayer is encapsulated in the report of a recently published case, *Effects of a Prayer Circle on a Moribund Premature Infant*. A baby girl, known as J. A., was born some two months prematurely to a black mother, aged thirty-six, who had three previous miscarriages and suffered from diabetes and hyperthyroidism (an overactive thyroid gland). The baby weighed just over 2.5 pounds. According to the case report: "She was blue and floppy with a heart rate of less than 100 beats per minute that was not increasing. The baby's skin was bruised and she was bleeding from both eyes." She was taken to the neonatal intensive care unit, a tube was inserted into her larynx and she was linked to a ventilator to enable her to breathe. Her condition was thoroughly examined and recorded and treated as far as was possible. After three hours her parents were told how sick she was and that there were no signs of improvement "despite maximum medical therapy." The outlook appeared hopeless. The parents agreed with the medical staff to withdraw support. They asked for the baby to be baptized first. "To show respect for the family the medical team retreated and no further therapies were initiated or withdrawn."

The baby was a little more than four hours old when the chaplain, the parents, the baby's nurse, and a respiratory therapist made a prayer circle around the bed. The baby was then baptized. Less than an hour later an improvement in her condition was recorded. Progress continued to be noted until nearly eleven hours after birth the baby was stable enough to be moved to an incubator.

Thereafter progress continued. On day twelve she began to feed and by day twenty-one she was feeding normally and breathing room air. A couple of problems yielded to solution and she was sent home with no medication and no oxygen. At the sixth-month follow-up visit J. A. weighed nearly twelve pounds and showed developmental skills "appropriate for a two- to four-month old infant." As of October 1998, all was going well and no treatment was needed.

The authors of this report, Shelley Cypher Springer, M.D., and Dorothea J. Eicher, M.D., of the Medical University of South Carolina, review the concept of non-locality of action and refer to the large number of studies of near and distant effects on plants, animals, and humans. They note that "most of the experiments exploring mental intention have not appeared in the traditional medical literature ... [but] there is evidence that the historically mutually exclusive relationship between medicine and spirituality is converging." Having reviewed J.A.'s case history they add, "It is quite intriguing that the baby's dramatic and rapid turnaround was temporally related to the initiation of only one additional intervention—the prayer circle." They continue: "The rest of this baby's clinical course continued to be unusually free of the typical complications seen in extremely premature, very low birth weight babies."

In their final paragraphs, Springer and Eicher describe the evidence in support of intercessory prayer as "provocative" although they admit that "compelling scientific evidence is lacking." They conclude as follows:

"Premature infants present a unique study opportunity into this question. Unable to pray for themselves, control groups composed of infants are free of this potential confounding factor. One could further assume that prayer from family and friends would be equally distributed among control and intervention groups, leaving the intervention group exposed to 'more.' Only further study, designed in randomized, controlled fashion, might determine whether intercessory prayer should be considered a useful adjunct to conventional medical treatment for critically ill premature infants." [60] It is worth noting here that in this case it was what Stannard described above as "the agonizing, involved prayers of loved ones and intimate friends," that appeared to affect the outcome. The scientific obsession for measurement, with randomized controlled studies, seems totally irrelevant here.

So we should ask ourselves whether further study is really needed. Does every healing process have to be subjected to

---

[60] *Alternative Therapies*, vol. 5. no. 2. March 1999.

scientific analysis and treated with suspicion unless the results are published in peer-reviewed journals? And should it be discovered after hundreds of trials that one distant healing process—let us say intercessory prayer—is statistically effective, what then? Should each hospital have a prayer manager and a praying team that springs into action, or falls to its knees, when a patient is seriously ill but has no relatives or friends able or even willing to pray for him? And should it be discovered after all those trials that there is no evidence that intercessory prayer works, what might the consequences be? For the parents of J.A., as for the parents of all sick children, it does not matter whether the effects of prayer are scientifically validated or not. All that matters is that anyone who prays for the welfare of another does not become fixated on results. For who can say with any certainty what the best outcome for another person is?

Yet, for the sake of our own future, it is vital that we discover all we can about the human capacity for healing. Reliance solely on mechanical medicine will in no way guarantee that future, and the cost of treatment in the mechanical regime is already rising alarmingly. Now that we are beginning to realize what less civilized societies have always known, that the *intention* of one person, whether expressed in words of prayer or not, may benefit the health and well-being of another, we owe it to ourselves and our successors to explore that realisation in every possible way.

Does it matter whether or not we know "how it works?" "In medicine we are often forced to dwell in a theoretical fog," says Dr. Larry Dossey. "For example, for the longest time we did not know how penicillin worked—or aspirin, quinine, colchine, and many other therapies. We often know that something works before understanding how it works. So it is with the distant effects of mental intentions. . . . Similarly, scientists have no idea how the brain produces consciousness or even if it does; yet no one favors ignoring either the brain or consciousness simply because we don't precisely know how they are related. Likewise, there is no reason to jettison the rich database of distant intentionality simply because we have not yet been able to integrate it with the rest of science."

This database includes thirty-seven experiments comprising 655 sessions held at the Mind Science Foundation in San Antonio, Texas. In these experiments, individuals attempted to influence the nervous systems of remote participants. Of these experiments, 57 percent produced significant results, where only 5 percent would be expected by chance.[61] A review of the Mind Science experiments, together with replications at the Universities of Edinburgh and Nevada, concluded that "across experiments the data show a relatively consistent effect size that appears replicable and robust. . . . Whereas the distant intentionality effect sizes are small, they are comparable to—or in some cases eight times larger than—those reported in some recent medical studies that have been heralded as medical breakthroughs."

The authors of the review noted that "various remote intentionality influences reviewed in the report may occur not only non-locally with respect to space (as these studies have already indicated) but also non-locally with respect to time." In their conclusion, referring to their search for "a better understanding of the mechanisms underlying distant healing," they raise what they describe as the most fundamental issue: "whether consciousness is *real* in some non-trivial sense. Can it be 'causal'? Results reported here and elsewhere suggest that consciousness may be causal, or that, in some ultimate sense, there may be no causality—only a whole system evolving. In the latter case, distant intentionality might not be an anomaly—but part of another order of reality."[62]

Another area of research was investigated by the Spindrift organization in Salem, Oregon, which conducted trials over eighteen years to assess the effect of prayer on growing organisms. In one series of experiments, to quote a statement on their web site: "Using hundreds of thousands of beans, seeds, yeast cells, mold, etc., and dividing them into control groups

---

[61] For references see Braud in *Body Mind Spirit*, edited by Charles Tart (1997), Charlottesville, Va.: Hampton Roads Publishing.
[62] *Alternative Therapies*, vol. 3, no. 6. summer 1997, pp. 62-73.

(non-prayed-for groups) and treated groups (prayed-for groups), Spindrift has subjected the above to stress and measured and compared the responses—the return to normal—of the organisms." The results appeared to show that the "prayed-for" organisms did better than the others by just over 3 percent, with a doubled treatment of prayer increasing the improvement by 5.4 percent. Spindrift also claimed that non-directed prayer, where the experimenter simply prays for what is best for the organism, seemed to produce better results than prayer directed towards a specific and stated goal.

The founders of Spindrift, Bruce Klingbeil and his son John, both Christian Scientists, hoped that their test results would "constitute a body of knowledge, never before available, applicable to the solving of problems including disease." Nevertheless they were heavily criticized by their own church for attempting to experiment scientifically with prayer, and voluntary helpers in their experiments who belonged to other churches also came under attack.

After twelve years of working with plant seeds but without obtaining any scientific recognition, Spindrift moved away from reliance on prayer and designed two tests intended to demonstrate "the power of thought apart from the mediation of the human nervous system." One test was called "Visual Image, Unconscious Response" and involved guessing the contents of twenty-four envelopes, each containing one of two pictures, one attractive and the other unattractive. The second test "consisted of the electronic generation of random binary sequences." The results they obtained, however, were not regarded as conclusive by those who refereed their work or studied their findings. Then in 1993, the Klingbeils published a detailed report of their researches, *The Spindrift Papers: Exploring Prayer and Healing through the Experimental Test.* In an interview they said, "There is really nothing more we can do on our own.... If anything comes of this, it will have to be by the replication and extension and revisions of others. We can do no more."

A month after their report was published, both father and son committed suicide. It is a sad story, which might have had a happier ending if Spindrift had received more understanding from the churches and more cooperation, especially from scientists experienced in data handling. The Klingbeils deserve recognition as pioneers in the field, and researchers who have examined their work generally agree with Dr. Daniel Benor that "there is sufficiently encouraging material here to warrant further study."[63]

A major problem with distant healing, as far as health authorities are concerned, is that many of the healers themselves have no medical training, belong to no recognized organization, and do not keep detailed records. There are exceptions however. A highly qualified retired professor of surgery, an examiner for the Royal College of Surgeons, went into private practice dealing with a variety of patients whose problems had defeated their regular doctors. He employed a number of unconventional means including an intriguing method of distant healing. In the evenings he would insert a card for each of his patients into a carousel on a photographic slide projector. He would set the timer for intervals of a minute or thereabouts and then switch on. My wife was one of his patients. From time to time, perhaps once a week, she would stop whatever she was doing and say, "Prof's coming through." We would note the exact time and check with him later. That was the time, it transpired, when my wife's card moved into the gate on the projector, which indicated to him that he should now direct his intention towards her. There was, however, no way of telling whether this or his other ministrations contributed more to the well-being of his patients. What can be said is that his success rate with "difficult patients," which he interpreted as patients whose doctors had difficulty in knowing what to do with, was remarkable.

The idea of using an electrically operated machine seems to have been loosely adapted from the healing modality

---

[63] For the Spindrift story see *Journal of the American Society for Psychical Research*, vol. 87, Oct 1993 and vol. 90, Jan 1996; also see Dossey *Healing Words*, and the Spindrift web site.

known as radionics. This method of treatment was launched in the 1920s and became moderately popular in the U.K., Canada, Australia, and New Zealand in the 1970s and early 1980s. Radionics was said to be able to "diagnose mental, bodily, and spiritual afflictions from a drop of blood or a lock of hair, photograph a diseased organ on a plate to which not a ray of light has been admitted, and cure a patient at a distance before the practitioner has become consciously aware of the case." Its practitioners developed reliance on a form of dowsing and on readings from electronic machines that produced diagnoses and indicated treatments. A numerical rate was ascribed to each disease and various books of rates were available for practitioners to consult. There was an attempt in all this to make radionics acceptable to orthodox science, an attempt that signally failed.

In 1982, *Radionics: Science or Magic?* was published by David Tansley, a leading radionics practitioner. Tansley was convinced that the method could work but for years had been heading in the wrong direction. By this time the term "radionic analysis" was being used instead of "diagnosis" and Tansley described how a practitioner would report on what he accomplished. "He would probably say that he had measured the functional integrity of each of a series of physical organ systems and determined the causes of any disease present in the patient at a distance. He might go on to further elaborate the states of the chakras and the subtle bodies according to the Theosophical construct of the occult anatomy, and to pinpoint their imbalances in relationship to the picture of the physical organs." Then Tansley adds, "The problem with this form of analysis is that there is no guarantee that the analysis is correct or otherwise accurate in physical terms."

Tansley believed that the instruments relied on by many practitioners did nothing. Mind and thought, he held, were the primary factors. "As long as we keep worshipping at the shrine of every new bit of instrumentation that appears, we are going to be pledging ourselves at best to a mechanistic view of radionics or at worst a mixture of physical and para-physical factors. What needs to be done is to place radionics once and

for all on a mental healing basis." Tansley posited two dimensions of reality: Dimension I, left-brain connected, is the
dimension of physical reality where life is governed by the
known physical laws; and Dimension II, right-brain connected,
is the dimension of transcendent holistic reality, "outside of
time and not conditioned by time" and "the area of consciousness in which the true processes of radionics function."
He saw distant diagnosis and treatment as Dimension II
techniques.

Tansley was a progressive thinker. In some ways he was
fighting a losing battle as radionics did not succeed in finding
a firm and respectable niche in complementary treatments.
But he did come to see that distant diagnosis and healing are
functions of human consciousness and do not have to be
made acceptable to orthodox science by explanation in terms
of radio waves or electrical forces running through a machine.

A healing modality that has become popular in the past
few decades is reiki, described as "an ancient healing art," and
claimed to be at least three thousand years old. It was revived
in Japan in the late 1800s, entering the U. S. via Hawaii in the
1930s and then moving into Europe. Practitioners are taught to
engage in distant, or absent, healing by using visualization,
"creating a representation in your mind of someone who
needs healing," as well as "sending" the reiki symbols they
would use if the patient were physically present. Reiki teaches
that according to "Natural Laws" the healing "energy" can be
transmitted regardless of distance, provided that the practitioner follows the approved procedures and the recipient is
aware that the process is taking place. Recipients of reiki healing do not have to be physically or mentally ill; the process is
intended for their general well-being. As with all reiki healing,
permission must be obtained from the recipient beforehand.
At the same time, the sending of absent healing is said to benefit the practitioner also.

The notion of "sending" is important to reiki. "Sending
energy, sending love, sending light or colors, praying, thinking
of someone, and imagining someone well are all distant healing techniques," comments Diane Stein in *Essential Reiki.*

However none of these is absolutely necessary. "Lighting a candle above the photograph of someone who needs healing is another method, or placing the picture in the hands of a Kwan Yin or Mary statue." It is the use of the symbols, which the practitioner has to learn from a master, that distinguishes reiki. "The reiki symbols add effectiveness and increase the power of psychic healing tremendously. Whatever method of distant healing you use is positive. Continue using it. Just add the reiki symbols, and it becomes a reiki healing."[64]

The popularity of reiki is instanced by the fact that in a recent issue of a "new age" magazine out of forty-two advertisements for various healing modalities, including such established methods as yoga and aromatherapy, nineteen were for reiki. With its three degrees, attunements, symbols, masters, world view, and, until recently, considerable charges for "initiations," reiki appears highly structured and complicated. It also appears to be based on a belief—that energy can be sent over a distance without diminishing as the distance increases—that runs counter to the findings of physics. Yet it is possible, as David Tansley suggested with radionics, that reiki distant healing is simply a function of human consciousness with the only requirement being the healer's intention. Everything else, including the symbols, simply acts as means of enabling the practitioner to focus intent and move into a state of consciousness in which healing may take place.

Recent years have seen a new interest in the ancient practice of shamanism, largely owing to the research of Mircea Eliade, and the practical and popularising approach of Michael Harner. It is easy to dismiss this interest as merely another aspect of new ageism, but not very sensible to do so. Harner makes the point that "Shamanism is the most widespread and ancient methodological system of mind-body healing known to humanity." Both he and Eliade refer to the similarities in shamanic methods and beliefs across the world, which Harner explains by suggesting that over thousands of

---

[64] Stein, D. (1995), *Essential Reiki*, Freedom, Calif.: The Crossing Press.

years "people in ecological and cultural situations that were often extremely different came nonetheless to the same conclusions as to the basic principles and methods of shamanic power and healing."[65]

To perform his task, whether it is to do with healing, prophecy, or ensuring adequate food for his community, the shaman, as Professor E. C. Krupp says, "recognizing that power is distributed throughout the cosmos ... must be able to travel supernaturally to wherever power resides. Usually this is accomplished by trance. The shaman enters an altered state of consciousness and interacts with the spirits, often assisted by spirit helpers, supernatural allies willing to endorse the shaman's case."[66] The shaman works through his own guardian spirit. In some shamanic cultures he may be assisted by several spirits, each of them performing a separate function.

Distant healing is frequently practiced in shamanic societies, especially where the sick person is in a hospital where shamans are not permitted to work. While practices differ in some details around the world, in a typical North American shamanic culture every tribal member has a guardian spirit in the shape of a power animal, which they acquire in the course of a shamanic journey to the "Lower World." If a person is seriously ill, it means that he has lost his guardian spirit. The shaman takes himself to a quiet, dark place, closes his eyes and sings his power song to himself, using his rattle. He calls on his own power animal to help. He faces the direction where the patient is located and visualizes the patient lying in bed. Once he has the patient in his sights, he starts a journey to the Lower World to recover a power animal for him. When he has it, he sends it mentally and emotionally to the patient in his hospital bed. Next the shaman calls on his own power animal. When he feels it near him, he sends some of its power

---

[65] See Eliade, M. (1972), *Shamanism*, Princeton UP, and Harner, M. (1980) *The Way of the Shaman*, New York: Harper & Row.
[66] Krupp, E. (1997), *Skywatchers, Shamans, and Kings*, New York: John Wiley.

into the patient's guardian to make it dance. He continues until he sees the animal jumping, dancing, or running around the patient. After the patient recovers, the shaman may ask him if he had any dreams or visions of any particular animal. Should the patient remain seriously ill, the process is repeated every few hours until he is out of danger.

The shaman sends power from his power animal only to the patient's animal, not to the patient himself. The power has to be filtered through the guardian. Also the shaman does not send his own energy as this would exhaust him. He uses his guardian's power instead. It is the guardian, the shaman's animal, that does the work. The shaman *is*; the guardian *does*. In this kind of shamanic distant healing, it is claimed that the patient does not need to believe in shamanism nor does he have to know what is being done for the procedure to work.

Soul loss, the loss of our vital essence or our spiritual being, is seen in shamanic culture to be a prime cause of illness. Sandra Ingerman, trained in counselling psychology and in shamanic practice, says that soul loss in today's world is often "a result of such traumas as incest, abuse, loss of a loved one, surgery, accident, illness, miscarriage, abortion, the stress of combat, or addiction." To track and retrieve the soul the shaman moves into a different state of consciousness and with the help of the spirits journeys into the non-ordinary world where the soul has fled. Ingerman says, "Shamans are just the instrument through which the power of the universe works. Therefore, asking the spirits for help and trusting that they will be there is the basis of the shaman's responsibilities."[67]

A variant of soul retrieval is practiced by Fawn Journeyhawk-Bender, a Native American shaman. Professor Stanley Krippner, writing in *Alternative Therapies*, 1997, describes what she does. "She often works with post-traumatic stress disorder, especially as experienced by Vietnam veterans whose souls were lost in Vietnam. She claims to "journey" to

---

[67] Ingerman, S. (1991), *Soul Retrieval*. San Francisco: Harper.

Vietnam and plead with the dead Vietnamese who have captured the soul to forgive and release it, so that the veteran—who is now filled with remorse and new understandings—can get on with his or her life." What a psychiatrist would describe as severe depression, Krippner points out, would to a shaman be a trivialisation of the problem. To a shaman, soul loss is worse than death.

Fawn also fights with the spirits of alcohol, cocaine, and heroin on behalf of addicts who have lost their souls to one or more of these. On such "expeditions" she takes her power animals with her as she herself is at risk. She sees these drug spirits as powerful individuals who must be defeated; they are too ruthless to be bargained with. [68]

Shamans move into the special state of consciousness in which they work by praying, singing or chanting, using rattles and drums. The guardian, the power animal, is always benevolent. It may be a fox, otter, monkey, bear, any sort of bird—whatever is met on the shamanic journey. It may be a mythological beast—a dragon or griffin. Lame Deer, of the Lakota Sioux, described his meeting thus: "All of a sudden I heard a big bird crying, and then quickly he hit me on the back, touched me with his spread wings. I heard the cry of an eagle, loud above the voices of the other birds. It seemed to say, 'We have been waiting for you. We knew you would come. Now you are here. Your trail leads from here . . . you will have a ghost with you always—another self.'" [69]

What is especially interesting in this type of healing is that the patient may be present or at a distance—and in the latter instance also ignorant of the shaman's activities. Hence the power of belief does not necessarily enter into the healing process. It can be argued that the patient might have recovered anyway—and, of course, there are no statistics available and no record of the percentage of patients who failed to recover. These are the same arguments that may be applied to almost all episodes and narratives of distant healing. In the last

---

[68] *Alternative Therapies* vol. 3, no. 6. Nov 1997.
[69] See Eliade and Harper, *op cit.*

resort, however, we may doubt whether statistics and percentages merit the importance we tend to ascribe to them.

We have seen that evidence is now beginning to accumulate that the *intention* of one person can affect the physical or mental well-being of another. We can suggest, as Jane Katra does, that this happens through the merging of consciousnesses. But this still does not tell us "how it works." Larry Dossey says, "We simply don't know how the mind of one person can engage in 'action at a distance' to bring about healthful changes in someone else." He feels it necessary to warn healers against describing their activities in the language of classical physics, when they say, as some do, that healing "energy" is employed. He adds: "Conventional forms of energy are an insufficient explanation for what we observe in spiritual healing experiments. In them the 'energy' does not fade away with increasing distance, and it cannot be shielded, as we would expect if ordinary forms of energy were involved."[70] All the same, physics does not have a monopoly on the term "energy" and if healers themselves feel that it is the most appropriate word available to describe what they do there is no reason to discard it in an attempt to avoid criticism from those who don't credit what they do anyway.

Another comment on this use of the term "energy" comes from Georgetown University research professor Candace Pert. In her recent book, *Molecules of Emotion*, she says, "Many ancient and alternative healing methods refer to a mysterious force we cannot measure with Western instruments, that which animates the entire organism and is known as 'subtle' energy by metaphysicians, *prana* by Hindus, *chi* by Chinese. Freud called it libido, Reich called it orgone energy, Henry Bergson called it *elan vitale*. It's my belief that this mysterious energy is actually the free flow of information carried by the biochemicals of emotion, the neuropeptides and their receptors."[71] The keyword here may be "information," for it would

---

[70] Scientific & Medical Network *Network*, no. 63, April 1997.
[71] Pert, C. (1997), *Molecules of Emotion*, New York: Simon & Schuster, p. 276.

seem that this is what is transferred whether by the sharing of consciousness, the biochemicals of emotion, or one of the forms of subtle energy mentioned above.

None of this implies that in contact healing—hands-on— there may not be a transfer or stimulation of what might be termed energy in orthodox scientific terms. But in distant healing both space and time are transcended. On this issue, biophysicist Beverly Rubik, director of the Institute for Frontier Sciences, Oakland, California, says, "According to conventional physical theory, acceptance of this hypothesis would require extending Bell's theorem of non-locality in quantum physics and the principle of causality to consciousness. A number of experiments on the effects of conscious intention, some relevant to healing, have demonstrated physical effects, offering precedents for extending Bell's theorem and the principle of causality."[72] That is one possibility, but conventional physical theory, as we have seen, is not the only path to follow.

It is misleading, however, to assert as confidently as some healers do that distant healing can be interpreted as involving "something" that is given or sent. Jane Katra believes that distant healing occurs "as a manifestation of a joining of minds, resonance, and entering into a universal consciousness. It involves a surrender of individual will on the part of the healer, with no personal effort exerted, no specific outcome designated on the physical level, and a state of being that is characterized by a 'letting' instead of a 'doing'. This letting is a willingness to be an instrument of the general well-being of another in an impersonal, non-emotional way. That state has been called a state of compassion or love, and it activates spiritual healing, which we believe is the manifestation of spiritual consciousness in human awareness." Katra adds: "I do not understand how it works, or why some people have instant relief from pain or other symptoms that lasts for years, while others experience only temporary or partial symptom relief, or no relief at all."

---

[72] *Hemi-Sync Journal*, winter 1997 (publication of The Monroe Institute) and *Alternative Therapies* vol. 1, no. 1.

In Katra's view, then, the healer "does" nothing. Nor does she think that, in distant healing, the healer is a channel for "healing energy," whether this comes from a divine or semi-divine source or just simply comes. All the same, whatever the individual healer, whether reiki practitioner or shaman, may believe, there is no reason why it should affect the healing process provided that, as Katra says, there is a surrender of individual will. Some of us are more comfortable when we function within a belief structure. The only proviso is that we do not seek to impose our belief structure on others. If we do this, it is as if we are telling them that they may listen to the radio provided that they are tuned only to the program of our choice.

Is it possible to arrive at any conclusions? A review of research in distant healing by Dr. Elisabeth Targ, director of the Complementary Medicine Research Institute, San Francisco, cast doubt on the design of many studies and concluded that more research was urgently needed. She commented that "in real-life situations, distant healing is rarely set up as the isolated 'treatment' we are attempting to study." In practice, she suggests, "it most likely functions as a potentate of other mechanisms including mind-body effects, patient expectation, and medical intervention." She noted that in many of the experiments that produce positive results "unselected volunteers" appear to be as effective as "designated psychic healers" and feels that "it is conceivable that distant healing largely functions unconsciously, subtly integrated into each procedure, each healing goal, and each intention as set by the medical practitioner."[73]

In another review published in 1997, the Dutch researcher Sybo Schouten, following an examination of recent data including both contact and distant healing, found "that treatment by psychic healing did have an effect on the health of patients. The effects were stronger for subjectively improved state of health than for objectively measured indicators of

[73] *Alternative Therapies* vol. 3, no. 6. Nov 1997.

health. It appeared important that the patient knew that treatment was being attempted; in only a few studies were effects observed when patients did not know that healing was being attempted....In none of the studies were strong indications of possible negative effects of the treatment found."[74]

There might seem to be a problem with patients who do not know that healing is being attempted, although in shamanic distant healing, as we have noted, the knowledge seems to make no difference. If we can accept Katra's suggestion that healing at a distance occurs "as a manifestation of a joining of minds, resonance, and entering into a universal consciousness," then, even if patients are not consciously aware that a healing process is activated, they may still be affected nevertheless. An exchange of information may still take place. In any event, we do not have to be consciously aware to contract an illness; similarly we do not have to be consciously aware to accept healing for it.

What spiritual healing appears to do, in most instances, if not all, is to stimulate the self-healing capacity of the patient. In *Coyote Medicine*, Dr. Lewis Mehl-Madrona, who practices both Western and shamanic medicine, quotes an Apache shaman who told him, "I'm about as powerful as a dead chicken." He added, "The patient must do 70 percent of the work of getting well. The Creator does 20 percent, and I do 10 percent, which is barely worth mentioning." Expressing this in another way, Daniel Wirth, speaking of spiritual healing generally, maintains that "since all healing is self-healing, the role of the spiritual healer then is not to cure the patient, but to activate through the healer's own love and compassion the healing potential within the patient." The necessity for love and compassion is echoed time and again in the reports of researchers and observers.

Distance is no barrier to intentionality. Nor is it a barrier to another possible manifestation of non-local consciousness in action—remote diagnosis. This in the past was largely the

---

[74] *Advances in Parapsychological Research*, vol. 8.

...nce of shamans and medicine men but in the twentieth century it has emerged into the Western world. Edgar Cayce, who acquired a considerable reputation as both a prophet and a healer, made thousands of distant diagnoses, known as "readings," and also produced treatments, mainly homeopathic and naturopathic in character, for his remote patients while in a trance state. There are individuals who, in a particular state of consciousness, seem able to "scan" a distant physical body and discern problems or "blocks" that affect its health. More recently, the work of Caroline Myss has become widely known. Myss is described as a medical intuitive. She has worked with several doctors in the U. S., but mainly with Dr. Norman Shealy, with whom she has written three books. She discovered this ability in 1983 and more recently has been concentrating on teaching it to medical students and others.

"No dramatic 'first event' ushered my intuitive abilities into my life," Myss writes. "They simply woke up inside me, easily, naturally, as if they had always been there, awaiting the appropriate time to emerge. . . . What's unusual about my intuition is that I can evaluate people with whom I've had no contact whatsoever. In fact, I prefer to have no previous contact, because looking directly into a frightened face interferes enormously with my ability to 'see' clearly. . . . I suspect I became extremely intuitive as a consequence of my curiosity about spiritual matters, combined with a deep frustration I felt when my life didn't unfold according to plan. On the other hand, it's equally possible that my medical intuition was simply the result of something I ate. Knowing how the gods work, I would not find it surprising in the least."[75]

Myss can diagnose in a hospital ward or over the telephone. Before she discovered this ability she had no medical training, but since working with Dr. Shealy she underwent an intensive course in anatomy to help her diagnoses become more precise. Shealy has estimated that she is accurate in nine out of ten instances—a far higher percentage than conventional methods

---

[75] Myss, C. (1996), *Anatomy of the Spirit*. New York: Harmony Books.

normally produce. She is not involved in prescribing or medical healing regimens but has developed her own approach to health and healing, which she describes in her books.

Although Myss's abilities are widely respected, remote diagnosis has the potential for harm unless confirmation from reliable medical sources is available. Dr. Benor, founder of the Doctor-Healer Network, reported the results of two studies, one with a group of eight healers, the other with four experienced healers who see auras. "Each group simultaneously observed a series of individuals with known diagnoses. Each drew a picture and wrote down their diagnostic impressions of what they observed. . . . No one was more surprised than the healers when each of their reports was as different from the others' as those of the blind men and the elephant. The next surprise was when the people who had been given the intuitive diagnostic impressions indicated that they agreed with all but one of the "readings." It appears that all but one of the healers resonated accurately with a different facet of the problems of the people they were observing. . . . Prior to these studies most of the healers had believed that they were perceiving the whole problem when they were giving intuitive diagnostic readings."[76] One of the healers reported that she felt depression in most of those she observed, which seems to indicate the possibility that she may have been projecting her own state of mind. Hence the necessity of removing "self" from the situation.

The removal of "self" applies to healing as well as diagnosing. Those healers—few, but they do exist—who instruct or advise their patients to cease taking their medication and to leave treatment wholly to them—are running the risk of causing more damage than benefit. It is far better for healers to work in cooperation with doctors than in opposition. Without seeking to denigrate the work of spiritual healers, it may be that what is needed most is a shift in the outlook and training of medical professionals themselves that would open

---

[76] Scientific & Medical Network *Wider Horizons, op cit.,* p. 132.

them to the possibilities of spiritual healing, both contact and distant. Incorporating this into their practice, making it as central as providing prescriptions, might help to restore medicine to its old tradition.

Daniel Wirth raises the question as to why modern medicine has "diverged so drastically from its roots of spirituality, holism, and compassionate individualized care, all championed by Hippocrates, Aristotle, Galen, and Paracelsus—the fathers of medicine." Wirth maintains that "modern medicine has become so scientific and focused on finding the biological cause of illness that the science of medicine has nearly eliminated the art of medicine and with it the very foundation of healing."

However, there are signs that more and more individual doctors are taking interest in holistic methods and there is some ground for hope that healing, not simply treating, may again become central to the practice of medicine. In the Netherlands, the Dutch Forum Health Care organizes biennial conferences on "The Hospital as a Temple," with the aim of working towards the integration of the sacred into medicine and seeking, in the words of the introduction to its conference papers, to reaffirm concern for the soul, and to restore its prior dignity within medicine as a healing art. In this context, intention and prayer would seem to be very relevant, and distant healing could also come into the picture. In Honolulu, one particular hospital adopts a strongly patient-centered approach. Each day begins with a Hawaiian prayer—and prayer, music, and art are essential components of the patients' daily life. Patients, for example, may each day choose which paintings they would like to decorate their rooms.

In Santa Fe, a local non-profit organization, the Santa Fe Forum, is working with the Santa Fe Indian Hospital to "heal the spaces" by creating a sacred area in the central courtyard where ceremonies and dances take place and patients can meet and sit with their relatives and friends. A ceremonial circle and wheelchair path have been created in the surrounding grounds, with spaces for farmer's markets, a children's playground, and the cultivation of medicinal herbs. Cooperation with a nearby complementary medicine center and with medicine men from the pueblos is also on the program.

These are just three examples of a change in outlook and approach. In each, the emphasis is on changing the environment to enhance the healing process. With distant healing, however, no change in the environment is needed. It costs nothing and involves intention, not effort. It may be that no matter how many trials and experiments are held the success of distant healing will never be subject to statistical evaluation. No matter how firmly the protocols are established there are still too many imponderables. Among these imponderables are the questions of how far the expectations of those administering the trials might affect the results, and the difficulty of distinguishing between the results of healing intention and the placebo effect. Also the beliefs, religious affiliations (if any), and expectations of the patients themselves have to be taken into consideration as they also may have some bearing on the outcome. With all this in mind, the success or otherwise of distant healing cannot be satisfactorily measured. But being able to be measured is not the only criterion of worth.

The studies referred to in this chapter show that there are good indications that distant healing works even though there is no evidence as to how it works. This is no more and no less than can be said about many kinds of medication. Moreover, distant healing has no negative side-effects so it accords with the Hippocratic injunction: "Do no harm." Some healers have a particular worldview, sometimes based on a religious faith or a conflation of faiths, in which an interpretation of the word "spiritual" plays an important part. But it is questionable whether the worldview of the healer affects the outcome.

Some consider that a source higher than themselves is responsible for the "power" or "energy" that they believe to be transmitted and that connects with the recipient's self-healing ability. Others may ascribe that "power" to a technique they have been taught or even to an object, a crystal perhaps, that they are holding. There are also those who, with no training or experience, join a "healing group" to participate in something they see as being of value. Many practitioners, whether trained or simply volunteers, cannot explain or even understand what it is that they do.

Here I would suggest that further exploration of consciousness might produce answers to some of the questions raised. The ability to heal may come to be accepted as a type of extrasensory activity; a variant of telepathic communication. Experience shows that physical contact between healer and patient is enhanced if there is contact between minds as well as bodies. When physical contact is not possible, it is consciousness alone that can transmit the empathy and compassion that lie at the heart of the healing process. If we can accept that the consciousness of an individual is not restricted to the brain but is independent of time and space, or if it can be understood more as a ripple in the ocean than as a single pebble on the beach, so that instead of there being six billion separate and independent consciousnesses they are all interconnected, then the means by which distant healing operates becomes clear. And if, as the poet John Donne said, "Each man's death diminishes me," then each birth adds to me also and strengthens that interconnection through consciousness that binds humanity together.

CHAPTER 4

THE NEAR-DEATH EXPERIENCE

The undiscovered country from whose bourn
No traveller returns ...   *(Hamlet)*

"Dr. Ross, I will share something with you if you promise not
to tell it to another human being." Long before near-death experiences (NDEs) were widely publicized, Dr. Elisabeth Kübler-
Ross heard words to this effect on countless occasions during
her work with dying patients. The first to describe this experience to her was a Mrs. Schwartz, who had been in and out of the
intensive care unit fifteen times. This inspired Kübler-Ross to col-
lect similar experiences. She amassed them from several countries and from patients of all ages and religions, as well as from
atheists and agnostics. However, she made no attempt to publish
them, because, as she says, "when they came back after having
had this glorious experience which for them was very sacred,
very private, and shared it with people, they got a nice little pat
on the back and were told, 'Well, you were under drugs,' or 'It is
very normal that people hallucinate at moments like this.'"[77]

The first major publication dealing with near-death experiences (NDEs) was Dr. Raymond Moody's *Life After Life* (1975).

---

[77] From a lecture delivered in Stockholm, reprinted in Kübler-Ross, E.
(1995) *Death is of Vital Importance*, Station Hill Press.

Johann Hamfe's German study, *To Die is to Gain*, followed soon after. Moody's book sold over two million copies worldwide, indicating the interest it aroused. He examined 150 reports of NDEs, seeking to make sense of them, finding out their common elements, and reaching towards some kind of explanation or meaning. From these reports Moody constructed a theoretically complete model, embodying all the elements of typical NDEs. This model has since been extended by other researchers but it retains its usefulness as a guide to definition. Here is the typical scenario:

A man is dying and, as he reaches the point of greatest physical distress, he hears himself pronounced dead by a doctor or nurse. He begins to hear an uncomfortable noise, a loud ringing or buzzing, and at the same time feels himself moving very rapidly through a long tunnel. After this, he suddenly finds himself outside his own physical body, but still in the immediate physical environment, and he sees his own body from a distance as though he is a spectator. He watches the resuscitation attempt from this unusual vantage point and is in a state of emotional upheaval.

After awhile he collects himself and becomes more accustomed to his odd condition. He notices that he still has a body but one of a very different nature and with very different powers from the physical body he has left behind. Soon other things begin to happen. Others come to meet and help him. He glimpses the spirits of relatives and friends who have already died, and a loving, warm spirit of a kind he has never encountered before—a being of light—appears before him. This being asks him a question, non-verbally, to make him evaluate his life, and helps him along by showing him a panoramic, instantaneous playback of the major events of his life. At some point he finds himself approaching some sort of barrier or border, apparently representing the limit between earthly life and the next life. Yet he finds he must go back to Earth, for the time of his death has not yet come. At this point he resists, for by now he is taken up with his experiences in the afterlife and does not want to return. He is overwhelmed by intense feelings of joy, love, and peace. Despite this strong emotional pull, however, he somehow reunites with his physical body and lives.

Later he tries to tell others but he has trouble doing so. In the first place he can find no words adequate to describe these unearthly episodes. He also finds that others scoff, so he stops telling other people. Still, the experience affects his life profoundly, especially his views about death and its relationship to life. [78]

Other elements of the NDE that Moody found in later interviews included glimpses of a separate realm in which all knowledge seemed to exist in a timeless state. "There was a moment . . . it was like I knew all things . . . communication wasn't necessary. I thought whatever I wanted to know could be known," said one report. Others describe visions of a beautiful countryside or cities of light. "I could see a city. . . . there were buildings . . . they were gleaming, bright. People were happy in there. There was sparkling water, fountains . . . a city of light would be the way to say it. . . . There was beautiful music. Everything was just glowing, wonderful. But if I had entered into this I think I would never have returned." [79]

Some reports mention seeing bewildered or depressed individuals who seemed unaware of anything, caught between the spiritual and physical worlds. "They couldn't make up their minds what to do . . . they didn't know whether to go on or to return to their bodies." Others tell of a voice, often identified as God or Jesus, that warns them not to proceed further or instructs them to return to life. Moody comments that all these features of the experience were told to him "by ordinary people who were not seeking these experiences, who had no previous interest in or knowledge of these matters and yet who, afterward, had absolutely no doubt about the reality of what they had seen."

Moody continued his research, interviewing more than a thousand people who claimed to have had NDEs. Working

---

[78] Moody, R. (1975), *Life After Life*, New York: Bantam.
[79] Ibid.

from all these accounts, he listed nine features that, he said, defined the near-death experience. Although very few reported all nine of these, most reported five or six. Moody considered that the presence of one or more was enough to bring the experience within the NDE definition. Here is his list: a sense of being dead (though this may not occur until later in the experience); a feeling of peace and painlessness; an out-of-body experience; the experience of moving through a tunnel, or through doors, or up a stairway; meeting people of light, often relatives or friends, also seeing countryside or cities; meeting a being of light, sometimes identified as God, Jesus, Allah—a holy being; a life review; rising or floating into the heavens, or into space; reluctance to return; also in some accounts time and space are compressed, seeming to have no boundaries.

Since the publication of *Life After Life*, many more books and articles (both academic and popular) dealing with NDEs have been published as well as a number of personal accounts. As a result of the opening up of the subject there is a lurking possibility that someone seriously ill may be influenced by previous reading to the extent that any experience he or she may have might be colored by such earlier narratives. Yet the range and variety of people who do report NDEs, coming from so many different backgrounds and cultures, would seem to show that any contamination would be so rare as to be of minor importance.

It is worth looking more closely at some of Moody's nine features. The sense of being dead sometimes comes from hearing what a doctor or medical attendant actually says, and sometimes from the seemingly inexplicable sudden shift out of pain and fear. The feeling of peace and lack of pain are clear enough; the individual is no longer conscious and all pain signals are cut off. The tunnel experience occurs rather less frequently. It has been suggested by the psychiatrist Stanislav Grof that this is a memory of the passage through the birth canal—as you enter life through a passage or tunnel, so you leave it in a similar way. The tunnel is also part of a medieval vision of passage into the afterlife and is so depicted by Hieronymous Bosch (c. 1460-1516) in *Ascent into the Empyrean*, part of an altarpiece in the Ducal Palace, Venice. Here the souls of the saved are conducted by winged angels into a large tunnel out of which they emerge into Paradise. In some accounts the sense of rising or floating upwards seems to take the place of the tunnel journey and most experiences include some sense of moving away from the body.

The out-of-body experience (OBE) is a common feature of many, if not most, descriptions of the NDE. This experience is not restricted to the NDE, but may occur spontaneously to anyone at almost any time. With regard to the near-death state, however, the OBE frequently follows a specific pattern, especially when, as often happens, the individual is in a hospital bed. Here the patient may observe his body from above, watching the medical staff at work, sometimes attempting resuscitation. Some patients report having observed the dust on top of the overhead lights, or, more rarely, the lack of dust. A lady in the intensive care unit of a Boston hospital found herself "up on the ceiling looking down at the bed, the IV bottles, the blood running . . . I looked around and I saw a beautiful, delicate cobweb, and there was some cracked plaster over the window. I thought to myself, 'My God, for $325 a day, why don't they keep the room clean and fix that plaster?'"[80]

The cardiologist Dr. Michael Sabom was among the first to make a detailed study of OBE reports. When possible he questioned his subjects as soon as possible after the event and he also noted information such as their religious beliefs, if any, and whether they had ever heard of NDEs previously. He also used the surgeon's notes, when available, comparing these with the reports of NDE patients. Dr. Sabom asked several cardiac patients who had not experienced an NDE to describe how they imagined a resuscitation to be carried out, and compared their descriptions with those of NDE patients who claimed to have witnessed their own resuscitations. The

---

[80] Ring, K. (1998), *Lessons from the Light*, New York: Insight Books.

descriptions of the NDE patients appeared much closer to eye-witness accounts. [81]

More recently, Dr. Peter Fenwick, consultant neuropsychiatrist of the Maudsley Hospital, London, undertook research into 350 NDEs. Here are three examples:

John Parkinson was being operated upon in the Blackpool Victoria Hospital when he had a massive hemorrhage and was given a blood transfusion. John reported feeling that he left his body and was looking down upon it and on the medical staff. One thing kept him from attributing this to a mere loss of blood from his brain. This was the fact he was surrounded by screens and was unable to see the rest of the ward. From his elevated vantage point, he watched the doctor enter the ward and visit another patient before coming to him. John realized he could not have seen this had he been lying in his bed (in his body, as it were). He confirmed his observation with the doctor.

Maurice James was in intensive care with cardiac arrest. "It was as though I was standing on the wall of the ICU defying gravity and looking down on my own body," he said later. The ugliness of his own corpse shocked him. He was nude and a nurse was removing a drip from his ankle. He was struck by how purple his face was and how blank his forehead appeared. Maurice also noted he had a black triangle from his hairline to his nose. Later his wife confirmed that his out-of-body impressions of himself had been accurate.

Lastly, here is the experience of Major Derek Scull, described by Dr. Fenwick as a very down-to-earth person. He was in intensive care after a heart attack, in a side ward with windows around the top of the wall. The door was closed. "I was lying there feeling terrible," he recalled. Then three women, who resembled witches to him in this state, descended upon him to insert a catheter. They gave him no warning, and as he had never experienced this before, he shouted out:

---

[81] Sabom, M. (1982), *Recollections of Death: A Medical Investigation*, New York: Harper Row.

"Who's that dreadful woman in the white coat?"Then he heard someone say it was the doctor.

"I felt this enormous tension as though I knew something was going to happen," Scull continued. He felt "absolutely airy-fairy," as if he were levitating serenely, outside of his body. He floated to the ceiling, looked back, and observed his own body, lying in the bed, eyes closed. He didn't feel surprised to be floating up around the ceiling. He looked through the window and saw the reception area in the ward. He became aware that his wife was waiting at the reception desk and that she was conversing with an attendant behind the desk. Scull noted his wife was wearing a red trouser suit. Then he thought to himself: what an inappropriate time for my wife to arrive. Visiting hours are past, I haven't shaved, I look dreadful, and I'm up here on the ceiling, and my body is down there in the bed. He wondered what would happen next.

"The next thing I was conscious of was being back in my bed. I opened my eyes and there sitting beside me was Joan in her red trouser suit." Scull wasn't surprised to see her "because I knew she'd arrived," he said. "I'd already seen her." [82]

Out-of-body experiences as part of an NDE are not confined to the hospital environment. Here is another example from Dr. Fenwick's records. It was reported by John Bowers, then aged thirty. He was serving with the Sudan Defense Force during the Second World War when his unit was attacked by a squadron of Heinkels. He lay down flat on the sand, made a hollow for his head, put his fingers in his ears and opened his mouth.

John noted that he was "enveloped in a cloud of beautiful purple light and a mighty roaring sound as if a great Atlantic roller was breaking over me." Then he felt he was floating, as if in a flying dream. He watched his body twelve feet below him, face downwards, on the sand. He did not see the two

---

[82] Fenwick, P. & Fenwick, E. (1995), *The Truth in the Light*, New York: Berkeley Books.

Sudanese lying next to him. He found himself talking to himself in a funny, quizzical way about rabbit hunting when he was younger, and had hunted with a farmer friend. Then he found himself gliding horizontally in a tunnel like a giant, round, luminous culvert, constructed of translucent material, at the end of which was a "bright pale primrose light." John liked the sensation of being without weight and the painless flying, and commented to himself that this was pretty dull stuff for death. Yet he sensed when he reached the lights, things would get more interesting.

John felt he was "being sucked back through the tunnel" and back into a body—his body—that seemed "rather unpleasantly heavy." Even though the Heinkels were still attacking, he had lost his fear. His back felt slimy and wet, and he discovered a mass of raw flesh and blood was the reason. He thought that if he wasn't already dead, he would probably soon be. Then he realized that all the blood and raw flesh was not his own but that of Osman the cook, who had been lying next to him. As the experience concluded, John said he felt "light-headed but quite happy."[83]

In contrast is what happened to Julie Chimes, a London business woman, who told her own remarkable story in *A Stranger in Paradise* (1995). She was attacked in her house in Surrey by a woman, Helen, diagnosed as paranoid schizophrenic who had ceased taking her medication. Helen called at her house saying she needed to talk to her. She got into the kitchen, took hold of a professional cook's knife and began a frenzied assault, stabbing Julie time and again shouting, 'Die! Die!' Julie struggled to pull the knife out of her chest. As she did so, Helen grabbed hold of it and stood staring at her. Julie describes what followed:

"Immediately I felt as if someone had plugged me into a giant switchboard in the heavens. Every conversation taking place on Earth was moving through me, and I could understand every single sound. The space I was swinging in

---

[83] Ibid.

became a vast screen on which worldly dramas were playing simultaneously. I watched it all—fascinated by the dance of humanity. Transfixed by the immensity and brilliance of creation. To my amazement I found that if I concentrated on any thought I was instantly transported within it. I could watch the screen, and take part in it at the same time. An entire planet scuttling about its business lay before me: past, present, and future. I thought of the Christ, and immediately found myself kneeling on a rocky hillside looking up at the cross from which he was hanging.

"'Master, where are you going? How will we find you when you are gone? Where will you be?' My heart splintered with shards of desolation.

"His head lifted. His eyes washed with a blue light, a light radiating from his entire being. A light which flooded the whole landscape, transforming all things solid into shimmering mirages.

"He spoke, 'Everywhere you look you will see Me.'

"The sound of his voice echoed across the skies. I understood.

"I flew back into the heavens; the screen before me was now filled with a light which shone with a brightness beyond anything I had ever seen. All the images of life blended into a sea of dazzling points of light, trillions of multifaceted gems reflecting a million suns. The cacophony of earthly sound exploded into one crystal-clear note and reverberated throughout the star-filled sky. It was breathtaking. Somehow everything was me. In me and out of me. Light and dark, good and bad, right and wrong. All encompassing. I was part of a magnificent whole. No thing was without meaning. All was one. For one exquisite moment I saw what was behind the physical masks.

"'Helen ... I ... love ... you!' I cried out into infinity.

"My tiny earthbound mind protested, with sarcasm dripping from its logical passageways, 'Are you totally bloody crazy too?' it demanded angrily. 'You are being murdered. . . . '"

A moment later the attack was renewed. Julie managed to fight her way from the kitchen into the hall, where Helen struck again. Julie crashed onto the stone floor of her tiny entrance hall, the knife embedded in her mouth. Blood oozed through her teeth. Using both hands, Helen yanked the knife out. It felt to Julie as if all her teeth went with it. She continues her story.

"I closed my blood-filled eyes and was immediately standing over my body, watching. Eerie whispers reverberated off the walls. No light. No music. No savior. No choirs. No angels, No friends. No voices. No space. No screen. No hope. No thing. No apparent way out. Perhaps this was hell ..."

Julie tried to will herself back into the light, but failed. Looking down at her bleeding body she thought she must be dead. Then she heard a voice telling her to go back.

"'I don't want to go back!' I informed the voice as I searched around me for a way out. I looked everywhere, but there was nothing, no arrow pointing to heaven or hell. What was I expecting? Perhaps an angel, or at least a dead friend or relative to come and meet me and show me the way. I tried again to go back to my vast space, but seemed to be stuck hovering in the hallway, forced to look down on my unconscious body which was still being subjected to the wrath of Helen-from-hell, as she stabbed, kicked and punched it.

"What on Earth was going on? I was not in a physical body because I could see it on the floor below me, but I knew it belonged to me," Julie continued. "This 'me' doing the watching did not seem to have any definable shape but I knew it was still 'me.' It was all so crazy.

"'Who am I?' I had no voice but somehow I cried out.

"'My friend ... you must go back,' came the immediate reply.

"'I do not want to go back into that shredded body. I'll be a cripple, I'll be a vegetable, come on ... nobody can survive that!' I answered angrily.

"'You will survive ... and you won't be a vegetable ... Go back.'

"'How can you be so sure?' I demanded.

"'Because ... my friend, I am you.'

"'I am so confused ... I don't understand.'

"'You will.'

"'Why can't I go back into the light? Why can't I stay in the vastness, the place where I know, the place where I understand? Why do I have to go back into that horribly limited body and life?'

"'Go back, my friend . . . and remember, I love you.'

"Instinctively I put my arm across my face, devastated to find I was once again in my torn and battered body."[84]

Julie needed over four hundred stitches in her wounds. She regained her health, married, and now travels widely in Europe "doing all sorts of things she would never have done before."

This account was written some years after the experience it describes. In it Julie is the observed and the observer as well as the narrator. She has shaped her recollections with touches of a wry sarcasm here and there to produce a dramatic and moving account of an experience which must, when it happened, have been shapeless, utterly terrifying, yet at the same time transcendent. Without seeking it, she attracts admiration for her courage and artistry.

Julie Chimes, John Bowers, and the patients in intensive care whose experiences have been described all eluded death. One who did not, however, was Sally, whose experience is recounted by Dr. Joan Borysenko, who was sitting with her while her parents went to have lunch in the hospital cafeteria. Sally was drifting in and out of consciousness. After a time, Dr. Borysenko asked, "Where do you drift off to, Sally? Your face looks so peaceful." Sally opened her eyes and said in a quiet voice: "You may have trouble believing this, but I've been floating around, touring the hospital. I've just been to the cafeteria, watching my parents eat lunch. Dad is having grilled cheese. Mum is eating tuna. They are so sad they can barely eat. I will have to tell them my body may be dying but I'm certainly not. It's more like I'm being born—my consciousness is so free and peaceful." She faded away for some minutes then spoke again. "It's so beautiful, Joan. I'm drifting up out of my body toward a

---

[84] Chimes, J. (1995), *A Stranger in Paradise,* London: Bloomsbury.

kind of living light. It's very bright. So warm, so loving. Don't be afraid to die," she added. "Your soul doesn't die at all. You know? It just goes on from here." A few minutes later she drifted out of consciousness for the last time. [85]

Light is of great significance in the near-death experience. Many of those who have written on the subject, whether as commentators or experiencers themselves, use the word in the title of their work: *Beyond the Light, Saved by the Light, Embraced by the Light, The Light Beyond, Closer to the Light, After the Light, Children of the Light, Reborn in the Light, The Truth in the Light* are among the examples. In his summary of the content and patterning of the NDE, Dr. Kenneth Ring synthesizes, in *Lessons from the Light*, many of these accounts regarding the encounter with light.

"You become aware of what is at first a pinpoint of light. This light quickly grows bigger and brighter and becomes more effulgent. It is an extremely brilliant light—golden-white—but it absolutely does not hurt your eyes at all. You've never experienced a light like this—it seems to be sourceless and to cover the entire vista before you. As you move closer to the light, you begin to be overwhelmed with the most powerful waves of what can only be described as pure love, which seem to penetrate to the very core of your being. There are no thoughts at all now—only total immersion in this light. All time stops; this is eternity, this is perfection—you are home again in the light.

"In the midst of this timeless perfection, however, you become aware that somehow associated with this light there is a definite presence. It is not a person, but a being of some kind, a form you cannot see but to whose consciousness your own mind seems now to be linked."

At this point, religious or cultural systems often take over. The being of light may be identified as the Godhead, as Jesus, Buddha, Allah, Vishnu, as an archangel, or simply as an enlightened being. In every major religion, light is of enormous significance; indeed, it provides a connecting link between

---

[85] Borysenko, J. (1990), *Guilt is the Teacher, Love is the Lesson*, New York: Warner Books.

the faiths. The being may impart information in response to questions or it may deliver a simple message. For those who experience it, the encounter with the being of light is usually the most memorable feature of the NDE. Interestingly, the vision of the being, whether it appears in human form or simply as light, owes little or nothing to the pictorial interpretations of divine figures—no crowns or headgear of any kind, no stigmata, no beards, nothing but light.

Light also appears to clothe the relatives and friends of those who meet them and to surround the landscapes and cities that figure in some of the reports. Lest suspicions arise that it has something to do with the bright lights above the operating table, it seems to make no difference where the experience takes place, whether on the battlefield, following a road accident, in the home, or out in the open. Light, whether associated with a being or simply as a quality of the experience, was reported in 72 percent of the 350 cases considered by Dr. Peter Fenwick in *The Truth in the Light*.

The importance of the light is emphasized in an experience recorded in the *News Bulletin of the International Association for Near-Death Studies* (Spring 1989). While being operated on for excision of the gall-bladder, Jean Sleath almost died. She recalled her experience as follows:

"Somehow, I was floating along a dark tunnel, being drawn slowly to the bright light at the end. When I emerged from the tunnel it was into a place of such utter beauty that mere words cannot describe it. . . . I felt I had discovered 'that undiscovered country' of which Hamlet spoke. There was utter silence, and a light that was more than light. I understood Plato's words: 'God is truth, and light his shadow.' The lesser light was all around. The greater light was in the distance waiting; condensed into an irregular shape. Both lights were without shadow, and the silence was sweeter than any music I had ever heard. The peace was that which passeth understanding. I was attuned to everything—it was 'normal.' Fear was an unknown emotion. Everything, everything, was so sublime—the scenery, the silence, the peace, yet I knew I had to go on—on towards that light which beckoned and would not be denied."

Jean then perceived a group of deceased relatives and friends who at first welcomed her but, as she approached them, suddenly stopped her, shouting "No, not yet! Go back!" She felt being pulled back into the tunnel and came to, finding herself on a trolley in a room next to the operating theatre with medical staff working on her and complaining about the anesthetist.

On the same page of this journal appeared a reprint of part of a near-death experience account by the philosopher, Professor A. J. Ayer, whose heart apparently ceased beating for four minutes:

"I was confronted by a red light, exceedingly bright and also very painful even when I turned away from it. I was aware that this light was responsible for the government of the universe. Among its ministers were two creatures who had been put in charge of space. These ministers periodically inspected space and had recently carried out such an inspection. They had, however, failed to do their work properly, with the result that space, like a badly fitting jigsaw puzzle, was slightly out of joint. A further consequence was that the laws of nature had ceased to function as they should. I felt that it was up to me to put things right. I also had the motive of finding a way to extinguish the painful light. I assumed that it was signaling that space was awry and that it would switch itself off when order was restored."

Ayer considered that, following Einstein's general theory of relativity, space and time could be treated as a single whole, so he thought he could cure space by operating on time. The ministers had moved away and he could not contact them. He began walking up and down waving his watch "in the hope of drawing their attention not to my watch but to the time which it measured." But he obtained no response and the experience suddenly ended.

This experience, Ayer thought, was probably delusive, but he added the following: "A slight indication that it might have been veridical has been supplied by my French friend, or rather by her mother, who also underwent a heart arrest many years ago. When her daughter asked her what it had been like, she replied that all that she remembered was that she must stay close to the red light."

Ayer firmly believed that the brain produced consciousness and that when the brain died consciousness died also. Yet he admitted later that this experience had actually weakened his hitherto inflexible attitude that there was no life after death.[86] It is worth noting how his own belief system shaped his experience; there was no sense of divinity, no being of light, just a couple of senior civil servants not doing their job properly.

However, of all the features characteristic of an NDE, the life review is the most intriguing. Here are three examples from Kenneth Ring's *Lessons from the Light*:

"It proceeded to show me every single event of my twenty-two years of life in a kind of 3D panoramic review.... The brightness showed me every second of all those years in exquisite detail, in what seemed only an instant of time. Watching and re-experiencing all those events of my life changed everything. It was an opportunity to see and feel all the love I had shared, and more importantly, all the pain I had caused. I was able simultaneously to re-experience not only my own feelings and thoughts, but those of all the other people I had ever interacted with. Seeing myself through their eyes was a humbling experience."

"Mine was not a review but a reliving. For me it was a total reliving of every thought I had ever thought, every word I had ever spoken, and every deed I had ever done; plus the effect of each thought, word, and deed on everyone and anyone who had ever come within my environment or sphere of influence, whether I knew them or not.... No detail was left out. No slip of the tongue or slur was missed. No mistake or accident went unaccounted for. If there is such a thing as hell, as far as I am concerned, this was hell."

"I was the very people that I hurt, and I was the very people I helped to feel good."

---

[86] International Association for Near-Death Studies, Bulletin, 7th issue, spring 1989.

Kenneth Ring comments that the presence within the light helps the individual through the life review with "the greatest and most tender compassion and love and even at times with humor. You are not being punished; you are being shown, so that you can learn." This seems to indicate a purposefulness within the experience, as if the being of light is not simply a presence but also a teacher.

Not everyone who has studied the NDE would necessarily agree with this. The NDE may turn out to be a learning experience, but the supposition that there is a teacher separate from the self who is actively involved in a teaching process moves the experience into a different area altogether. Nevertheless, many personal accounts of NDEs insist that there is a separate teacher. "I was given a lesson on how individual identity and consciousness evolve," declared Mellen-Thomas Benedict, describing his NDE in 1982. "I was being taught by the master teacher!" said Betty Eadie, looking back nineteen years on her experience in 1973. And the Lakota Sioux medicine man, Black Elk, who had a near-death experience at the age of nine, was told by the oldest grandfather, sitting among the clouds, "Your Grandfathers all over the world are having a council, and they have called you here to teach you."[87] Statements such as these may seem to echo particular religious beliefs. They are some distance from the many accounts where the being of light does no more than exude love and insists, with or without words, that the experiencer returns to the land of the living.

The life review often involves judgement, but it is the individual who does the judging, not the being of light. Phyllis Atwater, in *I Died Three Times,* described this process in detail:

"It was me judging me, not some heavenly St. Peter. And my judgement was critical and stern. I was not satisfied with many, many things Phyllis had done, said, or thought. There was a feeling of sadness and failure, yet a growing feeling of

---

[87] Quoted from excerpts in Bailey, L. & Yates, J., *The Near-Death Experience: A Reader,* New York: Routledge. This is a very useful introduction to the subject.

joy when the realization came that Phyllis had always done SOMETHING. She did many things unworthy and negative, but she did something. She tried. Much of what she did was positive and constructive. She learned and grew in her learning. This was satisfying. Phyllis was okay."

Dannion Brinkley, who had served with the U. S. Army in Vietnam and, he said, contributed to the deaths of dozens of people in South-east Asia, came to a different conclusion. "I had reviewed my life and what I had seen was a truly worthless person.... From the review I had just had, I could see that for every good event in my life, there were twenty bad ones to weigh against it. If guilt were fat, I would have weighed five hundred pounds." [88] From the being of light, however, Brinkley felt "a love and joy that could only be compared to the non-judgemental compassion that a grandfather has for a grandchild," and he felt the burden of his guilt being removed.

While several distressing or "hellish" experiences have been reported, there seems to be no mention of any being or figure pronouncing judgement or condemning the individual to punishment. There is a parallel here with medieval visions of journeys into the world beyond, where the traveller is usually judged by his deeds not by some external figure, deity, or devil, as described by Carol Zaleski in *Otherworld Journeys* (1987). I shall consider these "hellish" experiences in more detail later.

It may also happen, though rarely, that a vision of the future occurs during the life review. One such instance happened to a woman who saw herself with her son, although she was childless until many years after her NDE. There is also the case of a man who had his near-death encounter at the age of fifteen. He saw himself twenty years into the future as a married man with his wife and children in a room. He sensed an object behind him that he could not identify. Recalling the experience in later life he identified the object as a warm air-circulating heater, which had not been invented when he was fifteen years old.

---

[88] Brinkley, D. (1994), *Saved by the Light*, New York: Villard Books.

A third instance is recounted by Dr. Barbara Rommer, who practices internal medicine in Fort Lauderdale and is a director of the International Association for Near Death Studies: David, age 32, underwent a six-hour surgery during which complications arose. He was resuscitated after a period of 75 minutes of cardiac and respiratory arrest. During his NDE he was made aware that he would recover to raise and educate six children, although at that time he was childless. Some years later his brother and sister-in-law were both killed in a plane crash. By that time he and his wife had two children, and they raised their four nieces and nephews together with their own.[89]

The life review has a long-standing place in various religious and esoteric traditions. The Kabbalah, for example, holds that after death the psychological image of the person "reviews the whole of his life with every incident passing before him or her for judgement. . . . Nothing is missed, even those events that have been repressed or long forgotten are screened for the person to see and judge as a performance of his life. . . . Hints of this process are observed in old people approaching death and even in the young who come close to death during some illness or accident." The process is thought to begin "when the physical body is beginning to separate from the psychological body in anticipation of death."[90]

What is especially significant in the life review, however, is not so much the panoramic review itself but the identification with others, seeing through their eyes, feeling their pain and elation. David Lorimer, director of the Scientific and Medical Network, based in the U. K., suggests that the review involves what he calls "empathetic resonance," which he defines as "our capacity to experience another person's thoughts and feelings directly. It puts the subject in touch with the interrelatedness and interpenetration of all things—when what you've given

---

[89] Conference of the Academy of Religion & Psychical Research, Philadelphia 1999.
[90] Halevi, Z. (1977), *A Kabbalistic Universe,* Bath: Gateway Books.

out comes back to you exactly in measure. The first step is to be able to forgive yourself, and then start to forgive others."[91]

In attempts to "explain" the life review it has been pointed out that the neurosurgeon Wilder Penfield demonstrated that after he had stimulated the limbic lobe in the brains of epileptic patients a few of them reported "seeing their lives flash before them." But none of those whose experiences are quoted above was epileptic, and the identification with others was no part of the experiences that Penfield records. Furthermore, one common feature of these NDE experiences, including the life review, is their coherence. The great majority of the recorded instances form a logically sequenced narrative, even those reported shortly after the event.

The life review does not of course occur in the NDEs of children, although most of the other features have been reported. Until quite recently it was thought that children did not have such experiences, despite the fact that Dr. Kübler-Ross referred to them many times in books and lectures. Then in 1990, Melvyn Morse published *Closer to the Light: Learning from Children's Near-Death Experiences.* He interviewed eleven children shortly after they had recovered from cardiac arrest or had been in a deep coma. Of these, seven could remember what they had experienced while unconscious, six had out-of-body journeys, five recalled entering darkness, and four remembered travelling through a tunnel. These children could not have been affected by any expectations of what an NDE might be like. As Dr. Fenwick says, "Childhood experiences are particularly interesting because they are much more likely to be 'clean.'"

When interviewed by Pierre Jovanovic, a French journalist, Dr. Kübler-Ross was asked which NDE had influenced her most. She recalled the case of a little boy who had reacted very badly to an injection and had been pronounced dead.

"The mother went crazy and it took about an hour and a half to find the father on a construction site. And just a few

---

[91] *Noetic Sciences Review*, 32, 1994.

minutes before his arrival at the clinic, the little boy suddenly opened his eyes and said to his mother; 'Mom, I was dead.' Profoundly shocked, she didn't want to hear about it, and every time the boy tried to tell her his story, she told him to be quiet. But in the end he told her his experience: 'Mom, I have to tell you, you know, because Mary and Jesus came to look for me and they told me it wasn't my time. But I didn't want to leave and Mary took me by the hand and sent me down, saying to me, 'You must save your mama from hell.'

"The mother was plunged into depression because she believed she was going to burn in hell and that it was her son who would save her, all because the Church teaches fear and guilt. Then I asked her, 'But how would you feel if Mary had not sent back your son?' and she said without even pausing for thought, 'My God, my life would have been hell.' At that moment she understood. 'In the 1960s,' added Kübler-Ross, 'no one was talking about NDE.'"[92]

Many older people have given accounts of NDEs they recall happening to them when they were children. The out-of-body experience is the most common feature; indeed, Dr. Fenwick says that children seem to find it easier than adults to slip in and out of their bodies. These recollections, however, might be subject to the vagaries of memory; the experiences when recalled are fluent and shaped and not in the sort of language that a young child would use. What is evident, however, in all these recollections is that the experience was extremely powerful and had a long-lasting effect. The differences between children's and adults' experiences reflect their relative experience in the everyday world; the emotional content of a child's NDE is generally simpler and any people they meet, as might be expected, are more likely to be living than dead.

There has also been some investigation of NDEs reported by blind people. Kenneth Ring and Sharon Cooper have studied reports from thirty-one blind men and women, of whom some

---

[92] Jovanovic, P. (1995), *An Enquiry into the Existence of Angels*, New York: Evans & Co.

80 percent claimed that they could see during their NDEs. Some of these were blind from birth, while others had lost their sight comparatively recently. From this study, Dr. Ring suggests that the NDE "essentially affords another perspective from which to perceive reality. Furthermore, this perspective does not depend on the senses of the physical body or even upon an intact visual system. In fact, it occurs only when the senses are defunct. Under these circumstances, it seems, another kind of knowing, which I called *transcendental awareness* or, more simply, *mindsight,* is made possible and everyone—not just the blind—begins to see with eyeless vision."[93]

The experiences we have so far considered have been positive, usually peaceful, and full of hope. Earlier studies of the NDE included no exceptions to this pattern, possibly because people were reluctant to speak of them or it may be that the questions of the researchers did not open the door to negative experiences. However, Dr. Barbara Rommer found that just under 18 percent of the cases she examined were what she called "less than positive"—cases where the experiencer felt frightened because of terror, despair, guilt, or a feeling of aloneness. Yet even these unpleasant experiences seemed to reduce or abolish the fear of death. [94] Dr. Fenwick reported that some 15 percent of his cases included moments of terror, although the total experience was almost always understood as positive, and this seems to accord with the findings of other recent surveys.

In response to a notice in the newsletter of the International Association for Near-Death Studies, fifty people responded with accounts of distressing experiences. Analysis by Dr. Bruce Greyson and Nancy Evans Bush revealed that these accounts could be divided into three types: 1. prototypical NDEs interpreted as terrifying; 2. a sensation of ceasing to exist

---

[93] Ring, K. (1998). *Journal of Consciousness Studies* vol. 6, no. 5 has several articles on "Blindsight."
[94] Conference of the Academy of Religion & Psychical Research, Philadelphia 1999.

or being condemned to a featureless void; 3. an experience involving hellish imagery.[95]

Type 1 category reports indicated that the individuals experienced many of the features of the "normal" experience, such as the tunnel, the bright light, an out-of-body sensation, and a life review, but interpreted them as disturbing or frightening. Rather than accept what was going on some people tried to fight it but found that they were unable to control the experience and hence became more terrified of what might ensue. However in most instances, in the words of one report, "Slowly my ruffled feathers became smooth and I felt peaceful and calm." Professor Ayer's experience, recorded above, which he certainly found disturbing, might come into this category.

Greyson and Bush found that, although the sample was small, most of those reporting Type 2, featureless void experiences, were in childbirth under anesthesia. "The common themes include eternal emptiness, an experience of being mocked, and a sense of all of life being an illusion." In some instances the experience had depressing after-effects, with despair and a feeling of emptiness enduring for some time.

The "hellish" experience, Type 3, seems to occur seldom. Characteristically it involves "archetypal imagery, sounds of torment, and sometimes demonic beings." In this it resembles some of the medieval "back-from-the-dead narratives," although there is no evidence that those who report this type have come across these stories or are believers in religious fundamentalism. All the same, it is not impossible that these individuals may have been subjected to frightening tales of hellfire in their childhood. Fear instilled as part of religious instruction can have a long-lasting and powerful effect even when reason declares it is without foundation.

A Type 3 experience is recorded by Dr. Martin Israel, who is both a priest and a qualified doctor, in his most recent book. He recounts what he considered to be a near-death experience that occurred when he was seriously ill in the hospital.

---

[95] Greyson, B. & Bush, N. *Psychiatry*, vol. 55, Feb 1992.

He says he was not entirely unconscious because he could occasionally respond to comments. "During this time I felt that I seemed to descend into a vast pit of darkness where I could sense the souls of a vast concourse of people who were unknown to me personally. I seemed to be in hell and even now I believe that it might be possible that this was literally true. There was despair, darkness, and lack of communication between the souls that were there." Later he felt grateful for this experience. From it he became convinced that "we are all immortal." He no longer feared death and says he lost interest in "theories of the afterlife, heaven and hell, reincarnation, or the various promises made by different religions." He also considered that his personality changed, becoming more accepting, and noted also "an acquisition of self-confidence which was previously completely lacking in my character."[96]

It has been suggested that resuscitation practices, anesthetics, or attempted suicide may be responsible for distressing experiences, but it is hard to find evidence to support any of this. There appear to be no psychological reasons why some people, fortunately very few, should undergo such distress, and with such small samples currently available it is not possible to draw any firm conclusions. Greyson and Bush feel that there may be a connection between these experiences and the "more familiar post-traumatic stress syndromes" which further investigation may reveal. These distressing experiences, however, would appear to give the lie to those who theorize that near-death experiences are no more than a kind of wish-fulfillment.

Whether the experience is positive or distressing, the moment comes when a decision is taken about returning to life. In many accounts the individual feels that it is necessary to return to complete unfinished business or for the sake of spouse and children. Sometimes the being of light seems to say something like "Your time has not yet come." Others—guides,

---

[96] Israel, M. (1999), *Happiness That Lasts*, quoted in *The Christian Parapsychologist*, vol. 13, no. 7, Sept 1999.

angels, dead relations—may make the decision to send the person back. Often the individual is unwilling to return because the experience itself is so beautiful and peaceful that there is no desire to return to the world of work and pain. Yet, whatever the circumstances, the return takes place. Here are two examples that have been communicated to me recently:

Bella was a machinist in a sewing factory. While in the hospital she had a hypoglycemic attack and lost consciousness. In a subsequent interview, she recalled walking through fields with her first husband, Ron, who had died twelve years previously. He was wearing his favorite blue trousers and white shirt. She said, "He looked the way he used to when we were courting." She continues:

"There was no sound . . . there were flowers—primroses, violets, bluebells. I don't know if they are my favorite flowers or what but they were there. And we were just walking slow, through these fields and then came to this . . . stream, I'm not sure if it was a stream or a river. I wanted to go over the bridge to see the people on the other side because they were too far away for me to see who they were. They were all in white robes. But he wouldn't let me cross over, he said it wasn't time for me to cross. And he turned and said I had to go back, but I said I didn't want to go back, and he turned me around and it was all black. I could feel myself turning around and that's about it. It was all black and I could hear this other voice calling me and I could hear him telling me to go back. His voice seemed to go further away and quieter."

As Ron's voice faded, Bella heard another voice which she identified later as the doctor's. He said, "No we haven't, she's slipping away again," and then, "We've got her now."

In response to questions, Bella said that it was as if she and Ron "were mind reading each other." The experience was not like a dream, "it was like it was really happening . . . it was real to me." The colors were very clear; "the grass was really green . . . the yellows of the primroses were *yellow*, and the bluebells were *blue*." The stream was bubbly but there was no sound; she saw birds, but again there was no sound. Bella added that it didn't feel as if they were walking, "but we were moving, we were holding hands . . . just holding his hand as normal." There was no tunnel, but she did see a light when her husband turned her around to come back. "I seem to have shot through it. . . . it wasn't very big because it was getting bigger the closer I was getting to it." At no time had she felt frightened.

Bella recalled that Ron had told her she had to go back for the children, although they were grown up. She also remembered that she had already seen the place she visited in dreams that she had experienced more than once. In those dreams, she said, Christ was there, wearing brown robes of a rough material. "He had a beard on him and long hair, scruffy hair—all scraggy hair. . . . . He'd be holding his hand out, I've got my hand out . . . to hold his and then I fall back down to it. And when I get up he's still standing there waiting."

Asked about the effects of the experience, Bella said that she now helped people more. Her belief in God was "still as strong as ever." She was not afraid of dying, "because to me I can go where I was then and it doesn't worry me a bit. No, I'm not afraid of dying. To me that's where I'm going when I'm gone."[97]

The second example was sent to me by a man named Thomas who, like Bella, knew nothing of near-death experiences previously. He had to have surgery to remove his colon because of a five-year illness with ulcerative colitis. He writes:

"Although my surgeon was very experienced, a student intern was assigned to suture up after the more delicate surgery had been done. Apparently this part of the procedure was not done quite right and I learned later that while I was still unconscious in the recovery room I started having internal bleeding. I had to be rushed back into surgery and have virtually an entire body's worth of blood transfused.

"When I woke up it was a bit like waking from a dream. I was in an incredibly good mood and my earlier depression about facing life having an ileostomy had lifted. I then began

---

[97] I am indebted to Penny Sartori, a nurse in intensive care, for this account.

to recall the memory. The main thing I remember was the feeling of extreme happiness. I remembered getting close to an extremely bright, happy place and my father, who had died five years earlier from a heart attack, was waiting on the periphery. (While my father was alive we had a very strained relationship, but in this memory there was none of that, only love.) He was almost like a guide or protector and I really wanted to go over with him to this great place. But then there was a voice that said, 'No you're not ready yet. You still have things to do and accomplish in your life.' It was then that I felt as if a hand was on the top of my head, almost pushing me back under water, but instead of under water it was back to this world.

"Before I had this experience I did not truly believe in God nor had I heard of any other near-death experiences. To this day the memory is helpful to me both spiritually and creatively."

With regard to near-death experiences generally, we need to bear in mind that if the return did *not* take place there would be no story to tell—or rather, no story-teller—so there is no way of knowing how often the decision not to return is made. Also near-death experience accounts seldom refer to the role of the medical team in saving the life of the experiencer. It may be somewhat galling to the doctors and nurses, when they stand back relieved at the success of their efforts as the patient opens her eyes, to be greeted by the words, "Why did you bring me back?"

Before we consider the after-effects of NDEs, which often prove life-changing, we need to look at the questions that NDEs themselves give rise to. Professor Robert Kastenbaum, author of several books on aging and death, formulated seven questions: 1) Are near-death experiences real? 2) Are they significant? 3) Do NDEs constitute legitimate data for scientific and scholarly investigation? 4) Have studies been carried out to investigate NDEs? 5) Has it been found that NDEs sometimes are followed by powerful changes in thoughts, feelings, and attitudes? 6) Have theories been offered to describe or explain NDEs from a scientific perspective?

The answer he gives to each of these six questions is "yes." NDEs are real and significant to those who experience them; they have been studied and researched by scientists, doctors, and philosophers; investigation has produced many theories from a scientific perspective; there is evidence to show that they are frequently followed by marked changes in the experiencer.

Kastenbaum's seventh question, as he says, presents the problem. 7) Do near-death experiences prove survival of death?

Many people who have experienced an NDE, or who have read about them, would answer "yes," on the basis of this logical proposition: I was dead. While dead, I had a strange and beautiful experience. I came back to life (stopped being dead). Therefore death is not the end. They might add: I returned with the knowledge that "death" is nothing to fear, and since that time my life has been transformed.

To this seventh question, however, Kastenbaum's answer is "no." It is not the experience itself that is at issue here, he says, but the assertion that such experiences provide evidence for survival of death.[98] Belief in survival is a tenet of major religions and goes back to the earliest recorded times. That NDEs provide proof, however, is no more than an assertion, whatever explanation for them we may accept. What might be said is that for those who have experienced an NDE it may provide a window into the afterlife, and for many individuals, what they have glimpsed through that window takes away the fear of death. Even so, most people who have been close to death have no such experiences to report, and some of the features of the NDE have been recorded by people whose lives were in no danger, and the view through the window is not always hopeful or promising.

Returning to the logical proposition, we should consider the major premise—"I was dead"—before surveying the various theories that have been advanced in the attempt to

---

[98] See Bailey & Yates, *The Near-Death Experience, op cit*, p. 245 *et seq.*

explain or make sense of the NDE. Here are some quotations from accounts:

"In 1982 I died from terminal cancer." (Mellen-Thomas Benedict)

"I had been struck by lightning. I was dead." (Dannion Brinkley)

"I had indeed died." (Phyllis Atwater)

"Having worked as an LPN, I knew well the appearance of a dead body, and as I got closer to the face I knew at once that it was lifeless." (Betty Eadie)

"I was going to have to accept the fact that I was dead." (George Ritchie)

There are also the many instances when the patient hears the doctor, nurse, or hospice attendant declare that he or she is dead. Sometimes the phrase "clinically dead" is used. However, there is a conflict here between assertion and proof. For her book, *The Other Side of Life,* near-death researcher Evelyn Elsaesser Valarino interviewed, among other leading doctors, Paul Chauchard, professor of neurophysiology and author of *La Mort.* The discussion turned to the problem created by the term "clinically dead." Valarino quoted a passage from Chauchard's book: "Science does not resurrect, and never will resurrect the dead. But it can stop the process of death, and will increasingly do so in the future, by preventing the death of cells that would normally die, but are still alive." Valarino asked him if he concluded from this that individuals did not really die during the NDE, even if they were declared clinically dead, since they came back to life.

Chauchard agreed, saying that these persons were not dead and there was no resurrection. He added that regardless of whether one believed it or not it was only in the Gospel that he could see what might have been a genuine resurrection— that of Lazarus. That was something entirely different from resuscitation.

"Thus the term 'clinically dead' doesn't mean anything; it doesn't mean that the person is dead," said Valarino.

"You might look at it as a transition from life to death that doesn't reach completion," was Chauchard's response.

Elsewhere in the dialogue, Valarino remarked that during an NDE, brain activity was often thought by medical staff to be non-existent. She continued: "The subject is in a state of clinical death. However, this state is reversible, since the individual in question comes back to life and is able to relate his or her experiences. Does this mean that brain activity in such cases had ceased?"

"I would take it to mean that cessation of brain activity does not equal death," was Chauchard's reply. [99]

Dr. Moody, in his latest book *The Last Laugh*, is explicit on this. "By definition, death is a state from which one doesn't return. If a person is pronounced dead, no matter how sure the doctors were that their pronouncing it was correct, no matter how many dozens or hundreds of persons in that same condition they had pronounced dead, none of whom had ever snapped out of it, and no matter how stringently the standard medical criteria were applied, if that person subsequently resumed vital activities and regains consciousness, the logic of language still obliges us to say that person was not dead." [100]

It is more helpful to think of death as a process rather than as an absolute, but a process that eventually becomes irreversible. Once the body, including the brain, is buried and begins to molder or is consumed in an incinerator then there can be no argument that the process has been completed. The doctors who certify that the individual is dead will say that the process is completed sooner than that. Yet is that the end of the story? Wilder Penfield, pioneer in modern brain surgery, did not think so. In his last book, *The Mystery of the Mind* (1976) he wrote:

"When death at last blows out the candle that was life, the mind seems to vanish, as in sleep. I said 'seems.' What can one

---

[99] Valarino, E. (1997), *On the Other Side of Life*, New York: Insight Books. It has been pointed out to me that patients in intensive care are not necessarily hooked up to an EEG machine. Hence it is not always possible to be absolutely certain about the cessation of brain activity.
[100] Moody, R. (1999), *The Last Laugh*, Charlottesville, Va.: Hampton Roads Publishing.

really conclude? What is the reasonable hypothesis in regard to this matter, considering the physiological evidence? Only this: The brain has not explained the mind fully. The mind of man seems to derive its energy, perhaps in altered form, from the highest brain-mechanism during his waking hours. In the daily routine of a man's life, communication with other minds is carried out indirectly through the mechanisms of the brain. If this is so, it is clear that, in order to survive after death, the mind must establish a connection with a source of energy other than that of the brain. If not, the mind must disappear forever as surely as the brain and body die and turn to dust. If, however, during life, when brain and mind are awake, direct communication is sometimes established with the minds of other men ... then it is clear that energy from without can reach a man's mind. In that case it is not unreasonable for him to hope that after death the mind may waken to another source of energy."

Since Penfield wrote this, more and more evidence has accumulated to show that "when brain and mind are awake, direct communication is sometimes established with the minds of other men." If consciousness is not located in the physical brain, then there is no reason why it should be extinguished when the brain itself is dead. Hence the assertions made by those who believed they had in fact died during their near-death experience and yet had returned to life are not especially significant. The NDE is to be considered for what it is, as an experience that sometimes occurs during extreme physical conditions.

Nevertheless, the question is often asked as to whether NDEs provide any useful evidence of the survival of consciousness after physical death. In a paper published in the *Journal of Scientific Exploration* (vol. 12, no. 3) in 1998, experienced researchers at the University of Virginia listed three features of a typical NDE which they considered had the most relevance for the question of survival of consciousness. These features were: "normal or enhanced mentation when the physical body is ostensibly unconscious; seeing the physical body from a different position in space; and perceiving events beyond the normal range of the physical senses."

The researchers expressed their belief "that when these three features occur together they provide convergent evidence that at least suggests that consciousness can function independently of the physical body and hence may survive the death of that body."They agree that this evidence can only be suggestive because,"no matter how serious their condition, persons reporting NDEs were in fact still alive. . . . NDEs can therefore never provide conclusive evidence concerning what happens to consciousness when the brain and body are no longer revivable."

The researchers point out that almost all the cases they studied relied on memories of experiences that occurred many years before. In several instances those who might have provided corroborative evidence have died or have forgotten the precise details. For NDEs to contribute anything substantial to the evidence for survival of consciousness they need to be identified, recorded, and investigated as soon as possible after the event with details independently verified.

The Virginia researchers feel that a purely physiological explanation of consciousness may be inadequate to an understanding of the NDE. As they say, choosing their words extremely carefully: "Even a few well-documented cases of complex mentation occurring in conditions that are at variance with those predicted by a physiological model of consciousness may weaken that model." This is a pioneering study of an important, perhaps the most important, aspect of the NDE and we hope that this investigation will be only the first of many.

Some sixty books in English alone dealing with the subject of near-death experiences have been published in the past twenty-three years, plus twenty-five autobiographical accounts, several commercial films and innumerable articles in academic journals and popular magazines. Hence, this experience is well established in the public domain. Not surprisingly, many attempts have been made to explain the phenomenon from scientific, medical, and other perspectives. NDEs have been explained as hallucinations, possibly caused by oxygen deprivation; as created by "just imagination"; as the result of a flood of chemicals released into the dying brain; as types of mystical experience; as stimulated by drugs or anesthesia; as produced by unusual activity in the brain's right temporal lobe; and more.

Some of these explanations can be easily dismissed. For example, if NDEs are caused by drugs or anesthesia, how is it that they are also experienced by many who have reported them as happening outside hospitals, at home, in road accidents, in swimming pools, or on the battlefield, and with no medical attention at the time? The only possible connection between anesthesia and the NDE has been mentioned earlier; namely, the instances of distressing experiences in childbirth. As for drugs, Dr. Susan Blackmore, who has sought for a scientific explanation of the NDE for many years, says, "Apparently drugs taken near death are more likely to damp down the experience than bring it about." Other attempts to explain the NDE, however, merit attention as they may cast light on aspects of the experience even when they fail to provide a satisfactory explanation.

The hallucination theory has no evidence to support it. It is sometimes advanced by those who seek to reduce other people's experiences to the lowest common denominator, or who simply like to tell others that their experiences are illusory because they themselves know better. Professor Jean-Paul Girard, a professor of medicine in Geneva, Switzerland who experienced an NDE himself, was convinced that hallucinations had nothing to do with it. "Hallucinations imply a somewhat exaggerated, biased sensory functioning, but one that is nevertheless present," he says. There is *no* sensory functioning recorded for the majority of those who have NDEs in the hospital. Dr. Peter Fenwick asks, "Why should everyone have more or less the same hallucination in the same circumstances?" He adds, "Brains which are disorganized so that consciousness is lost do not produce coherent hallucinations. One is again driven back to asking how lucid experiences can arise in the disorganized brain of an unconscious person."[101]

---

[101] Fenwick, P. & E. (1995).

A thoughtful survey of some of the psychological, biological, and medical theories concerning the NDE can be found in Susan Blackmore's study *Dying to Live*, 1993. In her conclusion she claims that the "dying brain hypothesis," despite its shortcomings, is nevertheless sufficient to explain the consistency of reported experiences, the feeling of the reality of the experience, the paranormal or afterlife hypothesis, and the changes that occur in the outlook and priorities of the survivors. She bases her arguments largely on oxygen deprivation and stress on the brain leading to "the release of neuropeptides and neurotransmitters (in particular the endogenous endorphins)" which stimulate the limbic system. She suggests that the endorphins "could account for the blissful and other positive emotional states so often associated with the NDE."

In this, however, Blackmore is countered by another researcher, Karl Jansen, a neuropsychiatrist, who considers that "the brain produces its own blockers to protect the cells in the event of cardiac arrest or death." These "blockers," which he suggests might be a chemical called alpha endopsychosin, may in turn produce hallucinations and out-of-body sensations. Jansen has, for many years, been researching the effects on the brain of the anesthetic ketamine. He has claimed that ketamine can reproduce the effect of an OBE by blocking the flood of glutamate which surges into the brain in crisis and becomes toxic. Jansen maintained that glutamate and the "NMDA receptor" are chiefly responsible for the NDE. He described as "real reductionism," attempts by some writers to draw a "mystical shroud" over the NDE. [102]

However, Jansen has revised his views recently, now considering that drugs "do not create states of mind but render certain of them more readily accessible." In a recent issue of the *Journal of Near-Death Studies* Jansen writes:

"After twelve years of studying ketamine, I now believe that there most definitely is a soul that is independent of experience. It exists when we begin and may persist when we end.

---

[102] See Bailey & Yates, *The Near-Death Experience, op cit.*

Ketamine is a door to a place we cannot normally get to; it is definitely not evidence that such a place does not exist."

Blackmore and others attempting to explain the NDE through neuroscience run up against a major difficulty: neuroscience, although it has made some exciting discoveries, is still in its infancy. As Professor Susan Greenfield says, "the adventure is just beginning." She also makes the comment that neuroscientists tend to avoid the question of consciousness. As she remarks, "Consciousness brings the mind alive; it is the ultimate puzzle to the neuroscientist. It is your most private place."[103] Unless and until the relationship between consciousness and the brain is fully understood, it is impossible to come to a satisfactory *scientific* explanation of the NDE.

Another attempt to provide an explanation for near-death and other "paranormal" experiences is proposed by Dr. Melvin Morse. His studies include hundreds of accounts of NDEs, including four hundred Japanese experiences and fifty from Africa. As a pediatrician Morse was especially interested in children's accounts and he noted that, while cultural traditions clearly shaped much of the typical experience, the reports from Japanese children bore many resemblances to those from the American children he investigated.

Morse now proposes that the brain's right temporal lobe holds the key to all such experiences. He rejects propositions that the NDE has to do with resuscitation, drug treatment, hypoxia (oxygen deprivation) or hypercarbia (excess of carbon dioxide) and accepts the argument that there may well be "other realities to perceive" and that "theoretical physics contains the concept of a non-local reality, meaning that events can be independently linked even though there are no forces interconnecting them, implying that non-causal events can take place." Morse proposes that "our right temporal lobe allows for non-local interactions within the ordinary phenomenal world due to quantum non-locality," and claims that there

---

[103] Greenfield, S. (1997), *The Human Brain*, London: Weidenfeld & Nicolson.

are specific areas in this theory that can be proved by reproducible experiments.

Dr. Peter Fenwick, however, points out that "current neuroimaging suggests that it is wrong to be too specific about the brain areas involved in very ordinary activities." In the earlier brain model, certain faculties were categorically assigned to the right or left hemispheres. For example, reason—left; emotion—right: logic—left; intuition—right. However, from his clinical experience, Fenwick found that mystical experiences could be attributed to both right and left temporal lobes, and talking to God with marked emotional content could be left temporal, not right temporal. Fenwick's own hypothesis is that near-death experiences are consistent with mystical experience as far as the brain area is concerned. But even though Morse's focus on the right temporal lobe may not accord with all the evidence, his acceptance of the possibility of non-local interactions is a useful contribution to the debate.

Despite these, and other, attempts, scientific study of the near-death experience has not succeeded to date in providing anything more than untested hypotheses. This is no reflection on those who are striving to find a scientific explanation, having to work, as they do, with nothing more than subjective narrative accounts, often recalled months or years after the experience, and with the reordering, additions, subtractions, and interpretations that memory may provide. Such accounts are not good material for rigid scientific examination. Also this examination focuses on the functioning of the brain, the organ of the human body about which least is known. And, as we have seen, these attempts ignore the role of consciousness, or if they touch upon it they treat it as if it is simply and solely a function of the brain. So it seems that if we are to attempt to relate the NDE to other elements of human experience, to develop our understanding of the phenomenon or to seek to explain it, we may need to look elsewhere, than to the methods of conventional scientific enquiry.

In Moody's first book he used the expression "the experience affects his life profoundly" of someone who has had an NDE. As cases have accumulated and research has intensified, the profound effect of the near-death experience on the life of its survivors has emerged as perhaps its most striking feature. The after-effects so impressed Kenneth Ring that in 1984 he published *Heading Towards Omega* which dealt with these life-changing after-effects. In *Lessons from the Light* he writes that in all the cases he has studied, the individuals "though still diverse in their personalities, tended to share a common *psychological profile* afterward. In short, most of them appeared not only to be transformed by their experience, but transformed in much the same way."

Ring lists the elements of this psychological profile as follows:

- enhanced appreciation of everyday life
- greater feelings of self-worth and self-acceptance
- increased and compassionate concern for others
- reverence for animal life, for nature, and the ecological health of the planet
- rejection of materialist values and acquisition for its own sake
- an anti-competitive attitude
- a more universal and inclusive spirituality
- an increased thirst for knowledge
- a conviction that life is meaningful with a sacred purpose to everyone's life
- no fear of death
- a conviction that some form of conscious existence follows death of the body
- a deep, inner certitude that God (or the light) exists.

Other changes Ring recorded include an expanded mental awareness, increased paranormal sensitivity, and the gift of healing. While Ring notes that over 40 percent of a recent research sample mentioned that they had acquired healing abilities, other researchers (Phyllis Atwater and Cherie Sutherland) put the figure even higher. Ring notes that certain physiological and neurological changes emerged in some cases after an NDE. There are also reports from many respondents of belief in reincarnation following a near-death experience.

The findings of Moody and Ring about post-NDE life-changes are echoed in all the published reports and accounts dealing with NDEs. Even the critical Susan Blackmore admits that "there is no doubt that the NDE seems to transform people's lives." So marked and beneficial is this transformation that the near-death experience itself may come to be viewed as a learning experience to be desired, almost as if one is disadvantaged by not having had the experience. There is indeed a possibility—even Kenneth Ring has hinted at it—that the NDE may become a kind of cult, whose members (the experiencers, their loved ones, and readers of the NDE texts) may come to believe that they possess the innermost secrets of human existence. This, as can be imagined, is a dangerous path to follow.

At this stage it is timely to stop considering the NDE in isolation and to relate it to other manifestations of human consciousness. To begin with, let us return to the list of qualities making up the psychological profile that Kenneth Ring has compiled. There is no need to argue about the inclusion of any of these elements. Not only are there so many testimonies recorded by so many researchers but there is also the evidence of friends, relatives, and other observers. But is it necessary to have a near-death experience in order to undergo such a transformation? Or are there not other experiences that can produce a comparable and equally dramatic response?

One such experience is a close encounter with death where no "near-death experience" occurs. The brush with death itself is sometimes, though by no means always, enough to bring about a change of perspective, a new view of the important values, a heightened appreciation of the simpler things of life. The difficulty here is that the "non-event" is unlikely to be reported or recorded so it is not possible to gather any statistical information.

But it is not necessary to be close to death to have a life-transforming experience. There are testimonies from many people who have had one or more spontaneous out-of-body experiences who declare that these have affected their lives in a similar way. The same may be said of the transcendent experience, whether within or without a formal religious context, that may radically change one's outlook on life. In all such instances, consciousness seems to make contact with some other dimension and we see—somehow—eternity in a moment. The NDE is one type or variety of experience and we can make more sense of it if we do not study it in isolation but along with other experiences that "take us out of ourselves" into a realm where the physical body cannot enter but human consciousness can.

It is worth recalling some words of Schrödinger, quoted in an earlier chapter, in which he explains how science cannot deal with certain experiences. "The scientific picture of the real world around me is very deficient. It gives a lot of factual information, puts all our experience in magnificently consistent order, but it is ghastly silent about all and sundry that is really near to our heart, that really matters to us." The near-death experience, along with the other experiences we are considering in these chapters, takes us into that area where we find what is "really near to our heart, that really matters to us." The "us" that the NDE takes into that area is our consciousness, detached from the physical body with its brain lying senseless on the bed or the battlefield, amid the wreckage of a vehicle, or the debris of some disaster.

Now come the really difficult questions. Does the area where our consciousness takes us in the near-death experience, whether we have had the experience ourselves or simply read about it, have any sort of objective reality? Is it right for us to seek to console the terminally ill or the bereaved relatives with accounts of the journey through the tunnel, the meeting with the being of light, the life review, and the rest? Well, you may say, it's more credible than the old Biblical tales of judgement, heaven and hell, and so on. But is it enough?

In *Otherworld Journeys* Carol Zaleski writes: "Near-death literature is at its best when it is modest and anecdotal; pressed into service as philosophy or prophecy, it sounds insipid. There is no match here for the revelatory literature of the great religious traditions." The vision of Er, as told by Plato in *The Republic;* the Zoroastrian, Islamic, and Tibetan accounts; the visionary accounts narrated by the Venerable Bede—all these and many more are basically moral tales, telling of the rewards for living a good life and the punishments for being wicked. They are powerful teaching stories, impressive in their certainty. But the late twentieth-century experiences lack this strong moralizing. There is no evidence that the "good" person will have a positive NDE and the "bad" one a distressing time. The life review, when it happens, may give you an uncomfortable or even painful experience, but no divine judge pronounces sentence.

In a world of uncertainty, of holocausts, disasters—manmade and natural—brought vividly into our homes every day in pictures and print, the near-death experience may bring a form of consolation and—for some—hope. It may act as a signpost for future researchers investigating whether some element of consciousness does survive the death of the body and brain. Or perhaps this experience is a type or variant of a transcendent experience that some individuals may access in a state of extreme physical stress. Then, regarding it from another angle, it could be explicable as a construct of human consciousness, created through the interconnectedness of minds, in an age when the old religions have, apart from the fundamentalist believers, largely lost their hold on mankind. However we interpret the NDE, we can be certain that it adds to our understanding of consciousness as being able to function unrestricted by time and space. While not every NDE involves an out-of-body experience, it happens sufficiently often for us to be assured of the freedom of consciousness to operate outside the confines of the physical body, even when the brain itself is unable to function. We shall see this more clearly when we focus on the "ordinary" out-of-body experience, when the condition of the physical body becomes irrelevant.

But above all the NDE is a personal experience. It is memorably summarized in a medieval Sikh poem, translated by Dr. Maurice Roles and published in his *Voyage of Discovery*:

> *I looked at death, I viewed my end of life.*
> *The dying body that I saw was mine,*

> *Yet felt my spirit separate, calm and high*
> *On the wide ocean floating far and free,*
> *That ocean men describe as ecstasy*
> *Which all-pervaded is with light and joy*
> *And body's death is like the breaking of a toy.*

Finally, to keep the question open, it is not, I think, too far-fetched to suggest the possibility that the pattern of events reported in the typical near-death experience (Dr. Moody's nine features) might even lead us into a reality that has long waited to be discovered.

CHAPTER 5

THE OUT-OF-BODY EXPERIENCE

It was as if you were floating in warm soft clouds
where nothing exists as a separate piece of matter ...
(Robert Monroe)

In 1996 I had a phone call from a woman in Glasgow named Angela. Some twelve years ago, she told me, she started to have strange and uncomfortable experiences. Almost every night, soon after going to bed, she felt strong vibrations running through her body, accompanied by a sound that she described as resembling noisy air-conditioning machinery. The vibrations increased until she felt as if she was being pulled out of her body. While this was going on she could hear people talking in another room and the sound of a television. Angela struggled to overcome the vibrations and to remain in her body and in her bed. This experience sometimes occurred five or six times a night, she said. Sometimes she found herself a few inches above her body, looking down on it, feeling as if she was being pulled further away. She continued to struggle and eventually was able to lower herself back into her body as the vibrations weakened and stopped. Often it was early morning before she was able to sleep.

Angela was frightened and wondered if she was losing her sanity. She went to her doctor, who during the following months and years referred her to a variety of consultants, including psychologists and psychoanalysts. She was examined physically and mentally, scanned and brain-mapped. Someone suggested she approach the Department of Parapsychology at Edinburgh University, but whoever she spoke to there could not help her. The word "psychic" was mentioned, so she consulted a self-proclaimed psychic healer who told her the devil was trying to capture her soul. Although she says she did not believe this, nevertheless it added to her fear.

Then, twelve years after the first episode, she came across the phrases "astral travel" and "astral projection." No one she knew could explain what they meant. Deciding to do her own research, she went to the Mitchell Library in Glasgow and asked the librarian if there were any books on the subject. There was just one: *Journeys out of the Body* by Robert Monroe. Angela flicked over the pages. A few words caught her eye and she settled down to read a description of an experience identical to her own.

The book included the address and phone number of The Monroe Institute for further enquiries. The information was out of date but Angela persisted and eventually made contact. She was invited to visit the Institute but it was situated in Virginia and there was no way she could afford to go there. The secretary she spoke to then checked her files and came across a name and address accessible from Glasgow. Hence the phone call that begins this chapter.

Although the out-of-body experience (OBE) has not been documented so copiously as the near-death experience, except where the one is part of the other, it is still surprising that in twelve years of enquiry and examination not one medical professional recognized what Angela was talking about. The OBE is not uncommon; various surveys in Britain and the U. S. indicate that 20 percent of the population can recall at least one such experience, often from early childhood. However, researchers into consciousness or brain function generally ignore it or dismiss it as hallucination, dream, a consequence of mood-altering drugs, or a fantasy of the new age. Much of the publicity appearing in popular journals and newspapers is sensational, of the "he leaves his body and flies to the stars every night" variety. Hence many of those who have had an out-of-body experience tend to keep it to themselves lest they be laughed at or dismissed as suffering from some mental aberration.

Angela was relieved to discover that her experience was by no means unique, that it had nothing to do with her sanity or physical health or the forces of evil, that it was possible to learn how to control it, and that she could make use of it and even enjoy it. What had really troubled her for twelve years was fear: fear that if she allowed herself to leave her body, especially to move out of sight of it, she might not be able to return. This fear is shared by many who have had spontaneous OBEs. In one instance, a woman was so afraid of dying if she went out-of-body while asleep that she would sit up in a chair all night, refusing any medication lest it send her to sleep forever. Only when overcome with exhaustion did she close her eyes. When she awoke and found herself still alive, she ascribed this to luck. It made no difference to her when she was told that her autonomic nervous system, or her bladder, would protect her against dropping dead.

Gradually Angela succeeded in overcoming the fear of being, as it were, marooned outside her physical body. She was helped by exercises on tape, developed by Robert Monroe, which teach techniques to enable the listener to move into different states of consciousness knowing that it is safe to do so. Her OBEs occurred less frequently at the rate of once or twice a night and sometimes not at all. At last she was able to allow herself to move out of her body and to return at will. Since then Angela has acquired the confidence to participate in a research program on the OBE.

The expression "out-of-body experience" was coined by Professor Charles Tart, professor emeritus of psychology, University of California at Davis, who regards it as a particular kind of altered state of consciousness. He describes an altered state as "a qualitative alteration in the overall pattern of mental functioning, such that the experiencer feels his consciousness is radically different from the way it functions ordinarily."

An OBE could be defined as "an altered state of consciousness in which the subject feels that his mind or self-awareness is separated from his physical body and this self-awareness has a vivid and real sense about it, quite different from a dream." Monroe gives a detailed description of the OBE in his second book, *Far Journeys* (1985).

According to Monroe, in the OBE you are outside of your body yet completely conscious and able to see and act as if you were physically embodied. "You can move through space (and time?) slowly, or apparently somewhere beyond the speed of light," he notes. In the OBE, you can watch or participate in events, and make decisions based on your observations. You can pass through physical substance, such as a wall, a steel plate, concrete, the Earth, the ocean, air, even through atomic radiation, and you can do this with no effort or effect. Even more exciting, Monroe says, in the OBE you can go into the next room without ever opening the door; you can visit a friend thousands of miles away, or travel to far-off destinations, even the planets or the galaxy—anything or any place that interests you. "Or you can enter other reality systems only dimly perceived and theorized by our time/space consciousness."

Monroe provides a consensus view of the common characteristics of the out-of-body state. These comprise the following: Complete awareness—the ability to think logically, access memory, experience emotion, and so on—without the support mechanism of a physical body and sensory input. There's perception of both physical and non-physical environments and activities from a different perspective. There are physiological signs—temperature decrease of up to two degrees, drop in blood pressure to about ten below normal for the subject, loss of muscle tone, average 11 percent lowering of pulse rate, slow and shallow breathing—all similar to conditions of deep sleep.

Monroe also indicates two levels of activity, which he calls near and far reaches. In the "near reaches," the subject stays within the boundaries of the Earth. He can travel to China or next-door; he can pass through walls or mountains. In the "far reaches," he can make contact with other energy systems or non-physical worlds; time and space do not confine him.

In a way similar to how Raymond Moody's *Life after Life* sparked off public interest in the near-death experience, Monroe's *Journeys out of the Body* (1971) aroused interest in the OBE. Monroe, like Angela, knew nothing of any previous accounts or studies and believed at first that his experiences might be a sign of some mental derangement. "It is impossible to describe the fear and the loneliness that took over during these episodes," he said. To find an explanation, he turned to conventional medicine and orthodox science and had himself mentally and physically examined to ascertain there was nothing wrong with him. It was suggested, not wholly seriously perhaps, that he should go to Tibet to find an explanation. Instead he went to see Dr. J. B. Rhine, a well-known researcher in parapsychology at Duke University in North Carolina. Rhine could not help him, but as Monroe was leaving a graduate student, who had been sitting in on his interview, stopped him.

"Mr. Monroe, don't worry about it," he said.

"What do you mean, don't worry about it?" asked Monroe.

"Well," said the student, "I do it too."

This was the first time Monroe appreciated that his experience was not unique. Slowly he learned to control the process but it took him a year and some forty out-of-body episodes before he could accept the reality of the experience. [104]

The phrase "astral projection" that was mentioned to Angela in her search for an explanation was the precursor to Professor Tart's term "out-of-body experience." Like "astral travel," "astral body," and similar expressions, it involves a preconception or assumption about what is going on that otherwise has no rational justification. The term "out-of-body" has, in any event, a sufficiently distinguished history. It occurs in Paul's Second Epistle to the Corinthians (ch 12) in the authorized version and in Tyndale's earlier translation of 1534.

"I know a man in Christ above fourteen years ago (whether he were in the body I cannot tell, or whether he were

---

[104] Monroe, R. (1971), *Journeys out of the Body*, Garden City, NJ: Doubleday. The prime classic of out-of-body literature.

out of the body I cannot tell, God knoweth) which was taken up into the third heaven. And I know the same man (whether in the body, or out of the body, I cannot tell, God knoweth) how that he was taken up into paradise, and heard words not to be spoken, which no man can utter."

Paul himself was the "man in Christ." He regarded this experience as among "visions and revelations granted by the Lord" and affirmed to the Corinthians that it gave him authority for what he said and did.

Among the Buddha's teachings in the *Anguttara Nikaya* are descriptions of what resemble out-of-body activities:

" …unhindered he goes through walls. … . He dives in and out of the earth as if it were water. Without sinking he walks on water as if on earth. Seated cross-legged he travels through the sky like a winged bird."

In the early 1670s the English poet Thomas Traherne received a letter from his brother Philip, then living in Smyrna, describing what must have been an out-of-body experience. Thomas turned the experience into a poem:

> *On Earth he seem'd to move*
> *Yet Heaven went above.*
> *Up in the Skies*
> *His Body flies*
> *In open, visible, yet Magick, sort:*
> *As he along the Way did sport*
> *Over the Flood he takes his nimble Course*
> *Without the help of feigned Horse.*

Philip flew over a highway, crossed a river and soared up until "he o'er leapt the Moon." [105]

The noted religious scholar Mircea Eliade writes of the shaman's ability "to pass out of his body and undertake mystical journeys through all the cosmic regions." He refers to the

---

[105]Traherne, T. *Poetical Works*, 3rd edition 1932.

Eskimo shamanic practice of undertaking "ecstatic journeys to the sky, to the land of the dead, 'for joy alone.'"[106] The eighth century Anglo Saxon monk and scholar, the Venerable Bede, describes Drythelm's visionary journey, at the end of which his guide instructs this pious family man who appeared to have died "to go back to the body and live among men again," and the Irish missionary Fursa's vision "when he left his body and was carried by an angel to a great height."[107] There are references to varieties of OBEs in records from Egypt, India, China, and Tibet and among Hindus, Hebrews, and Moslems. Almost all of these early accounts, however, have a didactic purpose; they are shaped into teaching stories for the betterment of those who are to hear or read them. But they are introduced in such a way that we can assume the hearers or readers were able to accept the notion of the out-of-body journey without debate as to whether this type of experience was even possible.

A recent survey found that 41 out of 44 non-Western societies believed in the occurrence of OBEs, and the anthropologist Erika Bourguignon discovered that 437 out of 488 world societies had a tradition concerning some form of out-of-body experience. The experience itself is known by different names: the Oneida tribe of Native Americans, for example, say that "the process of going somewhere when your body stays here is known as Spirit Walking—because that's what happens. It feels like moving forward, like walking."

There is extensive literature dealing with the OBE. The bibliography to Robert Peterson's *Out of Body Experiences* (1997) lists over 150 titles dealing primarily with OBEs. About forty of these have the word "astral" in the title. Unlike books on the near-death experience, however, the major publishers, with very few exceptions, seem to shy away from these offerings. The largest contributor to the list is Dr. Robert Crookall, with twelve titles, although the single best-selling book is still

---

[106] Eliade (1972).
[107] Zaleski, C. (1987), *Otherworld Journeys*, Oxford: Oxford University Press.

Monroe's *Journeys out of the Body*, which has been translated into several languages. Most of the books are either narratives of personal experience or come into the category of "how-to" publications. Scientific studies barely figure at all and there are few attempts to relate the OBE to other manifestations of human consciousness. Today there are several web sites on the Internet offering instruction on OBEs, and an organization was founded in 1988, tongue-twistingly entitled The International Institute of Projectiology and Conscientiology, that offers programs "of theory and practice designed to make an OBEer out of those willing to put in the effort." The site has an Online Out-of-Body Experience Survey "motivated by the highest scientific spirit, with the objective of producing a comprehensive, unbiased analysis of the OBE phenomenon." It may be that it is possible to achieve regular out-of-body experiences by following such instructions and programs but I have seen no evidence of this so far.

A pioneering study that has been reprinted several times is *The Projection of the Astral Body* by Sylvan Muldoon and Hereward Carrington, first published in 1929. This includes Muldoon's descriptions of his many out-of-body experiences, edited and commented on by Dr. Carrington, himself a psychic researcher, together with analyses and suggestions as to how this state may be achieved. Carrington provides a definition of the "astral body" which many subsequent commentators have adopted.

"The astral body may be defined as the Double, or the ethereal counterpart of the physical body, which it resembles and with which it normally coincides. It is thought to be composed of some semi-fluidic or subtle form of matter, invisible to the physical eye . . . The broad, general teaching is that every human being 'has' an astral body just as he has a heart, a brain, and a liver. In fact, the astral body is more truly the Real Man than the physical body is, for the latter is merely a machine adapted to functioning upon the physical plane."

Carrington describes the astral body as the "vehicle of the Soul." It coincides with the physical body when awake, but in sleep it withdraws, "usually hovering just above it, neither conscious nor controlled." When the subject is unconscious for any reason the astral body withdraws—this is "involuntary projection." "Voluntary projection" occurs when the subject wills to leave his physical body and does so. "He is then fully alert and conscious in his astral body; he can look upon his own physical mechanism, and travel about at will, perhaps viewing scenes and visiting places he has never seen before. Subsequently he can verify the truth of these experiences by visiting the scenes or places in question. While fully conscious in the astral body, he seems to be possessed of extraordinary, supernormal powers. He can at will return to his physical body, or may be drawn into it again automatically by reason of some shock, fright, or vivid emotion."

Like many other writers on the topic, Carrington maintains that "the astral and physical bodies are invariably connected by means of a sort of cord, or cable, along which vital currents pass. Should this cord be severed, death instantly results.... This cord—which is the silver cord spoken of in Ecclesiastes—is elastic, and capable of great extension. It constitutes the essential link between the two bodies." There is no evidence that the author of Ecclesiastes was referring to this specific "essential link," but a cord or string linking the physical body to the spiritual or astral body is often mentioned in the more esoteric accounts of transitional states. When the OBE is part of a near-death experience, however, I cannot recall any references to a cord.

While Carrington's account of voluntary projection is similar to Monroe's and to many other descriptions of this state, his, or rather Muldoon's, insistence on the cord raises a problem. This means of connection which, if broken, results in death is seldom referred to in recent accounts. Yet Muldoon goes into great detail in several pages, discussing the dimensions of the cord, which seem to vary from the thickness of a hose to a single strand of a spider's web, depending how far the two bodies are apart. He declares that, "regardless of the apparent deadness or laxity of the cord," which occurs when projection is extended, "there is necessarily an intrinsic flow of cosmic energy from the astral, or animate, to the physical, or inanimate." Robert Monroe mentions that he felt a cord on one of his early experiences but does not refer to it in later accounts. [108] Some other accounts speak of the cord as being "non-physical" altogether.

Dr. Crookall found that a majority of 380 individual reports of OBEs mentioned a cord connecting them to their physical bodies, but a methodical survey by Stuart Twemlow, M.D., Glen Gabbard, M.D., and Fowler Jones, Ed.D., presented to the American Psychiatric Association in 1980, revealed that only 21 percent of their OBE respondents reported any form of connection with their physical body. An English researcher, Celia Green, found that hardly any of her respondents were aware of a cord. [109] It may be that the presence of such a connection is a construct of the mind to overcome any fear that the two bodies may be unable to reunite without it. That it is mentioned so rarely in the more recent accounts could be because in current thinking its presence is no longer considered necessary.

So what do we make of this? We need to remember that Muldoon was physically ill while his OBEs were occurring but without knowing the clinical details it is impossible to say how much and in what ways his illness affected his perception. We should also bear in mind that, in general, people see what they expect to see, and once Carrington and Muldoon's account was published—and it is an impressively thorough study—it might well have had an effect on the ways in which other out-of-body travellers interpreted their experiences.

Carrington and Muldoon are trying—and how hard they are trying—to make sense of Muldoon's experiences. Also, and generously, they provide instructions for others to learn how to project. Then, towards the end of their study, Muldoon's pessimism, doubtlessly driven by his illness, becomes clear.

---

[108] Monroe (1985), p. 5.
[109] Green, C. and Sanford, W. (1993) *Out-of-Body Experiences*, Hillside, N.J.: Enslow.

"For my part I see *life* as the curse. I regret that life exists. . . . I regret that death does *not* end all. I wish that death would bring one long and dreamless sleep. But, alas, my experiences have proved conclusively to me that 'dust thou art and to dust returneth' was *not* written of the Soul." His experiences gave him a firm belief in immortality—alas, as he says, for this was not what he wanted.

Some remarkable accounts of OBEs appeared in William Gerhardi's autobiographical novel *Resurrection*, published in 1937. It seems almost certain that Gerhardi was writing from personal experience, although he may have read Carrington's book. His descriptions certainly carry the ring of truth. Here are some extracts from his second experience:

"It was nearly five o'clock when I turned out my light in my bedroom and fell asleep. When I felt myself waking I was alarmed at not being able to move a muscle, always associated in my mind with the danger of being buried alive. But I remembered Lord Herbert's injunction to keep calm, to dissociate myself from my benumbed body, held stiff in catalepsy, and to welcome my other freedom as I had experienced it the previous day with all its adventurous possibilities. And my wish came true. I did not this time surprise myself floating above my bed and then being placed on my feet. I was only conscious of whirling blindly—it was something between swimming and flying—through my rooms. My consciousness was so dim that it did not occur to me that anything singular was happening to me. Even though, as the contours of my room came into focus, when I stretched out my hand to soften the impact of my body with the wall or, taking no heed, passed through them, I still felt too dim to realize what was happening. Only when my own face looked back at me in dull but recognizable reflection was I sufficiently startled to say to myself: 'But I am hanging on to the stained-glass fanlight over my dining-room door'. . . . How was it then that now I managed to hold on by my finger-tips without any effort at all, and behold my reflection in the stained glass of the fanlight?

"The answer flashed across my mind: it was another 'astral' projection. And the proof? The proof was to see my body in bed.

"No sooner thought than complied with. But how queer! I saw myself in bed. My hair was differently ruffled from what I remembered of the previous occasion. My face was disconcertingly distinct. But how queer that the bed seemed to be in an unfamiliar corner. Was I dreaming, perhaps?

"And suddenly I awoke. I was standing by the door in my bedroom facing the large mirror reflecting the bed with my sleeping body. I turned away from the mirror and faced the bed; so it was. I approached my sleeping self, bent over my breathing body, lowered my hand to touch the brow of the sleeper. But an inch from it my hand halted. I could not touch that head. I cannot say what prevented me. Was there some real resistance? It may have been the fear I had that at that touch something terrible, a kind of fuse would ensue, causing my death. I turned away."

Later in his story, Gerhardi develops his out-of-body experience to the outer limits of metaphysical speculation.

"I, who had left my natural body on the bed, could now overtake the millions of untenanted bodies once mine, and tune in with them. Catch up with the waves, the vibrations which made me—millions of them, catch up, identify myself, or stand a little beside and outside, as a singer might listen to his own record or join in if he wished. . . . Time ran at right angles on this new four-dimensional plane. It ran at odd angles on the further plane. Space, too. And so I could appreciate space and time as interpenetrable and near at hand, and there was no distance I had to go to overtake the army of William Gerhardis marching away in single file, while I hovered over them like a hawk choosing his prey." [110]

Robert Crookall, who was a doctor both of science and philosophy, a leading geologist and botanist, author of such works as *The Kidston Collection of Fossil Plants* and a contributor to several scientific journals, was deeply involved in researching the OBE. In one study he recounts more than 150 instances of OBEs, concluding that "in the present writer's

---

[110] I am indebted to John Pick for these three references.

opinion, the theory of survival, the case for a non-physical body, and the reality of OBEs can all be accorded a very high degree of probability. They seem to him to be as well established as the theory of evolution."[111] But the evidence he presents, the personal narratives, may not be totally convincing. Many of Crookall's cases seem to be part of a near-death experience, some are admittedly dreams, some occur under the influence of drugs or hypnosis, and others appear to be examples of clairvoyance. Several of them are taken from published books and journals, where they are likely to have been subjected to an editing process. Here is one, and there are not many like this, that falls neatly within the OBE definition.

"I have at different times, without any conscious wish, found myself leaving my physical body and travelling through space to some scene in which I was present and heard and saw what was taking place at the time. One night I found myself leaving my body and floating towards the house of a friend. At that period of my life she was a great deal in my thoughts. I stopped at her house and wandered around outside, and then suddenly found myself in the scullery where I found my friend walking up and down in great pain and very ill. I felt very distressed and tried to help but found I could not do so. I was so frightened that, with a violent rush, I was back in my body, shaking violently and suffering from shock. The following day I called upon my friend, and, on being questioned, she admitted that she had been ill precisely in the manner at the exact time that I had visited her in my Astral Body." (Case No 96, *The Study and Practice of Astral Projection*, 1960.)

In a later book, *Intimations of Immortality* (1965), Crookall draws together the evidence, as he sees it, from OBE accounts, near-death experiences (although that term was not then current), communications with the dead, testimonies from "mediumistic" and "non-mediumistic" people, and from other sources to make a case for post-death survival. What is missing from

---

[111] Crookall, R. (1961), *The Study and Practice of Astral Projection*, London: Aquarian Press.

Crookall's work, however, as it is from Carrington and Muldoon's and other researchers of the period, is any attempt to relate his material to the workings of human consciousness. This does not imply any failing on their part. We need to remember that at that time the study of human consciousness was in abeyance; one might as well criticize Crookall and others for ignoring this as for ignoring the human genome project. At times one can sense the desperation of the researchers as they strive to find explanations for these phenomena. Back they have to go to *Ecclesiastes*, to Theosophy, to communication with discarnates, to lengthy discussions about the texture of the "astral body". It is as if everything has to be explained. Yet with the evidence and information they had before them they did the best they could.

While the majority of near-death experiences follow a similar pattern, it is quite different with OBEs when they are not associated with the near-death state. The narratives vary from the mundane to the ultra-bizarre, from moving into the next room to travelling among the planets and stars, or meeting with creatures weirder than any Hollywood script writer could imagine. Here are a few examples of spontaneous out-of-body experiences:

"One day when I was ten years old I was living at my uncle's house, a major in the Army Medical Corps. I was reclining on my bed quite awake and was looking at the ceiling beams of the old Spanish building where the living quarters were located. I was saying to myself many questions such as what was I doing there and who was I. All of a sudden I got up from the bed and started walking into the next room. At that moment I felt a strange sensation in me; it was a sensation of weightlessness and a strange mix of a sense of a feeling of joy. I turned back to go back to bed when to my big surprise I saw myself reclined on the bed. This surprising experience at that very small age gave me the kind of jerk which, so to say, shook me back to my body."[112]

---

[112] Monroe (1985), Appendix III, p. 276 (from a paper by Stuart Twemlow, M. D., Glen Gabbard, M. D. and Fowler Jones, Ed. D. presented at the 1980 Annual Meeting of the American Psychiatric Association in San Francisco).

Michael Talbot, author of *The Holographic Universe*, reported a spontaneous OBE as a teenager: "After recovering from the shock of finding myself floating over my body and staring down at myself asleep in bed, I had an indescribably exhilarating time flying through walls and soaring over the treetops. During the course of my bodiless journey I even stumbled across a library book a neighbor had lost and was able to tell her where the book was located next day."

Carl Gustav Jung recorded the following picturesque experience: "I found myself at the edge of a cosmic abyss. It was like a voyage to the moon or a descent into empty space. First came the image of a crater, and I had the feeling that I was in the land of the dead. The atmosphere was that of the other world.

"Near the steep slope of a rock I caught sight of two figures, an old man and a beautiful young girl. I summoned up my courage and approached them as though they were real people, and listened attentively to what they told me. The old man explained that he was Elijah and that gave me a shock. But the girl staggered me even more, for she called herself Salome! She was blind.

"They had a black serpent living with them, which displayed an unmistakable fondness for me. I stuck close to Elijah because he seemed to be the most reasonable of the three, and to have a clear intelligence. Of Salome I was distinctly suspicious. Elijah and I had a long conversation which, however, I could not understand."[113]

Jung also recorded a spectacular experience following a heart attack in 1944 when he seemed to find himself high in space viewing the Earth in all its beauty, "bathed in a glorious blue light" below him. Then a Hindu temple manifested in space. As he moved towards it, a strange thing happened: "I had the feeling that everything was being sloughed away; everything I aimed at or wished for or thought, the whole phantasmagoria of earthly existence, fell away or was stripped

---

[113] Jung, C. (1963), *Memories, Dreams, Reflections*, London: Collins & RKP.

from me—an extremely painful process. Nevertheless, something remained; it was as if I now carried along with me everything I had ever experienced or done, everything that had happened around me. I might also say: it was with me and I was it."

Later in the experience Jung met an image of the doctor who was treating him "in his primal form." He realized that this meant the doctor would shortly die, and indeed it turned out that Jung was the last patient he attended, for the doctor died of septicaemia shortly afterwards. [114]

In a very few reported instances a witness claims to have seen someone who was actually travelling out of body. Dr. Charles Wise, a lawyer by profession and a trustee of the Academy of Religion and Psychical Research, writes as follows:

"My brother in New Orleans had a night-watchman job and between rounds was studying to be a Southern Baptist minister. Required to write a paper on Buddhism (in a course on comparative religions), he felt out of his depth and said out loud: "I wish my brother Charles were here; he could really help me with this." (I had studied Buddhism.) Immediately I was standing, fully formed and dressed, before the desk at which he was working. Without preliminary greeting or question, he tells me, I gave him three excellent suggestions which really helped him to finish the paper. Without waiting for thanks or other comment, I turned and walked through the closed door of the room. I have no memory of this contact. . . . Do many of us travel at night and awaken without memories of it? Are some of our dreams OBEs? Are some of the answers to problems we possess on waking gained from distant sources while we slept?[115]

Robert Monroe would have answered "yes" to all of these questions.

---

[114] Ibid.

[115] *Journal of Religion & Psychical Research,* vol. 22, no. 1. January 1999.

Most OBEs, once the initial fear of leaving the body and being unable to return has been overcome, appear to be positive, interesting, often enjoyable, and sometimes informational. A few experiences, however, are frightening:

"Sometimes I feel, and still do occasionally, a terrible danger and overwhelming evil. On such times there comes a moment, when I know I must return to my body and wake up. This is instantaneous, but sometimes a strong feeling of the presence of evil persists for some seconds after waking."[116]

A patient under an anesthetic "saw herself lying on a marble slab, high up in the sky." She was approached by an evil woman carrying a stiletto who said, "If I cut her in the side she will die." Prompted by the voice of her dead daughter, she managed to roll off the slab and down snowy slopes into oblivion.[117]

The English writer and broadcaster Melvyn Bragg recalled having out-of-body experiences between the ages of twelve and fifteen. They frightened him so much that he was unable to go to sleep. What made it worse was that he could not bring himself to talk to anyone about them. "They were terrifying because I was going out of my mind, which in a sense I was," he said. "They were like those out-of-body experiences people have while on an operating table." He conjectured that they were caused by anxiety about his father's safety during service with the Royal Air Force and they ceased after his father's return.[118]

Robert Monroe recorded some frightening experiences but devised techniques to help him deal with them before returning from his out-of-body journeys. On one occasion when he was on the way back to his body he ran into what seemed to be a solid wall made of steel plates welded together. He could not push through it nor could he find a way round it. He struggled and prayed but to no avail. "I panicked. I clawed, screamed, and sobbed," he said. Then, as a last resort,

---

[116] Quoted in Jakobsen, M. (1999), *Negative Spiritual Experiences*, Religious Experience Research Center, Oxford, Occasional Paper.
[117] Ibid.
[118] *The Daily Telegraph*, London, Sept 5, 1999.

he turned and moved back the way he had come. Seconds later, he was back in his body, in bed.[119]

In some instances the individual takes on a different personality in the out-of-body state and appears to move into a different time period also. Professor J. H. M. Whiteman, a mathematician from Cape Town University, South Africa, conducted an intensive study of mystical and psychical experiences. He travelled out-of-body on many occasions. In that state he frequently saw himself as a woman. Here is an example that occurred in 1954. He was lying on his bed, fully awake, when he passed into what he calls "secondary separation."

"I am in the cabin of a boat and have just got ready to go down to dinner, having been delayed. . . . I am the recently married wife of the captain, and am travelling with him on the boat as if taking a kind of delayed honeymoon trip. Thought of our relationship brings an indescribable contented feeling to my heart.

"I go down the stairs rather quickly, enter the dining saloon, which is not very large, and come up to a table where the people are sitting, approaching from behind my husband, an empty seat for myself being on his left. Before sitting down, I lean forward and kiss him on his left temple.

"Just at that instant I become conscious of a man on the opposite side of the table, and I look up to find him staring at me with a peculiarly fixed gaze. The intensity of human contact brings the scene into an extraordinary sense of reality. The expression on the man's face, though vivid and intense, is barely describable in words. It seems to me that he is holding in check a kind of resentment of me (perhaps for a woman being on a boat of that kind), covering a reluctant personal interest, as a man might have for a woman in that situation. The impact of his mind on me leaves me rather shaken, and I return to a more normal state, living again less vividly the feelings and perceptions in the experience."[120]

---

[119] Monroe (1971).
[120] Whiteman, J. (1986), *The Meaning of Life*, Gerrard's Cross, Buckinghamshire: Colin Smythe.

Whiteman suggests that here he has entered into the life of another person who is not physically alive and is acting out events "in a corresponding body and with memories relevant to the situation." In other OBEs he has seen himself as a woman wearing clothes subsequently discovered as resembling a fashion worn in Florence in 1460, and as being present, again as a woman, in four scenes, two in the Forum in ancient Rome, one in a crowd 'far from Rome,' and one in a small boat approaching the southern coastline of England. Of this episode he says "all four experiences seemed to be vividly 'my own' and of the same period in the past." Then in two successive days in 1974 he was an apprentice Minoan priestess. Three years later he found a picture of the type of skirt he had been wearing. [121]

There are some similarities between Whiteman's experiences and those of Monroe. Once he had gained confidence in handling the out-of-body state, Monroe made several visits to a world he refers to as Locale 3, which he describes as a physical-matter world almost identical to our own. "There are trees, houses, cities, people, artifacts ... homes, families, businesses, and people work for a living. There are roads, railroads, and trains." But there are no electrical devices, lights, radios, televisions, or electric power. No internal combustion, gasoline, or oil were found as power sources. The engines were steam-driven; the automobiles were large, without pneumatic tires, steered by a single horizontal bar, and limited to about 20 mph.

On his out-of-body visits to this world, Monroe melded with a man who was a sort of architect-contractor, a lonely man with little money. On later visits he met a wealthy woman with two children, whom he eventually married. Later they parted. Monroe took over this architect-contractor from time to time at various stages in his life. He says it was not the sort of life he would choose to live.

Locale 3, Monroe suggests, might be a memory of some earlier Earth civilization, or another Earth-type world located in a

---

[121] Ibid.

different part of the universe. Or it might be an anti-matter dupli-cate of our world where we are the same, but different. He quotes Dr. Leon Lederman, professor of physics at Columbia University: "Basic physics is completely consistent with the cosmological conception of a literal antiworld of stars and planets composed of atoms of antimatter, which is to say negative nuclei surrounded by positive electrons. We can now entertain the intriguing idea that these antiworlds are populated by antipeople, whose antiscien-tists are perhaps even now excited by the discovery of matter."[122]

This hypothesis might account for the experiences of those who appear to lead double or multiple lives. One woman, the wife of a university lecturer, would from time to time shut herself away in her room for two or three days. During this period she claimed to be living the life of a younger woman married to a wealthy businessman in Switzerland. She could report on this life in the closest detail. It seemed to her more real and much more exciting than her life in this reality, full of luxury living and adventure with much criminal activity, sometimes violent. Another woman followed an alternative life as a male medical student, living in a town she had never seen before. Indeed, she claimed to have five alternative lives into each of which she was moved from time to time with no effort or will on her part. These are not instances of multiple personality. These alternative lives do not seem to co-exist; they are kept quite separate, and it is as if the two, or more, personalities do not meet or affect each other. For many years, however, the first woman earnestly hoped that her Swiss husband would come to join her in this reality. To date he does not seem to have done so. [123]

The popularity of his books—the last of them, *Ultimate Journey*, was published in 1994—led to Monroe becoming closely associated with the OBE. At his institute in Virginia, Monroe experimented with sound patterns to see if they could bring about an OBE. His team, which included

---

[122] Monroe (1971).
[123] Personal communications.

physicists and psychologists, found that certain combinations of very low frequency sound signals might induce an OBE, but generally only in those people who had previously experienced one or more episodes. The signals helped the listener to move into a deeply relaxed state and then to roll or lift out of the physical body. [124]

Monroe's participants work either in a sensory deprivation unit in his laboratory or in single units with controlled temperature, shielded from outside interference. They are connected via headphones and microphone to a monitor, who observes certain elements of the participants' physical condition (body temperature, galvanic skin response, skin potential voltage), controls the input of the sound patterns and helps to guide them through whatever they are experiencing. They are also able to record their experience on tape. This facility makes a useful contribution to any study of what has been happening, whether it is an OBE within the terms of the definition, a peak or transcendent experience of some kind, a pre-arranged mission to investigate a particular question or problem—or simply nothing much. These live recordings have an immediacy that is lost when experiences are recollected, sometimes months or years later, and are not subject to editing for the sake of grammatical or syntactical accuracy. Here is a transcript of a tape made by a woman called Elizabeth during such a session.

"It's night-time and I'm in a boat approaching a rocky coast—it might be the west coast of Ireland, or Cornwall. The rocks are tall and upright, with water slapping against them. I might be just above the boat. Ahead there is a cleft or shaft in the rocks. I'm going into this—I'm not afraid. The walls are black with wetness shining on them. I'm turning into a tunnel or narrow cave ... now I'm in a cave ... there's light reflected off the rocks so I can see.... I'm going down—there's a fissure in the roof above.... There's the little dog that I've seen before. (This little dog had manifested in a previous OBE.)

---

[124] These exercises may be found on cassette tape or compact disc in The Monroe Institute's course "Waves of Change."

"I've come through a long, narrow tunnel—so narrow, how could anyone get through here? Now I'm being shown what it's like to have the weight of a rock on my chest—it doesn't hurt but it's as though a big piece of rock is lying across me. It's showing me what someone would experience if a mine shaft or something like that collapsed on them. . . .

"Energy is pouring in . . . I must relax . . . I'm being shown what it's like to be trapped in a confined space deep inside a rock formation. . . . It feels as if someone is holding my left hand . . . there may be somebody there, if I can reach him . . . . Yes, his name is Gregory—he's coming loose from a place he's been stuck in, low down to my left in the rocks. He's sliding out—he's very relieved to come out. He didn't think that anyone would find him . . . he's thirty-one years old . . .

"I feel he was climbing on the rocks and the tide came in. He found the opening, like I did, and went down. I feel that because I was shown the compression of rock—the weight—that there must have been a rockfall and he was trapped.

"He's still holding my hand. I'm trying to find out . . . Black—is that his surname? He wants a hug—he's been there a long time . . . since 1948. . . .

"What shall I do? Take him to the Center? But how do I know . . . ? Fix the idea of the Center in my mind, extend for it. He'll be comfortable there and looked after—he understands.

"He's leading me now. He knows where to go. I tell him I love him and he's free to go . . . he's moving away now . . .

"I'm being taken to a more comfortable place . . . . It's strange—when I asked to be moved after Gregory had left I picked up on the fear he'd experienced when he entered the cave . . . when he died. It was as though his fear had permeated the rocks, and after he left the fear left also—I felt it brush past me, as if I were in its slipstream. . . . Now it's time for me to return. . . ."[125]

There is an intriguing postscript to this story. Elizabeth's daughter had died the previous year. A few months later Elizabeth was a participant in a seminar that included a

---

[125] Monroe (1994), pp. 263-4.

holotropic breathing session. This is a process developed by the psychiatrist Stanislav Grof in which guided, controlled over-breathing may achieve an altered state of consciousness which sometimes leads to an out-of-body experience. An acquaintance of Elizabeth's, Carol, was also on this seminar. Here is an extract from her journal.

"Towards the middle of the exercise I found myself at the level where I usually commune with my guides. As I walked across the bridge instead of my guides I saw a woman walking towards me. Simultaneously I had a flooded feeling that I had not spent sufficient time with Elizabeth at the seminar and I made a commitment to remedy that after the exercise was over. The woman approached me and spoke in a decidedly English accent: "Tell Mummy hello for me." Then she added: "Ask her, how is the little dog." The woman was very happy and surrounded by light—very radiant. I agreed to tell Elizabeth and then moved on into another experience. . . . After the session I sought out Elizabeth but felt foolish telling her of her daughter asking about the dog. Finally I did so, and both of us shared in the meaningfulness of the message."

Contact with someone who has died happens quite frequently in OBEs. It may be a loved one, a relative, or a person quite unknown before. In another account from the records at The Monroe Institute a doctor when out-of-body met a little girl about eleven years old. She told him she had recently died of leukemia at a hospital in Ohio. He explained to her that he was there to help her "in her transition to another level." The account continues: "She seemed to understand me and trust me. I did the same, and as we hugged I suddenly experienced an overwhelming feeling of love that engulfed my whole body. It was a feeling I have experienced only a few treasured times in my life."

He guided the girl to the level where he knew she should be and left her there. After the experience, he wrote the following:

"I never checked to see if the name and address she gave me were real. The experience was real and meaningful beyond measure." The doctor understood afterwards that he had been offered the chance to finish an episode from his life that had remained unresolved for decades. It had started when he was a medical student and had befriended a girl who had leukemia. During the three years he knew her, the girl was hospitalized off and on. One Sunday, at the end of a busy workday in his pediatric internship, the doctor was approached by the girl. He was so busy writing orders in charts that he told her he couldn't talk to her then. She went back to her room. Soon after a nurse reported that the girl had died in her bed. The doctor lamented: "Had I taken just a few moments, I could have helped her in the transition that I knew was coming." Now, twenty-five years later, he was given another opportunity to help. This time he made good use of it. [126]

Sometimes attempts are made to validate events in experiences such as these, with occasional partial success. But those who have the experiences are usually not interested in validation. For them, the experience itself is enough. In some instances it gives a different perspective, seen in comments such as "I have a new realization of truly being part of a whole"; "This has truly freed me from my emotions surrounding this loss (mother's death) and I believe it has freed her"; "There's no more question in my mind where I will go when I die and what I will be doing the rest of my life." There is much value here for the individual without the need to draw any general conclusions. [127]

In Monroe's nightly journeys he moved further and further from home until he found himself in what he called "other energy systems." "Exploration out-of-body is a prime means for functioning outside the physical universe," he writes in *Ultimate Journey.* "The 'second body' of the [out-of-body] state is certainly not physical. It is part of another energy system that commingles with the Earth Life System but is out of phase with it." The barrier that prevents some people from allowing themselves to move out-of-body or, if they have managed this,

---

[126] Ibid, p. 262.
[127] Ibid.

to explore the "far reaches," he believes, is fear. Taking exploration one step at a time, as he did himself, enables you to discover that these changes are not dangerous or threatening to physical life.

The matter-of-fact approach that Monroe took to learning to travel out-of-body dispenses with such terms as "astral projection," "traveling clairvoyance," "astral," or "etheric" body, and avoids belief systems with talk of doubles or soul-bodies. This serves, at least in part, to demystify the process. An OBE is most likely to occur spontaneously, when you are in a different state of consciousness from the normal, everyday state in which most us spend most of our time. The hypnagogic state, when you are between awake and asleep, or the hypnopompic state, between asleep and awake, may provide opportunities. Being totally relaxed or, in contrast, totally focused, are also states in which an OBE might occur.

Sometimes the OBE, especially when it involves moving into a non-physical world, is confused with what is known as lucid dreaming. A lucid dream is a dream you know you are having. You are dreaming, but you are aware that you are dreaming. You may be able to alter or control your part in the dream. With practice, you may be able to plan or pattern your dream before you go to sleep. This does not mean that you can control every element in the dream, only your own contribution to it. You are in a dream world where anything can happen.

The non-physical world that you visit out-of-body is, to all intents, a real world while you are in it. You are unable to affect or alter it except insofar as yourself or the character you are inhabiting can do so in the course of daily life. Unlike the dream world, this world appears to have a logical structure of its own. You may enter it voluntarily or you may suddenly find yourself there without any intention on your part. Others may enter it also. Monroe himself discovered the "Park," which he described as "an artificial synthesis created by human minds, a way station designed to ease the trauma and shock of the transition out of physical reality." Following the route he mapped out, others claim to have discovered it also.

Because it is extremely difficult to prove an OBE, it is often dismissed as "imagination," a type of hallucination or simply a dream. It is possible that some reported "experiences" may fall into one of those categories, but nevertheless sufficient evidence has accumulated to reject these hypotheses as explanations for OBEs in general. Don Eldridge, an Australian researcher who has had several OBEs, says he feels "sorry for philosophers totally trapped in their bodies who construct their theories of consciousness from reading the theories of other philosophers, also trapped in their bodies in what mimics an infinite regress. Without the hard evidence of personal experience to go by, I can understand why these 'rationalists' refuse to believe those of us who have been out of our bodies, and why they say, with the absolute certainty that comes only with a complete lack of evidence, that we have been hallucinating."[128] The Monroe Institute has details of hundreds of individuals who have experienced out-of-body episodes under laboratory conditions while their brain activity is being recorded by EEG. While some OBEs occur while you are asleep, this provides the clearest evidence that they may also occur when you are wide awake.

Various experiments have been set up to ascertain whether individuals out-of-body were able to visit specified places and report back particular items of information. Charles Tart tells of an experiment he conducted with a young woman he calls Miss Z. At this time he was concerned about the relationship between OBEs and the near-death experience and wondered whether Miss Z, who had frequent OBEs during her sleep, was near death when she moved out-of-body. She slept in his laboratory for several nights, attached to an EEG machine. When she was ready, Tart moved to another room, selected at random a five-figure sequence from a book of random numbers, wrote it on a piece of paper and placed it on a shelf near the ceiling in the room where Miss Z was to sleep. He told her the number was there and asked her to memorize it and also memorize the time from a clock in the room.

---

[128] Scientific & Medical Network, *Network* 64, August 1997.

The EEG reading showed that she was not near death but was in a brain wave state he had never seen before, a mix of theta and slow alpha. On all nights except one she said that while she had gone out-of-body (she describes it as "floating") she could not see the target number. "On the one occasion when she said she saw the number," Tart says, "she correctly reported that it was 25132. Now that is odds of a million-to-one to guess correctly like that on a single try." He adds that a single experiment proves nothing, "but this does make the question of whether an OBE can sometimes indeed be what it seems to be, the mind being located in space elsewhere than the body, a most interesting question!" That is precisely what the out-of-body perception in many near-death experiences appears to confirm: that the mind—or consciousness—during the experience is located in space elsewhere than the body. [129]

Another report throws further light on the OBE. Keith Clark was thirty-five when it happened. Nine years previously he had fractured three cervical vertebrae in an accident and thereafter was classified as a quadriplegic with no sensation or control below his neck, including his fingers.

Keith was taking part in a weekend workshop, listening to taped exercises using the Monroe audio technology mentioned previously. Because of his disability, Keith was lying on a bed in a room adjacent to that where the other participants were gathered. On the Saturday evening the exercise employed was called "Living Body Map." This is designed to enable the listener to balance and strengthen the body, visualizing a symbolic map of the body to help focus attention.

As he listened to the tape, Keith began to sense what he described as a freedom and ease of movement. "It was indeed freedom from the long-felt constraints of paralysis that my

---

[129] Tart, C. (ed) (1997), *Body Mind Spirit*, Charlottesville, Va.: Hampton Roads Publishing. Introduced and with two contributions by Professor Charles Tart, the doyen of investigators into altered states of consciousness, this volume contains essays by several notable researchers into the relationship between science and spirituality.

body had been subjected to for the past nine years." He continues his account:"Gently and smoothly, with great intention, I sat upright. And, in what seemed so effortless a way, I rose to my feet. With a brief hesitation, I carefully took my first step. Well, perhaps it wasn't a step but more of a shuffle. But at any rate I was standing erect. Not only was I standing, but I had movement!"

Keith began to move toward the door, gradually gaining confidence. He could feel the carpet beneath his feet and the coolness and texture of the wall as he steadied himself. He was, he says, being bombarded with sensations. In ten slow steps he reached the doorway into the next room, and entered. He moved around the room and stopped, looking down on the face of the workshop leader who was a long-time friend of his."As I looked down upon her face, I had a sense of how tall I was. My injury had reduced me from my one-time height of six feet, two inches down to four feet, six inches—but now I had moved back again. As I continued looking down, I noticed that she was becoming more distant. Suddenly I realized that I was floating—that I was being led or taken to another place. A place that is here and now while being beyond here and now. And there I met with what I have heard the Hawaiians, and perhaps the Native Americans, refer to as 'your Council.'"

Keith could not find words to describe what followed. He was aware of receiving definite communication, an "imparting of knowledge," and of a presence that he sought to describe as "an unlimited source of love." He felt that this experience resembled the planting of a seed that would eventually flower and that in time his understanding of the information he received would become usable and complete.

He insisted he did not want to return to the confines of a paralyzed body and tried as hard as possible to bring back with him "whatever would allow me to repair the damage to the physical body that I had chosen and was identified as belonging to me. I remember saying over and over again, 'I am not going back without full recovery; I am not going back into physical limitations. . . . ' Then a bit of what I would call 'a sense of caring, parental reassurance' came over me—and I was back in my body."

The tape was ending. Keith thought how he wanted to get up—to open his eyes, swing his legs up and over to the right, place his feet firmly on the floor, sit upright and stand. Recalling his recent vivid experience, he opened his eyes and began to focus on the room. As he did so, his legs began to move."And with one graceful movement both my right and left legs simultaneously swing up and over the right side of the bed. My hips were in alignment, and from almost any angle it would appear that I was ready to get out of bed."

He continues:"Now it is true that I did not physically stand that day. However, my body did respond in the exact way in which I had asked it to. This was the first time since my accident nine years before that I had intentionally moved my legs to exactly where I wanted them. A week later I repeated the "Living Body Map" tape. I again finished the tape, opened my eyes, and moved my legs over, placing my feet once again upon the floor."

Keith's story has not yet ended. He claims to be getting gradually stronger and achieving greater control of his body. One day he hopes to walk. [130]

Of course it is easy to provide a materialist or reductionist "explanation" of Keith's experience. But why seek to do so? No one knows more about the "reality" of the experience than Keith who experienced it. It speaks for itself.

Although being out-of-body is a consciousness experience, the word "consciousness" very seldom appears in OBE narratives. One account, from the archives of the Religious Experience Research Center, is an exception.

"One afternoon while I was at home alone, just relaxing, I started thinking about the universe, how big it must be, perhaps never ending. I was wondering about that. How could something never end? Suddenly, it was as if a funnel were in the top of my head and my consciousness went out into it,

---

[130] Russell (1993).

spreading wider and wider as it went. This went on for quite some time until I suddenly realized that I was conscious of everything that is, and that I was part of it all. Then I became aware of it from a different aspect. I was everything that is.

"It seemed curious at first, but then turned into a feeling of being very much alone. I thought surely there must be something or someone outside of me, but I searched and searched and could find nothing that was not a part of me. Desperately I wanted someone to share my existence. Finally the loneliness became overwhelming and I snapped back into my usual little self. . . . It changed my life, giving me a strong feeling of empathy for all the people around me and even all those I have never met. We are all in the same boat." [131]

This account comes into the category of a transcendent experience but the expressions "went out" and "snapped back" indicate that the woman to whom this experience occurred was aware of something, which she defined as her consciousness, that left her body and returned to it.

Another experience from the same archives has similar transcendent qualities. In this case the woman had stopped talking about it "because the response (even from my husband) has been embarrassment tinged with worry about my mental state." She was in church one Sunday, not attending to the service but "worrying about the things that preoccupy most mothers of three adolescents (e. g., would my eldest son fail his A levels/fall off his motorbike/sleep with his girlfriend/take drugs/dye his hair pink, etc.)." She continues:

"Suddenly I was 'taken out of myself' (I can't think of any other way to express it but I felt disembodied) and taken up and felt that I was at the edge of a tremendous crowd surrounding a bright light. The ones nearest were drenched in the light and all I wanted ('yearned for' would be nearer) was to be drawn into the light too. There was no 'Christ figure'—just light.

"Suddenly I knew I was back 'inside' myself, but was left with a feeling of peace, which lasted for several weeks. Not

---

[131] Quoted in Maxwell & Tschudin (1990).

that the things that I was worrying about would not happen, but a feeling of assurance that even if they did, it didn't matter—ultimately all would be well.... I was not asleep (in fact we were standing at the time) and I was not day-dreaming.... I was not on drugs and my health was good. I could find no explanation for what I felt was a glimpse of another dimension of existence."[132]

The words "taken out of myself," "disembodied," and "back inside myself" define this as an OBE. The "I," the consciousness, is away from the physical body, on its own journey. One wonders what the minister would have thought had he known what was happening to a member of his congregation.

"The validity of the out-of-body experience as a genuine phenomenon of consciousness has gained credibility," says professor of physics Amit Goswami.[133] To begin with, his scientific training made him regard the OBE as an illusion, but once he was able to relate the experience to remote viewing he rejected this idea. Now he was able to conclude, "Here was an explanation of the OBE that could satisfy the skepticism of a scientist. The nonlocality of our consciousness is the key to resolving the paradox." Goswami contends that quantum mechanics provides crucial support for the nonlocality of consciousness. Clearly this has to be considered, although there is always the tendency for the specialist to see a solution to a problem within his own specialization.

Another sort of specialist would approach this phenomenon from a very different angle. While the belief system of the materialist, whether scientist or not, may balk especially at the notion of non-physical worlds, such as Monroe's "Park" or Keith Clark's visit to his "Council," non-physical worlds are articles of faith for most religions. What are the Kingdom of Heaven, the Paradise of Indra, al-Jannah, Elysium, the Kingdom of Inexhaustible Light except non-physical worlds? Visits to such exalted areas are not unknown in the accounts of OBEs.

---

[132] Maxwell & Tschudin (1990), p. 65.
[133] Goswami (1993).

The out-of-body experience challenges the conventional view of reality as being necessarily visible and tangible. Hence for some of those striving to construct a science of consciousness it is tempting to deny or dismiss the experience rather than to accept it and consider its implications. But no science of consciousness can be anything like comprehensive unless it takes subjective experience into account, not simply as an addendum, but as a central part of the study.

In the meantime, what are we to make of the out-of-body experience itself? It may alter one's perspective on life, and perhaps also on death, but probably, and not surprisingly, less so than a full-scale NDE. It demonstrates that you are more than your physical body, but in this it is only one of many other phenomena. Its importance lies in what it can tell us about human consciousness: that it is not confined to the brain or the physical body but can operate effectively in another dimension unrestricted by our constructs of space and time.

CHAPTER 6

COMMUNICATION WITH THE UNBODIED

The voice of the dead was a living voice to me ...
(Tennyson)

"The principal reason human consciousness is so much richer than the consciousness of other animals," said Peter Russell in *The Consciousness Revolution*, "stems from the fact that we have evolved the capacity for speech." But what if the speech comes—or appears to come—not from other human beings but from those who are physically dead, or who have never been in physical existence, or who manifest themselves as voices inside our heads? In this area, it is not what we say but what is said to us—the quality and value of the communication—that we have to consider. So what does this sort of speech, coming from non-physical sources, add to our exploration of human consciousness?

First, there is the type of communication that comes from inside one's head, This is known as "hearing voices"—voices inside your head that give information or instructions and may also pronounce judgements. It has a very long history. Much of Biblical prophecy seems to be in this category. Mystics of different faiths heard voices and saw visions. Joan of Arc based many of her actions on messages from God and the saints that came to her as voices in her head. Carl Jung heard voices frequently and at one time conversed, to his advantage, with Philemon, a mythological Greek sage. But the divine or the mythological do not have to be involved. Professor E. D. Starbuck, a leading psychologist of religion in the late nineteenth century, cites an instance where prayer and resolutions had failed. He tells of a woman, Louisa, who tried to quit smoking her pipe but found the desire too strong:

"I cried and prayed and promised God to quit, but could not. I had smoked for fifteen years. When I was fifty-three, as I sat by the fire one day smoking, a voice came to me. I did not hear it with my ears, but more as a dream or sort of double think. It said 'Louisa, lay down smoking.' At once I replied, 'Will you take the desire away?' But it only kept saying, 'Louisa, lay down smoking.' Then I got up, laid my pipe on the mantel-shelf, and never smoked again or had any desire to. The desire was gone as though I had never known or touched tobacco. The sight of others smoking and the smell of smoke never gave me the least wish to touch it again." [134]

It may not be profitable to try to interpret this type of experience. Many people will recognize something similar happening—a voice in your head uttering a warning or command that is to your advantage or benefit. It may be a type of premonition or it might originate from a deeply felt wish or intention that for the moment is submerged yet somehow takes verbal form without your being aware. In these instances the "voice" appears to know more than you do and you are inclined to trust it. In some instances the voice accompanies you for many years. You may come to regard it as a guardian spirit, a companion, or friend. One woman who had been hearing voices for eleven years said, "I suppose they help me think things through a bit. It is like people doing your reasoning for you in your head." Another woman, now in her sixties, had been hearing voices since

---

[134] Quoted in James, W., *Varieties of Religious Experience.* James frequently refers to the work of Professor E. D. Starbuck who was a pioneer investigator into the psychology of religion.

childhood. "Although it can be difficult, I have learned to take notice of these voices, because they have invariably been proved right," she says. "I have adopted them as travelling companions."[135]

With some people the voices seem to alternate between good and evil. The story of a woman named Marian, who recorded her experience for a Hearing Voices self-help group in the north of England, illustrates this. Marian had a troubled childhood and was sent for psychiatric treatment after self-injuring and overdosing. After leaving high school she lived with an austere and disciplined religious group for about a year. Towards the end of that time she began to hear voices. She describes what happened:

"I felt no surprise; it seemed natural to me. I was not shocked but in awe. What sounded like baby angels was soothing; they sounded sweet and loving. They comforted me. But the demons were chilling and I was terrified. Sometimes I had to go to bed with the light on I was so frightened. The demons mocked and scorned me and sounded menacing. Even though the voices told me to do things, I never did what they said. Sometimes the voices came from machines. A running vacuum cleaner called me filthy names. Laundry machines, air conditioners, cars, and motorcycles all taunted me. The flame on the gas stove also spoke. Sometimes I thought I heard the footsteps of huge invisible men following me. When I read a book the words became audible. And when I walked my footsteps were words. As the wind blew, it whispered messages in my ear."

Then, without warning, there was a change. The voices, now emanating from insects and birds, became melodious and loving. In a heavy downpour, Marian heard a voice in the rain saying "Believe in Jesus Christ and you will be saved." This, she says, helped her through subsequent psychiatric treatment for schizophrenia by convincing her that life had meaning

---

[135] Romme, M. & Escher, S. (1993), *Accepting Voices*, London: Mind Publications.

and purpose. Her condition has improved dramatically through a change in her belief system and a combination of medical science and religion. [136]

Another aspect of this phenomenon is demonstrated by the experience of Sharon, age 32. She was illegitimate, black, and when very young was put into care. Here is part of her story in her own words:

"I first began to hear voices at the age of about 13. I endured much racial abuse at school. As I lived in a white area people stared and I grew up paranoid and lonely. I had no friends to mix with. Other children's parents told them to keep away from me. I became withdrawn, confused, sad, and suicidal. The first time I can recall hearing voices was when they ordered me to kill myself; they were so persistent. They called me 'nigger,' 'coon,' and 'wog.' I was so depressed with all this going on that I finally couldn't take any more. I took an overdose of forty pain-killers and was discovered and rushed to the hospital for a stomach-pump. I did it to escape the voices. I wanted to die to make it all end."

A few years later Sharon enrolled at a college. She was still hearing voices and could not concentrate on studying. She suffered a breakdown and was sent to a psychiatric hospital. "I longed to be punished," she says. "I really couldn't cope with life any more." In the hospital she was described as "emotionally unstable" and given drug treatment, enforced injections, and electro-convulsive therapy which, she claims, induced petit mal epilepsy for which she is still on medication. She received no other therapy at all. The treatment did not stop the voices and she still had to take drugs.

Sharon continues her story:

"I only wanted someone to talk to. I felt lonely. I hated myself for being a person trapped in a black body. I didn't

---

[136] Sheffield Hearing Voices Group, Newsletter No. 1. (reprinted from Schizophrenia Bulletin 23(3):541-543, 1997). This is a self-help group with an education and training section and a resource center. There are several similar groups in the U. K.

understand why I was born, or why people hated me so much. Again voices ordered me to kill myself. I was in the hospital for nearly fifteen months and then discharged myself with only six pounds in my pocket and nowhere to live. The voices were taking over. I was homeless in Leeds, found rough hostels, and was sexually abused. I was desperate and vulnerable. The voices were worse than ever. In the end I was so unhappy, the voices told me to set a fire in another hospital. I heard the Devil screaming inside my head: "You are an evil black whore!" So I was sent to Styal Prison for five and a half months. At last I was being punished. I felt relieved to be safely locked up away from society. Prison was easy and I didn't want to be discharged."

Subsequently Sharon had to spend more time in the hospital and was labelled "paranoid schizophrenic," a label that she does not accept. In a drop-in center she met and later married a man who also heard voices. They both help at the Hearing Voices Network where she has made friends and feels accepted "as a valid human being" not as "a mad, crazy nutter."

Sharon has formed a theory about her voices, which she believes are memories and recollections from her early childhood when she suffered depression as well as racial abuse and was the butt of ignorant jokes. She adds: "But it is worse than that. This pattern has remained in my mind, and I am destined to hear constant reminders of terrible emotional trauma. What is the cure? There is no cure because I do not have a biological illness. I am bruised and hurt by earlier experiences, and this is part of my roots."[137]

Sharon may be correct in asserting that there is no cure, although in a shamanic society she would be treated with more understanding than she received in a psychiatric hospital. Her experience would be understood as "spirit possession" and would be dealt with in a way appropriate to the particular society. The ground between shamanism and psychiatry is

---

[137] *Voices* Magazine, no. 17, summer 1996. Sharon de Valda is now Women's Officer for the Hearing Voices Network, Dale House, 35 Dale Street, Manchester M1 2HF, England.

something of a quagmire, as what shamanism regards as spiritual experience, however unpleasant it may be, psychiatry treats as psychosis. It takes a brave man to cross that ground, and in Sharon's case there was none available. While there is no guarantee that shamanic methods would get rid of the voices, they might have been effective in helping her to handle the problem in a way that would promote her self-esteem and self-respect.

Nevertheless, Sharon was able to give a common-sense explanation of what created the "pattern" in her mind and she may be correct in that. Yet there are many cases of individuals who hear voices that denigrate and criticize them, abuse them, and order them to harm themselves, even to kill themselves, who have never suffered anything comparable to what Sharon had to endure in her earlier years. There is some evidence that severe stress may trigger an onset of voices and there seems to be a connection between stressful events and auditory hallucinations but more research is needed before any firm conclusions can be drawn.

What relevance do these instances of hearing voices—or auditory hallucinations as they would be technically described—have to the exploration and understanding of consciousness? Despite Sharon's rejection of the schizophrenic label, if we can accept the diagnosis for the time being we can consider the comments of Dr. Benjamin Wolman, a highly experienced clinical psychologist and psychoanalyst in New York.

"In most instances, schizophrenic patients hear voices when they expect to hear and, possibly, when they wish to hear them. When a patient told me he heard voices telling him to assault the nurses, he somehow knew in advance what he would hear. It took a period of intensive psychotherapy to discover not only the patient's expectation, but also his awareness of what was going on. The voices were a projection of his hostility. This projection on outside forces that told him to act aggressively was a defense mechanism that protected him against, or at least reduced, unbearable guilt feelings.

"The auditory hallucination was neither entirely conscious nor entirely unconscious. It was a protoconscious state.

The projection was unconscious; the insight gained in psychotherapy was conscious. The voices came from the unconscious, and the patient's listening to them without being able to control them was protoconscious." [138]

Wolman explains the protoconscious as "the bridge between conscious and unconscious phenomena; the so-called altered states of consciousness occur on the protoconscious level." It is hard to say how much substance there is in his theory. It does not seem to have been taken up by others in the field. But it is not impossible that it may provide a clue to the understanding of such phenomena as auditory hallucinations as well as indicating the possibility of yet another dimension to human consciousness.

Wolman, perhaps automatically, uses the term "schizophrenic" when he refers to his patients. In orthodox psychiatry, drug treatment is the usual method for "managing" those who hear voices and are given the schizophrenic label. There is an alternative approach, however, that takes this phenomenon into quite different territory. It is put forward by gerontologist Ingrid Elfferich who came across many terminally ill people who revealed that they were hearing voices, often voices of friends or relatives who had died.

Elfferich suggests that contemporary research into both physics and consciousness "appears to offer confirmation of the metaphysical view of the world: namely, that a human being may transcend his or her physical existence and find access to other dimensions which are as much a part of the reality of creation as is the visible world." This metaphysical perspective, she says, "opens up the possibility of the voices representing a phenomenon that transcends the individuality of the hearer. This model places our perceptions in a broader framework of understanding, one which implies a capacity to make and maintain contact with other planes of being. In the case of negative voices, this would suggest that one may be

---

[138] Wolman, B. & Ullman, M. (1986), *Handbook of States of Consciousness*. New York: Van Nostrand Reinhold.

fighting something which actually exists, even though its reality is not perceived by others." She adds that hearers of negative voices need to develop "the mental power and capacity to shut themselves off from these perceptions. . . . The harmony resulting from self-acceptance may be the best protective shield one can have when confronted with these negative energies."[139]

If there is substance in this theory, then "the capacity to make and maintain contact with other planes of being" is another indication of the non-locality of consciousness. Some who hear voices would support this idea; for them the inner voice is a gift, a spiritual guide, perhaps a link with their "higher consciousness" or with another order of being. For others it is a curse, a disorder of the brain that requires careful and sympathetic therapy or, as very much a last resort, psychiatric treatment. In both cases, further exploration of altered states of consciousness might lead to a better understanding of what is actually happening, whether manifesting as gift or curse, to those who hear these disembodied voices.

Whatever interpretation we prefer, there is agreement that these "heard voices" come without warning and without being sought. Their messages are entirely personal, relevant only to the hearer. They are very different in kind and quality from those other voices that have been attracting much attention, especially in the West, in recent years. Here are two messages to illustrate this.

"This planet upon which you dwell has the possibility of becoming one of the great planets of your solar system. In truth, when this structure which the Grand Architect is now building is complete, it will create a glistening Light Absolute emanating forth from the planet Earth, blending with the Sun Absolute, creating paradise itself on Earth. Thus, Earth will become one of the great jewels of the kingdom of the heavens." So spoke the fourth-dimensional avatar, Rabindra Matori, through the channel Carol Bell Knight.[140]

---

[139] Romme & Escher (1993), p. 105.
[140] Knight, C. (1985), *Passing the Torch*, Walpole, NH: Stillpoint.

"Only by raising the level of this planet and the level of consciousness of this planet, perfecting the love and perfecting the core that is inside each human, can we go on and perfect other planets in the galaxies. This planet is one of the lowest that a soul comes to, in order to learn a lesson. The tragedy is the density of this planet—it is like a mire, it is sticky, and these beings get trapped in this stickiness. We are going to raise the level of this planet with your help, which will make this planet a lighter planet. The energy then coming from this planet will be sent into the universe, and will help raise the level of consciousness and the levels of other planets." This is part of a message from Tom, spokesman for the Council of Nine, relayed through the channel Phyllis Schlemmer.[141]

Communication with discarnates (beings not, or no longer, in physical form) might, if we can accept that discarnates actually exist, be considered a variant of telepathy. In our time such communication is usually known as channeling. This term is now almost exclusively used to cover, in the words of researcher Jon Klimo, "the communication of information to or through a physically embodied human being from a source that is said to exist on some other level or dimension of reality than the physical as we know it, and that is not from the normal mind (or self) of the channel."[142] Professor of Anthropology Michael Brown, author of *The Channeling Zone* (1997), provides a slightly different definition: "[Chanelling is] the use of altered states of consciousness to contact spirits— or, as many of its practitioners say, to experience spiritual energy captured from other times and dimensions."[143]

Channeling in its present form is widely practiced in both North America and the U. K. It has, however, a long historical tradition. Messages from the gods or spirits are written in to the

[141] Schlemmer, P. (1993), *The Only Planet of Choice*, Bath: Gateway Books, p. 67.

[142] Klimo, J. (1982), *Channeling*, Los Angeles: Tarcher.

[143] Brown, M. F. (1997), *The Channeling Zone*, Cambridge, Mass: Harvard University Press.

history of ancient Egypt and Greece and similar communication is recorded in the early history of China, Japan, and in shamanic societies around the world. The receivers of the messages, who might be priests, oracles, or shamans, operated in an altered state of consciousness, sometimes with the use of drugs or hypnosis, or by moving into a trance or meditative state, or receiving the information in a dream. Looking at the reports of channeling through the ages, Klimo points out the importance of belief in the afterlife and reincarnation.

"At the center of the story much channeling has to tell us is the odyssey of the human spirit as a slowly evolving, death-surviving, multi-lived being operating within and transmitting from more than just the physical realm" says Klimo. "And with this picture comes the belief that other, non-human, beings also exist within other dimensions and are capable of communicating to us."[144] At the same time, channeling is hardly ever referred to in studies of consciousness. What proof there is of its validity depends almost entirely on personal testimony and very few outside the channeling circles take it seriously at all.

There are parallels between channeling and a phenomenon that attracted much public attention a century and more ago. In the second half of the nineteenth century something like one million people in the U.S. and U.K., across all ranks of society, became involved with Spiritualism. There was much interest in the claims of mediums to be in contact with the dead and to be able to pass information and messages to their living relatives and acquaintances. Sometimes mediums operated through a "spirit control"; sometimes with no intermediary between the spirit of the deceased and themselves. The principal message of Spiritualism was that humanity was essentially divine and that eternal life was a reality. Later in the century much of this public attention moved to the newly formed Theosophical Society founded by Madame H. P. Blavatsky, who considered herself as receiving thought transference from a number of "Masters" and "Mahatmas" who

---

[144] Klimo (1982).

conveyed through her their wisdom and ideas. A significant amount of the content of her two major works, *Isis Unveiled* and *The Secret Doctrine*, described as an amalgam of occultism and Eastern philosophy, percolated through into the late twentieth century's new age.

While Spiritualism sought to bring science and religion together and generally taught that the individual should be free to make up his own mind about the great issues of life rather than accept the dogma of established religion, Theosophy quickly developed a hierarchical structure with authority vested in the masters and their disciples. Echoes of the concerns and teachings of the spiritualist movement and of Theosophy could be found in the pronouncements of many late twentieth-century channels. [145]

The final three decades of the twentieth century saw an extraordinary revival of activity and interest in communication with discarnates. Hundreds of books, tapes, and videos devoted to channelled material poured onto the market and the names of such as Seth, Ramtha, Maitreya, Lazaris, Michael, Bartholomew, Emmanuel, and Mafu became widely known in the West. People changed their lifestyles, their philosophies, and their abodes through following channelled messages, especially those uttered by Ramtha, said to be a great spiritual leader from Lemuria 35,000 years ago, and speaking through the medium of that accomplished—and wealthy—performer J. Z. Knight. The Seth books—there are more than a dozen, together with tapes and videos—channelled by Jane Roberts over a period of twenty years proved extremely popular and still attract much serious attention. Seth's communications have a coherent philosophic content providing what amounts to a useful psychotherapeutic guide to daily living. The well-known Findhorn Community in Scotland was founded and developed as a consequence of channelled messages from God, nature spirits, and various entities, transmitted through the

---

[145] Brown, M. (1998), *The Spiritual Tourist*, London: Bloomsbury. This includes an account of the author's visit to Sai Baba (see ch. 2).

Caddy family and their followers and friends. Its courses and conferences continue to attract people from all over the world.

Perhaps the most influential of all the channelled publications was *A Course in Miracles* totalling twelve hundred pages. This was dictated to, or through, Helen Shucman, a psychologist, who claimed that she neither understood the process of its composition nor who its author was. (The actual author was said to be Jesus.) The major theme of the *Course* is to assist its readers in moving from fear to love as the aim of spiritual existence, and it uses a number of psychological exercises to help effect this transition.

Other well-known twentieth-century channels include Eileen Garrett, founder of the Parapsychological Foundation, Alice Bailey, who channelled material to fill twenty volumes mostly from teaching, received from "The Tibetan," otherwise known as Djwhal Khul; Grace Cook, channel for "White Eagle," from which developed the well-known group "White Eagle Lodge;" Ruth Montgomery, whose "Lily and the group" helped her to write several best-selling books; and Ruth Norman and her "sub-channels" responsible for sixty volumes of material including information from a multitude of philosophers and scientists from Plato to J. Robert Oppenheimer. Other sources include Silver Birch, Grey Eagle, Little Owl, Kryon, Hilarion, the Pleiadians, Archangel Michael (a "recombined entity" also called plain Michael), Josephes (a cousin of Jesus), the Lion people, Enoch, various ascended masters (including the unlikely but popular St. Germaine), Sothis ("a loving light-being originating from the star system Sirius"), Mary, Raphael, Tesla, Gildas, Orin, Melchizedek, Jesus (or the Christ, whose dialogues with a lady in Texas are recorded on twelve audio cassettes), and God Himself, who has conducted numerous early morning conversations with Neale Donald Walsch, now set down in three volumes with a guidebook and a set of questions and answers. Several instructional texts are available on how to channel.

In addition there are also the hundreds of "local channels," many of whom charge considerable sums for sessions where their guide or control gives advice on a variety of topics of personal or universal import, sometimes peppered with archaic phrases or delivered in unusual accents. Almost all guides conveniently speak in some form of English or the language of the country where the channeler is functioning, no matter from where they themselves claim to originate. Seth in particular, to whose material a magazine, *Reality Change,* is devoted, seems to have exerted much influence over the content of recent channelled information and advice from other entities. The quality of this material may possibly be due to the psychological training and personality of Jane Roberts herself.

Professor Brown describes contemporary channeling as "a well-established form of religious exploration that is likely to be with us for a while," although some might query his use of the word "religious." He continues: "Its practitioners believe they can use altered states of consciousness to connect to wisdom emanating from the collective unconscious or even from other planets, dimensions, or historical eras. They apply their insights to financial affairs, career issues, relationships, and the resolution of emotional problems." As well as nineteenth-century Spiritualism, Brown mentions the personal recovery movement and woman-centered spirituality as among the influences that seem to affect channelled teachings.[146]

What are we to make of this? Do we take it, or any of it, at face value, accepting that this type of communication—with spirits or "entities," some of whom are identified as the spirits of deceased individuals while others are claimed to be divinities, ascended masters, beings from outer space, or members of the ruling council of the universe—is possible and valuable? Do we assume that all the material comes from the higher consciousness, or the unconscious, of the channeler? Or do we simply dismiss it all as rubbish, self-delusion, or a means of making easy money from gullible seekers after truth?[147]

Arthur Hastings, Ph.D. professor at the Institute of Transpersonal Psychology, Palo Alto, California, and author of

---

[146] Brown, M. F. (1997), p. 6.
[147] Ibid. p. 153.

With the Tongues of Men and Angels: A Study of Channeling, (1991) who has had wide experience in parapsychological research and is one of the very few to have studied channeling closely, believes that most channelled communication "draws on the mind of the channel for information, vocabulary, and often even the material itself, but there are also messages that seem inspired and informed beyond the individual personality of the channeler. . . . In the best of the messages there is an intelligence and perspective that can contribute to social values and personal guidance. But channeling also can express the trivial, fallacious, and pretentious and be given credence that diverts attention from authentic transpersonal communication. As with many other sources of spiritual teaching, there is a place here for discrimination along with open-minded consideration."[148]

Jon Klimo goes further still, maintaining that "Channeling holds out to us the possibility of an incredibly complex, multileveled universe, filled with fellow consciousness, a universe with which we can *all* interact in new and meaningful ways, each of us taking ultimate responsibility for our respective growth. Rather than following some voice of authority from beyond ourselves, most of the channelled sources stress self-determination, guided from the highest levels within ourselves. We are given messages of self-empowerment, love, and the oneness of all beings, of all Creation."[149] It is fair to add that many thousands of people obtain hope, useful advice, and sometimes consolation from channelled messages, whatever their source.

Dr. Jean Houston of the Foundation for Mind Research, Pomona, New York, and advisor for UNICEF, introduced the channelled text *Vision*, by Ken Carey, also author of the well-known *The Starseed Transmissions*. Dr. Houston says that "the channeler is he or she who is able to tune the electronic structure of his or her brain-mind to listen deeply for knowledge

---

[148] Tart (1997).
[149] Klimo (1982).

that gives the great patterns of reality, and then to structure them through the lenses of his or her own cultural conditioning so that these patterns make sense and wisdom in local space and time out of the immensities available for knowing." Houston also warns against "the great garbage heap of the unconscious, sanctified to the channeler and his duped disciples as the word of God. Indeed, a great deal of what passes for channelled information is just that—the flotsam and jetsam of the unconscious minds of inflated egos." Once the flotsam and jetsam have been identified and discarded, we can attend to the real stuff. All the same, Houston insists that "the nervous system and the brain have to be re-educated in order to open the doors of perception on the strange and beautiful country of channelled knowing."[150]

If channelled knowing is as significant as these researchers suggest, then why is it ignored in almost all studies of mind, brain, consciousness, and contemporary wisdom? Why is it mentioned only in publications displayed in book stores under the heading "New Age?" Dr. Hastings makes the point that "if the material does come from the unconscious of the individual, then we still have to explore how the unconscious can create the more sophisticated and exceptional channelled material." To date, this exploration has not been seriously attempted. It is understandable that frequent repetition of words such as "self-empowerment," "love," and "the oneness of all beings," which have become buzzwords of the "new age," may act as deterrence to scientifically-minded investigators. But it seems as if a sort of academic snobbery or exclusivity is at work here (as elsewhere in the field of consciousness exploration).

We can always begin with ourselves. Perhaps most of us in a variety of situations have heard ourselves say something pertinent or even profound without any forethought or even being aware that we were saying it. "Who said that?" "Did I say that?" are typical reactions. Many of us will have carefully

---

[150] Carey, K. (1985), *Vision*, Kansas City: UniSun.

prepared a speech or address of some kind and stood up before our audience with a sheaf of notes—and, disregarding these notes, have said something quite different from what we had planned. Almost all our audience has responded with interest and enthusiasm far beyond our expectations.

To quote from my own experience, it was my task some years ago to address a gathering of six hundred boys and girls, ages eleven to sixteen, before they dispersed to their classes. Only when I discarded my notes and thoughts and allowed "something" to take over did I succeed in stopping the yawning and neighbor-whispering, sometimes even eliciting a spontaneous burst of genuine applause. So, what was that "something?" Was I channeling some aspect of my consciousness that in the normal daily routine I was unaware of? Was I "inspired," whatever that may mean? Did I move spontaneously into an "altered state?" Or did some unknown force trigger a neuronal response that switched my brain into, as it were, another gear?

Some people in attempting to answer questions such as these will talk of their angel or guide; others may refer to their "inner self-helper." Only through metaphor, it seems, can we attempt to explain these moments of illumination. Those who believe that they have the ability to channel may deliberately move into a non-normal state of consciousness, perhaps through meditation, in order to make contact with that part of themselves, or that "entity" as they may see it, which feeds the advice or information through them. But if the message arrives instantaneously we have to consider whether such a deliberate consciousness shift does in fact occur. All that has been found by examining the brain wave patterns of channelers is that a frequency in the region of 8 Hz is most often recorded, similar to that occuring in a light meditative state. However, this does not take us very far in understanding what is going on.

The consciousness explorer Robert Monroe worked with several channelers in his laboratory in Faber, Virginia, and succeeded in inducing states of consciousness in which they claimed to connect with various sources of information.

Messages, recorded on tape, ranged from the cosmically bizarre to straightforward advice on how to improve your life. Using this method, many who had never before channelled in their lives found that they too were able to make contact with a guide, whether visualized as outside or within themselves, and to record information that often proved of significance to themselves and that sometimes provided valuable insights.

Some of the channelled sources themselves have commented on the channeling process. Lazaris, who was something of a celebrity amongst channels, says that they "transmit through the cosmos in the various levels that enter your reality through the mental planes, then drifts down on its way to the physical plane, much as the television signal to the antenna, and then it is amplified. We transmit blips and bleeps that through their amplification sound like words. You absorb the ideas and thus we communicate." Others talk of having to reduce the frequency band within which they operate so that they can be understood, and words like "frequency" and "vibrations" are often used. Vishnu, a channelled source, declares, "I am but the spiritual energy upon the sounding board of all vibratory forces throughout the universe." A cherub speaks of "The Spirit of God flowing in the instrument [to] irradiate another brain cell in which will vibrate a word that comes close, in its frequency of light, to the meaning the Spirit wants." It would seem from these and other examples that the sources are no better at explaining than are terrestrial beings. None of them can compare with the way that the prophet Jeremiah expresses what happened to him: "Then the Lord stretched out his hand and touching my mouth said to me, 'See, I put my words into your mouth.'"

An especially interesting account of channelled communication was published in Paris in 1976, and translated into English under the title *Talking with Angels* (1988). Four young Hungarians, a married couple, Hanna and Joseph, and two single women, Lili and Gitta, were living and working together. The women were graphic artists and Joseph was a teacher. During World War II, they moved into a small house in the village of Budaliget in Hungary. Gitta Mallasz, the only non-Jew, was also the only survivor of the Nazi occupation and it was from the notes she kept that *Talking with Angels* was put together. It consists of over eighty dialogues with forces that the four of them came to understand as angels. These angels spoke through Hanna, and the dialogues, most of them with Lili and Gitta, began in June 1943 and took place nearly every Friday at three P.M. for seventeen months.

In her introduction to the dialogues, Gitta writes: "We felt ourselves to be standing before a world of lies, brutality, and all-pervading evil. At the same time, we were convinced that the meaning of our lives must be buried somewhere, and that the cause for our not finding it must be in ourselves. With this in mind, we decided at one point that each of us should write down as clearly as possible our particular problems, so as to better be able to discuss them together." Discussing her questions with Hanna, Gitta is made aware of their "blatant superficiality." Gitta continues:

"Hanna is about to say something but suddenly stops as she senses that it is no longer she herself who is about to speak. She just has time to warn me; 'It is not I who will speak to you.' And then I hear the following words:

"'Enough of your shallow questions! It is time for you to assume responsibility for yourself!'

"It is Hanna's voice that I hear, but I am absolutely certain that she herself is not speaking.... I am filled with a bright light but there is nothing joyous about it. On the contrary, it illuminates my darkest interior with merciless clarity and I am compelled to see myself without deception."

The dialogues continue, mostly personal at first as if building up the spirits of the human participants. After the Nazi occupation of Hungary, the quartet moved into Budapest, hoping they would be safer there. The messages then became more general. The English translator, Robert Hinshaw, summarizes their content:

"The angels taught Gitta and her friends—and continue to teach us—that earthly existence is only a part of a whole: and if we are aware of this, we no longer need fear death. Eternal is not the eternally repetitive but the *eternally new*. We are encouraged to become aware of the ever-moving, the undogmatic, *Light.* The more light we are able to bear, the more aware we become, and the closer we can come to our 'peak.' At the same time, our individual angel strives to descend and meet us at this same 'peak.' Thus, we are not alone in this endeavour, even if our way of going about it is very individual. *How* each of us goes through this experience is not important: only *that* we go through it, each in his or her own individual way."

As the situation worsens, Joseph is sent to a work camp where he dies. The women work in a clothing factory, where Gitta, as a non-Jew, is put in charge of a section and does all she can to ease matters for the Jewish workers. With the advance of the Russian Army, the Germans and the Hungarian Nazis prepare to clear out. Some of the workers escape but thirteen remain, including Hanna and Lili. They are deported to Ravensbruck where only one of the thirteen survives. Later, this woman told Gitta that when the guards were shaving the heads of the prisoners one said to Hanna "Hey, what are you doing here with your blue eyes, your straight nose, and your long blonde hair? Are you an Aryan?" Hanna replied: "I am a Jew." Gitta comments, "She had conveyed the word of truth for seventeen months and must have become incapable of uttering even the smallest lie."

Hanna and Lili died in Ravensbruck within an hour of each other. Gitta struggled on in poverty for fifteen years. Eventually she moved to Paris, with the notes of the dialogues wrapped in bed sheets in her suitcase. She married and resumed her career as a designer and began to translate the dialogues into French. In April 1976 she was interviewed about them on a radio program and they were published later that year. Since then the book, which carries no author's name on the jacket and was never advertised, has been translated into at least ten languages.

The dialogues are interspersed with Gitta's commentaries on their effect on the four participants and on the events affecting their lives. It seems clear that the dialogues enabled them to face the horrors of the Nazi occupation with remarkable courage, and gave them an unyielding inner strength. Focusing on personal responsibility and embracing the importance of spiritual life, the messages from the angel are powerfully expressed with vivid imagery and impressive conviction. Whatever spoke through Hanna, whether some spiritual force or an inspired aspect of her own consciousness—or perhaps a combination of both—it effected a major transformation in its hearers.

Talking with Angels stands apart from other published channelled communications. It does so not only because of Gitta's eyewitness account of the appalling events that overtook and eventually destroyed the lives of three of the quartet, but also because of the extraordinary spiritual quality of the dialogues themselves. Gitta Mallasz insisted that "No one has the right to teach about the contents of the dialogues simply because no one has lived them. Because it is a personal experience, all comparison with known religions or other spiritual teachings is useless and out of place." With their many references to God and Jesus the dialogues relate to Christianity, but not to Christianity as taught or preached by any known Church.

As a contrast to *Talking with Angels* in style, material, and claimed origin, but equally impressive in its sincerity, *Testimony of Light* by Helen Greaves, a British writer and co-founder of The Group Meditation for World Goodwill, is a good example. This book, first published in 1969 and running into nineteen printings up to 1996, consists of communications received by the author "by telepathy and inspiration from the surviving mind of Frances Banks, who left this world on November 2, 1965." Frances Banks was a nun who spent much of her life in South Africa where she obtained a degree in psychology and taught in a Teachers' Training College. She was a student of mysticism and extrasensory perception, an author, and was involved with the British Churches' Fellowship for Psychical and Spiritual Studies. She is described by Alan Paton in the foreword to Greaves's book as "a woman of tremendous force of character and tremendous willpower."

Frances Banks died from cancer at age seventy-two. Her last words to her friend Helen were "It's all right, my dear. The Change has started." Then, some three weeks later, Helen was sitting alone when, she reports, "I gradually became aware of a

Presence. . . . Slowly my whole being seemed to be caught up into a peace and beauty that I cannot describe. . . . Almost imperceptibly I passed into a state of deep meditation in which I was conscious of being immersed in light. I was part of the Light yet the Light issued from beyond me. I felt a Oneness with all that was highest and best and with the eternal self within me. . . . Gently and with great reverence, it was borne in upon me that I was not only in touch with my own immortal soul, but also with the soul of Frances Banks."

Helen continues: "It was some days later when I felt Frances' *mind* impinging on mine as it had often done in our time together on earth. Words dropped into my thoughts which did not come from my consciousness. I knew that her discarnate mind and my incarnate one had linked together again in telepathic communication." Helen began to write, not, she says, automatically but perfectly in control, feeling that Frances' mind was using hers. This resulted in a number of scripts in which Frances describes the Rest Home in which she found herself, run by Sisters of her Order, and recounts stories of the many people she meets, both residents of the Home and visitors. She moves into a cottage by the Home, with a garden of her own. She is taken to visit Halls of Learning and Higher Spheres but is not yet ready to proceed further. As she learns and experiences more, she sheds many of her earthly ideas and feels that she is beginning to merge into a spiritual body, a Body of Light. She talks of "the next step in progression, the stepping out of illusion into the consciousness of the functioning of the Higher Self, an emergence into a wider consciousness and an awareness of Spiritual beings and of Forces from the All-Creating Mind of God."

After the receipt of the script in which this passage appears there was an interval of seventeen months. Then, with scant warning, five more communications followed. Frances was now a member of an extension group, one of several, whose speciality was studying "what you would term 'mysticism' but what we here ennoble by the title of Reality." Now she shared "a beautiful estate with others of the Group. This place has wide sloping grasslands, trees, and flowers of the most exquisite beauty, and avenues of light. I have no other words for this, for meditation and contemplation." She visited the halls of learning, attended meditation groups and meetings and sought to contact the minds of old friends still in physical existence. She said that she was learning "a joyous apprehension of the vast wonder of the unity of Creative Mind in which all, every atom, every soul-fragment, every Group Soul, every creative thought, is One. . . . If there is a message in these writings it is the simple statement that all is Unity and that Unity is Light." Readers may well feel that if there is an afterlife it would be both comforting and exhilarating if it should be as Frances Banks describes it.

Testimony of Light leads into the question of survival. In this area the classic study is *Human Personality and its Survival of Bodily Death*, by F. W. H. Myers, first published in two large volumes in 1903. Myers believed, to quote a review by Willis Harman, "that we live two lives: the planetary life in this material world and a cosmic life in the spiritual world which is the soul's native environment; he felt confident that he had deduced from the research findings of himself and his colleagues that communion between this and a discarnate world is, if not established fact, strongly intimated." Myers maintained that if anything was to be known about an unseen world it had to be discovered, to use his words, "by experiment and observation—simply by the application to phenomena within us and around us of precisely the same methods of deliberate, dispassionate, exact inquiry which have built up our actual knowledge of the world which we can touch and see."

Included in the research agenda Myers set out for this inquiry were: sleep and dreaming, hypnotism, phantasms of the dead, genius and creativity, the disintegrations of personality, and what today would be called extrasensory perception. Science, however, as Willis Harman says, went in the opposite direction, "towards the positivism and behaviorism of mid-twentieth century academic science. Only now does the climate of tolerance appear to be moving in the direction that might make such a research program acceptable."[151]

---

[151]*Noetic Sciences Review,* Spring 1996.

Science in general has not yet moved very far in that direction. For the great majority, scientists, and laymen, claims of communication with the dead, with the implication that something of the human being survives physical death, are matters of belief or non-belief rather than a question of proof. An afterlife is an essential belief of Christianity while reincarnation is equally essential to Hinduism and Buddhism.[152] But as far as evidence for possible survival of bodily death is concerned, this, according to the very experienced psychologist and ESP researcher Dr. Karlis Osis, sometime president of the American Parapsychological Asssociation, "comes mainly from research on the following phenomena: apparition experiences collectively perceived, some types of out-of-body experiences, certain aspects of near-death experiences, selected communication ostensibly coming from the dead, and reincarnation memories." Osis points out that assessments of the evidence ranges from those who find none of it convincing to others who "find certainty."[153] It seems possible that the assessment largely depends on what the assessor himself tends to believe before consideration of the evidence begins. And evidence as any judge, lawyer, or scientist will tell you, is not the same as proof.

If we can engage in "the willing suspension of disbelief" it may be worth considering this: if anything of the human being does survive physical death, what might it be? It is not the physical body, nor any part of it. Frances Banks, awakening in her otherworldly Rest Home, realized that her physical body was being burnt and that death was no more than "life separated by density." Her mind continued to exist, her consciousness

---

[152] Scientific & Medical Network (1999) *Wider Horizons.* In his contribution to this volume, George Blaker tells the story of a little Indian boy, a recent immigrant to Britain, who was asked at school to write an essay on what animal he would prefer as a pet. He chose a cat and wrote as follows: "The cat is a square animal with four legs, one at each corner. It also has nine lives, but it doesn't use these in Europe because of Christianity."

[153] Tart (1997) p. 210.

continued to exist, and developed, in her account, to become part of a group soul.

Several groups and individuals devote time to working with those in the afterlife in a kind of mutual aid process. Often this involves helping those who have suffered sudden death, perhaps through violence or accident or some natural calamity. In some instances the "spirits" advise or assist in problems concerning those still in physical existence. Many of these groups work in a religious context although some, while not necessarily rejecting religion, consider that it does not have all the answers.

In 1970, Geoffrey and Barbara West, a married couple living in Yorkshire, England, in their own words, "were contacted by a Spirit Reception team, all of whom had earlier been biological relatives." This contact came through Barbara West's ability to receive directed writing. They soon found themselves involved in the work of helping souls "who were either recovering from the shock of sudden death or finding their way, with a great deal of sympathetic help, from distress or misery resulting from suicidal situations." They came to realize that "the whole exercise, under Christ, was planned within the spiritual family, to which we already belonged, and that it had been a task for which we had volunteered before we were born."

The record of their communications, most of them taken down in writing by Barbara West, occupy 3,500 pages, divided into twenty-six photocopied volumes under the title *Losing Fear of Death: Learning How to Live.* Their work with the Reception Team ended in 1972, but communication continued with their spiritual family on matters relevant to their own and their living relatives' concerns. When in 1995 Barbara West died, she communicated fourteen days later with her husband through his brother. The Wests did not seem to have the problems mentioned in a *post mortem* statement from Frederic Myers in which he related the difficulties of communicating with people on Earth: "The nearest simile I can find to express the difficulties of sending a message—is that I appear to be standing behind a sheet of frosted glass—which blurs sight and deadens sounds—dictating feebly—to a reluctant and somewhat obtuse secretary."

Geoffrey West comments more generally on the nature of communications received from "the other side." "Discarnates can perceive what we are thinking. Even the 'resentful' uncooperative spirits of the spirit underworld can do this. And they can communicate purposely misleading material to psychically open enquirers, if the latters' motivation does not earn protection, i.e., if it arises out of pure curiosity or simply out of skepticism towards religious ideas. . . . They can easily use the ideas in the medium's own mind; or, for example, the 'expectations' of a person practising hypnotic regressions. In the first months of our own psychic experiences, we did learn what can be achieved by mischievous spirits in this way, before our protection in Christ was 'earned' by rejection of the idea of 'manipulative research.'"

With regard to survival, West maintains, on the authority of his discarnate father, that conscious life continues after physical death but develops into a more expanded awareness. For him the family connection seems essential. One family member who communicated with the Wests was named Cecily. She recalled various existences, once as a twelfth-century nun and also as the late wife of Geoffrey's brother Gordon. There was also Adam who had become a Christian in ancient Rome and died in the gladiators' arena. In the eleventh century Adam had lived in India with Irene as his sister. Later he and Irene had been the twin children of Gordon and Cecily. West draws a distinction between members of spiritual families and others, believing that spiritual family members reincarnate every 400 to 500 years while others reincarnate only at far longer intervals and may never remember previous existences. He presents his experiences, and those of his spiritual family, in a matter-of-fact way as if there can be no question of their authenticity. [154]

Dr. Arthur Guirdham, a retired consultant psychiatrist, gave closely detailed accounts of reincarnation in three books

---

[154] From a letter in the *Quarterly Review of the Churches Fellowship for Psychical & Spiritual Studies,* no. 179, spring 1999.

published in the 1970s. He maintained that he had a previous existence as Roger-Isarn de Fanjeaux, a Cathar. Then, through what appeared to be a chance encounter, he met a lady he refers to as Miss Mills and through her came across a group of people living near Bristol, England, all of whom claimed to recall past lives as Cathars during the siege of Montsegur, in the Languedoc region of southern France around 1242-1244. Guirdham claimed to have found the thirteenth-century names and families of seven of the eight individuals in the group. Miss Mills herself was at that time Esclarmonde de Perella, who had been burned at the stake. In a dream she recalled being struck on the back by a burning torch on her way to the stake; she had, Guirdham observed, several small protuberances on her body above her left hip that appeared, to him, to resemble semi-solid blisters.

Guirdham says that the characters in the group "tune in with remarkable precision to the siege, to the evacuation from the castle of the Cathar treasure, probably rare books, and above all, to the last celebration of the Consolamentum before the Cathars perished at the stake after the capitulation. The Consolamentum was the only sacrament recognized by the Cathars. It signified a voluntary renunciation of the flesh and of attachment to the things of this world." He believed that there was a purpose behind what he described as "an operation so well devised and so perfectly executed" as the reincarnation of this group. It was "to disseminate the knowledge of Catharism" and in particular its dualist principles. This early Christian cult was strong on the need for healing and on the belief in reincarnation and on the two opposed energies of good and evil. [155] Guirdham went on to claim that his Cathar group had shared other reincarnations, in Roman Britain and Napoleonic France. It has, however, been suggested that what Guirdham really desired was corroborative evidence of his own belief in reincarnation. It may be that through his strong

---

[155] Guirdham, A. (1974), *We Are One Another,* Jersey, CI: Neville Spearman.

personality and sense of conviction he was able to induce others to share his beliefs and thus provide him with the "evidence" he required. [156]

The most intensive and methodical study of the possibility of reincarnation is contained in the research of Professor Ian Stevenson of the University of Virginia who has collected well over two thousand instances of young children who appear to remember past lives and in many cases seem to reproduce birthmarks and scars that were apparent in the same physical locations on those who "preceded" them. His massive work, *Reincarnation and Biology: A Contribution to the Biology of Birthmarks and Birth Defects,* deals in close detail with 225 cases. He includes children's memories of "past lives" and accounts of dreams relevant to reincarnation. In a recently published study of cases of the reincarnation type in Turkey involving ninety children, sixty-one "gave information about how the previous personality had died." Most of the deaths were violent, with the mean age at death being about twenty-nine. [157]

In this study, as in larger studies carried out in India, Burma, and other Eastern countries, while much evidence derived from young children points in the direction of some form of reincarnation, Stevenson is careful to utter no definitive conclusion. His research is mostly, though not entirely, restricted to countries where a belief in reincarnation is culturally acceptable and to accounts from children between the ages of two and five who seem spontaneously to refer to lives they have previously led. The interval between the death of the "previous

---

[156] See Fenwick, P. & Fenwick, E. (1999), *Past Lives,* London: Headline, for an account of Guirdham and his ideas. This book is useful for anyone with an interest in past lives. The Fenwicks point out that much of the Cathar material that Guirdham recounted had appeared some years previously in *Massacre at Montsegur,* by Zoe Oldenbourg.

[157] Keil & Stevenson, "Do Cases of the Reincarnation Type Show Similar Features Over Many Years?" *Journal of Scientific Exploration,* vol. 13. no 2. summer 1999.

personality," as Stevenson describes it, and the birth of the child being interviewed is usually about fifteen months.[158] The sheer volume of documentation and references that Stevenson presents, together with his own reluctance to force his readers into making judgements, add to the impressive nature of his research.

A story that reveals the strength of belief in reincarnation is told by author and psychologist Dr. Sukie Miller. She was visiting Nigeria with a colleague when they were invited to a meal at the home of a professor. "'Ah, here comes father,' he announced as we were having drinks, and we all stood up, expecting, judging from the professor's age, a frail old man in his eighties. Into the room scampered a three-year-old, full of energy and curiosity. My host, noting my confusion, showed me a mark on his son's forehead—a little mark, to be sure—and explained his father had had the very same mark in the same place.'He is a part of all our family meetings, all our decision making, sitting where my father sat. He is my father,' he told me. 'The return of the spirits who leave us through death is not a concept as you would call it,' said the professor, 'but a reality in our lives. They leave and they return. It is a cycle. '"[159]

Tibetan Buddhism views reincarnation rather differently. Sogyal Rinpoche, Tibetan Buddhist meditation master and author of *The Tibetan Book of Living and Dying,* explains as follows: "Most people take the word 'reincarnation' to imply there is some 'thing' that reincarnates, which travels from life to life. But in Buddhism we do not believe in an independent and unchanging entity like a soul or ego that survives the death of the body. What provides the continuity between lives is not an entity, we believe, but the ultimately subtlest level of consciousness."

His Holiness the fourteenth Dalai Lama elaborates on this: "According to the Buddhist explanation, the ultimate creative principle is consciousness. There are different levels of consciousness. What we call innermost subtle consciousness

---

[158] See *Advances in Parapsychological Research,* vol. 7.
[159] *Noetic Sciences Review,* no. 42, summer 1997.

is always there. The continuity of that consciousness is almost like something permanent, like the space-particles. In the field of matter, that is the space particles; in the field of consciousness, it is the Clear Light. . . . The Clear Light, with its special energy, makes the connection with consciousness."

The Dalai Lama gives the following example: "The successive existences in a series of rebirths are not like the pearls in a pearl necklace, held together by a string, the 'soul', which passes through all the pearls; rather they are like dice piled one on top of the other. Each die is separate, but it supports the one above it, with which it is functionally connected. Between the dice there is no identity, but conditionality." [160]

If we are looking for an "explanation" of what seems to be some type of reincarnation, it may be that Tibetan Buddhism, with its emphasis on the indestructibility of consciousness, provides the most fruitful material for research.

Although Christianity formally rejected the idea of reincarnation at the Council of Nice in 553 A.D., in the West it is estimated that twenty-five percent of people polled believe in the concept in some form or another. Moreover, it seems that belief in past lives is increasing, possibly because certain "new age" ideas and beliefs, including those transmitted by channelers, have moved in to take the place of orthodox religious doctrine. There is also a sort of nervous shift away from the concept of free will and the responsibilities this brings with it. However, blaming aberrant behavior or some undesirable physical condition on something that happened in a past life can be no more than an attempt, however sincerely imagined, to avoid personal responsibility. There is a similarity here to the defense put forward by a murderer that it was his inherited genes that were responsible for his violence, to which the State of Texas responded by declaring that such a defense meant that the convicted man was incurable and hence should be executed forthwith.

---

[160] Sogyal Rinpoche (1992), *The Tibetan Book of Living and Dying*, London: Rider.

As another view of reincarnation there is the theory of the late noted mythographer Joseph Campbell expressed in his televised dialogues with Bill Moyers. Campbell declared that reincarnation was a metaphor, specifically an Oriental metaphor, deriving from a belief that if you died still fixated on the things of the world you had to return to have further experiences that would clarify until you were released from those fixations. Campbell continued:

"The reincarnated monad is the principal hero of Oriental myth. The monad puts on various personalities, life after life. Now the reincarnation idea is not that you and I as the personalities that we are will be reincarnated. The personality is what the monad throws off. Then the monad puts on another body, male or female, depending on what experiences are necessary for it to clear itself of this attachment to the field of time."

"And what does the idea of reincarnation suggest?" asked Moyers.

"It suggests that you are more than you think you are," Campbell replied. "There are dimensions of your being and a potential for realisation and consciousness that are not included in your concept of yourself. Your life is much deeper and broader than you conceive it to be here. What you are living is but a fractional inkling of what is really within you, what gives you life, breadth, and depth. But you can live in terms of that depth. And when you can experience it, you suddenly see that all the religions are talking of that."

In the West, investigation of past lives mostly comes within the orbit of past life or regression therapy, in which the therapist seeks to help the client, often under hypnosis, to recover past life memories and traumas in order better to deal with current problems. This therapy, according to Jungian analyst and author Roger Woolger, depends on the assumption that tragedies in an earlier life "leave the imprint on the soul, the subtle body, whatever it is that's passed on." Many individuals claim to remember past lives while undergoing this therapy, recalling places and situations they feel familiar with and that trigger a variety of memories, some highly detailed, frequently involving some traumatic experience such as a severe injury or even a violent death. In one published example, a woman claimed to have had eighty-six previous existences.[161] Sometimes couples or friends claim to have shared experiences in past lives and are able to corroborate various details. Significant historical events and major disasters often figure in past life recollections.

The neuropsychiatrist Dr. Peter Fenwick, with his wife Elizabeth, published a study of "past lives" in 1999. They record that out of three hundred people who told them about their past life memories "eight had memories of dying in the *Titanic*. None had memories of any other maritime disaster."They add, perhaps slightly with tongue-in-cheek: "This does suggest that *Titanic* memories are over-represented in our sample and that, on a worldwide scale, the number of *Titanic* reincarnees is probably greater than the 1,500 who actually went down with the ship."[162]

The biochemist Dr. Rupert Sheldrake of Cambridge University and Harvard tentatively suggests that the "hypothesis of formative causation," which proposes that memory is inherent in nature, may provide an explanation for past-life memories. He indicates that an individual, in most instances a young child, could possibly "tune in by morphic resonance [the non-energetic transfer of information] to a person who lived in the past." He continues: "This might help to account for the transfer of memories without our having to suppose that the present person *is* the other person whose memories he or she can pick up." The possibility of memory transfer via "the subtlest level of consciousness" is a tempting area for investigation. Sheldrake also feels that morphic resonance may help to explain how telepathy works, either by enabling an individual to make some form of mental contact with another or to tap into a kind of pooled or collective memory.[163]

It has to be said, however, that some past life recollections tell us more about the power of memory than anything else.

---

[161] Weiss, B. (1988), *Many Lives, Many Masters*, London: Piatkus. Interestingly, the lady who claimed to have lived 86 past lives was able to date some of them B.C.

[162] Fenwick & Fenwick (1999), p. 49.

[163] Sheldrake, R. (1988), *The Presence of the Past*, London: Collins.

Before attempts are made to verify such recollections it is essential to examine the contents of books and films that the individual has come across previously. It is surprising how much fine detail has been absorbed into memory and hidden away (cryptonmesia), to be brought out again under hypnosis even though the individual in the normal waking state does not recall having read the book or seen the film at all.

Channeling, communication with the dead (or with "discarnates"), reincarnation (in the physical sense) and past-life memories fall at this time outside the concerns of orthodox science and, in some reported instances, also outside the bounds of common-sense. But many of those who have had these experiences are convinced of their veracity. Do they inform us about the human capacity for self-delusion, or the power of imagination, or do they possess a genuine objective reality? Is there, as the twelfth-century Sufis maintained, "a world created solely out of the subtle matter of *alam almithal*, or thought ... a plane of existence *created by the imagination of many people*, and yet one that still had its own corporeality and dimension, its own forests, mountains, and even cities"? Henry Corbin, an authority on Sufi thought, called it the "imaginal realm," a world that is created by imagination but is ontologically no less real than physical reality."[164]

Robert Monroe, who is unlikely to have read about the "imaginal realm," created a series of audio guided exercises designed to permit "the individual mind-consciousness to travel safely beyond the transitional point [between life and death] and to return when the task was accomplished." The task was to be of service to those "who have recently left physical existence but who either have not been able to recognize and accept this or are unable to free themselves from the ties of the Earth Life System." This involved helping such "lost souls" to find what Monroe called the Park, "an artificial synthesis created by human minds, a way station designed to ease the trauma and shock of the transition out of physical

---

[164] Talbot (1991).

reality. It takes on the form of various earth environments in order to be able to be acceptable to the enormously wide variety of newcomers."[165]

Monroe's "Park" seems almost identical to the Sufis' "plane of existence created by the imagination of many people." Most of those who have followed Monroe's exercises claim to have helped others no longer in physical existence to find the Park, which usually resembles an environment that they themselves feel comfortable with. One person who underwent this experience reported that the most important thing he had learned was "the experienced objective reality of the imaginal realm, which I had 'believed' was only a metaphor for personal issues in need of integration. The several retrievals [of those no longer in physical existence] were so unexpected and palpable they have forced an opening through experience (I always thought and behaved as if they were real) into other realities." Others reported the names and various personal details of those they had helped, most of them complete strangers. One of the consequences of taking part in this exercise was that almost all participants claimed that they no longer had any fear of death. They had made the journey, or part of it, into the realms beyond physical life and they had seen what it was like, or might be like, to be dead.[166]

There is another phenomenon that for some people indicates that communication from some non-physical source is possible. This is an echo of nineteenth-century Spiritualism and is sometimes known by the elegant term "clairaudience." It used to be, and perhaps still is, applied to mediums claiming to receive verbal information from "the other side." Whatever is going on here—and the more one examines the topic and discounts the many proven instances of fraud the more conflicting evidence one finds—the information tends to be trivial with much of it concerned with events, often quite insignificant, in the daily lives and histories of those attending a

---

[165] Monroe (1994), p. 258.
[166] Ibid., ch 18.

séance. There are, of course, exceptions, one of the more notable being the sessions of the trance medium Eileen Garrett (1893-1920). The psychologist and author Lawrence Le Shan worked with her many times and came to know her well. On one occasion, after a session in which Le Shan found himself arguing with a man who had been dead for five years, he discussed with her what had occurred.

"'Never forget, Larry,' Garrett said, "that awake or in trance, I am very telepathic, and that the stage lost a great actress in me.'" Le Shan continues: "Here was one of the greatest psychics ever known to science, a deeply serious woman who spent the last thirty years of her life trying to understand what her mediumship was all about, a woman who, during those thirty years, worked almost entirely under experimental conditions with any scientists who would work with her, saying she did not know whether her paranormal information was derived from spirits of the dead or telepathy."[167]

On the whole, however, while mediumship sometimes produced interesting information it does not provide much insight into the afterlife other than suggesting that it largely resembles this life without the inconveniences and the necessity to work, apart from spending time and effort in trying to contact one's erstwhile relatives with the help of a middle-aged lady.

This chapter has taken us into strange territory. If we look for objective reality here we will have a hard job to find it. Leaving "hearing voices" out of the account, these phenomena—channeling, communication with the dead, memories of past lives, reincarnation, clairaudience—depend largely (some would say entirely) on belief. They certainly raise more questions than they answer, and until more answers become clear, if they ever do, the best we can do is to keep an open mind and continue to ask the questions. Continually we seek evidence for the survival of some part of

---

[167] Le Shan, L. (1987) *The Science of the Paranormal*, Wellingborough: Aquarian Press.

ourselves, some element of our consciousness, after physical death. Ignoring these phenomena, or dismissing them out of hand, does nothing to add to our knowledge or further our search for truth.

Interestingly, none of the topics in this chapter are referred to in professor of psychology Steven Pinker's popular and bracing study *How the Mind Works*. In his preface, Pinker describes the "big picture": "that the mind is a system of computation designed by natural selection to solve the problems faced by our evolutionary ancestors in their foraging way of life." His interpretation of the mind confines it to the brain, possibly because in any computational theory there is nowhere else to put it. The skull, after all, is just a box made of bone, with a number of sockets and connections. Inside it, in this interpretation, is what has been described (although not by Pinker) as "a computer made of meat."

Now mind and consciousness do not define each other, but they do appear to go, as it were, hand in hand. If they are not then confined to the brain, where else might they *be?* Candace Pert, author of *Molecules of Emotion*, says, "We are all aware of the bias built into the Western idea that the mind is totally in the head, a function of the brain. But your body is not there just to carry around your head. I believe the research findings . . . indicate that we need to start thinking about how the mind manifests itself in various parts of the body and, beyond that, how we can bring that process into consciousness."[168]

Striking examples of recent research findings are described in *The Heart's Code* by Dr. Paul Pearsall, a psychoneuroimmunologist, researcher, and international lecturer based in Hawaii. Pearsall tells the story of Glenda, a family physician, whose husband David was killed in a car accident at night and whose heart had been used in a transplant. She had asked to meet the young man who was the recipient of her husband's heart. As she and Pearsall waited in the hospital

---

[168] Pert (1997) p. 187.

chapel, she suddenly said: "He's here in the hospital. I felt him come about thirty minutes ago. I felt my husband's presence." A moment later the young man and his mother entered the chapel. "Sorry we're late," he said in a heavy Spanish accent. "We got here half an hour ago but we couldn't find the chapel."

After they had been introduced, Glenda asked if she could put her hand on the young man's chest and feel his heart. He agreed and she did so. Pearsall's narrative continues:

"Glenda's hand began to tremble and tears rolled down her cheek. She closed her eyes and whispered, 'I love you David. Everything is copacetic.' She removed her hand, hugged the young man to her chest and all of us wiped the tears from our eyes....

"Speaking in her heavy Spanish accent, the young man's mother told me, 'My son uses that word 'copacetic' all the time now. He never used it before he got his new heart, but after his surgery it was the first thing he said to me when he could talk. I didn't know what it means. He said everything was copacetic. It is not a word I know in Spanish.' Glenda overheard us, her eyes widened, she turned towards us and said, 'That word was our signal that everything was OK. Every time we argued and made up, we would both say that everything was copacetic.'

"The young man went on to say that before his transplant he was a vegetarian and very health-conscious, but he now craved meat and fatty foods. His taste in music had changed to rock-and-roll and he often dreamed of bright lights coming straight for him. Glenda replied that her husband loved meat and junk food, had played in a rock-and-roll band, and that she also dreamed of the lights heading for them on the night he was killed."[169]

This is one of several instances of a connection between a donor's heart and its recipient that Pearsall has collected from

---

[169] Pearsall, P. (1998) *The Heart's Code*, New York: Broadway Books, pp. 76-77. This is an intriguing study. Dr. Paul Pearsall is a brilliant lecturer, worth travelling many miles to hear.

more than a hundred interviews. In some cases a marked change in sexual behavior seems to occur, especially when the implanted heart comes from a much younger donor. It can be argued that there may be other reasons for this, in particular as it seems that more than half of heart-attack victims report no sexual activity in the year preceding their attack. But what other reasons could there be for a heart recipient, whose wife's name was Karen, calling her "Sandy" when they subsequently made love—Sandy being the bedroom name of the wife of the donor of his heart?

Pearsall points out, "By bioscience's own measurements, the heart is five thousand times more electromagnetically powerful than the brain. By the twenty-fifth day of life, when a woman may not even know she is pregnant, the embryonic heart has already formed and started to beat.... Some form of subtle, non-local energy we cannot yet measure causes a tiny clump of cells to begin to beat together in the rhythm of life that will resonate within us until our death. In the first few days after the heart begins to beat, it is already pumping blood manufactured in the liver throughout the fetus, and along with this measurable substance comes an immense amount of as yet immeasurable life information." After reviewing recent research in the field of neurocardiology, Pearsall concluded that the central role of the heart in our consciousness was much more than metaphor and that continuing research would reveal complexities of a conscious heart at present unimaginable.[170]

What Pearsall's findings suggest is that some degree of memory can survive physical death. He sees this memory as enshrined in the heart but there are also indications from the after-effects of other transplant surgeries that it may also reside in other organs. At the present time this research is in its infancy and covers only a relatively small number of cases, but as it develops it may throw another beam of light on research into the possibility of some form of survival. The philosopher Michael Grosso expresses the idea slightly differently:

---

[170] Ibid pp. 65-69.

"On the one hand, if it could be shown that memory is tied in some exclusively localized way to the brain, then personal survival, in the sense of continuance of personal memories, would not seem to be the sort of thing we could ascribe to an afterlife. On the other hand, there might be levels of mind intrinsically independent of the personal brain-memory that might survive the destruction of death."[171]

Looking at the current state of survival research, Grosso remarks that he feels himself "pulled toward belief in probable extinction." This, he thinks, has to do with his education at Columbia University where he studied philosophy and classics in the 1960s, as the model of reality that was in the air then "was simply not congenial to belief in postmortem survival."[172] For many others, however, this model will not do.

Most of the phenomena we have discussed in this chapter—channeling, communication with the dead either directly or through mediums, reincarnation and past lives—depend on a belief system that holds that some sentient part of an individual survives physical death. This part or element appears for a time to retain memory of life in physical terms as well as a degree of interest in what continues to happen in physical reality. It may find a role to play in the afterlife or it may undergo preparation for a return. This belief has largely supplanted an earlier one that envisaged the "soul" as surviving the death of the body to be subjected to judgement by some divine agency and rewarded or punished according to its record on Earth. We have seen from many reports of near-death experiences that a kind of judgement may still be pronounced but in these cases the judge is the individual himself.

In the areas we have been exploring in this chapter, we have to make up our own minds about the meaning and validity of the experiences that have been quoted. The unbodied (as I would like to call them) who are reported as

---

[171] *Noetic Sciences Review,* no. 32, 1994
[172] Ibid.

communicating with the living appear to be self-aware in that they can identify themselves. Hence they must retain some element or facet of consciousness. If the materialist/reductionist view is correct, that consciousness is solely a function of the brain and that when the brain dies consciousness therefore dies also, then everything in this chapter can only be the result of vivid imagination, fraud, self-delusion, mistaken interpretation, or some form of mental derangement. Well, it may be. It may also be that in all the areas we have touched on, aspects of human consciousness operating in an altered state are revealed. If consciousness is indestructible, if it is true that, as Joseph Campbell maintained in *The Power of Myth*, "the whole world is informed by consciousness," then the materialist/reductionist view cannot stand.

This does not imply that what is perceived in an altered state is necessarily truthful in the terms of the reality in which we lead our daily lives. Anyone who has used mood-altering drugs or is addicted to alcohol can attest to this. It is possible that there is a reality in which Tom and the Council of Nine exist and operate, and another reality inhabited by the fourth-dimensional avatar Rabindra Matori, but neither is the reality in which we currently live.

At the beginning of an essay on "Altered States and the Survival of Death," Charles Tart expressed the essence of the ideas he was about to share:

"After some initial shock and confusion resulting from the process of dying, I will not be too surprised if I regain consciousness. On the other hand, I will be quite surprised if "I" regain consciousness. To put it more precisely: I will not be too surprised if I regain some kind of consciousness after death, but that consciousness may be of quite a different kind than the ordinary state of consciousness to which I am accustomed. And I doubt that "I," in the sense of my ordinary self, will be the self that regains some sort of consciousness."[173] Tart

---

[173] Tart, C. (1989), *Open Mind, Discriminating Mind*, San Francisco: Harper & Row, p. 333.

continues, "The question: 'Will I survive death?' cannot really be answered except as a subset of the larger question, 'Who and what am I?'"

In another essay, Tart reviews the different perspectives that contribute to answering the question, 'Who am I?' He focuses on one very important aspect: "I am a psychic being who at times is not limited by the ordinary barriers of time and space." Whatever may happen to us in the next life, should there be one, it is on those occasions in this life, brief or fragmentary though they may be, when the barriers of time and space disappear that we come nearest to defining our essence—our soul or spirit, call it what you will. It is then that we cease to be "I," or any variant of "I" that we can recognize, and become a part of something immeasurably greater. It is in the transcendent experience that we come nearest to knowing who and what we really are.

CHAPTER 7

TRANSCENDENCE

When you have learned to see yourself in all beings,
in all creation, in the earth, the trees and the flowers, the
birds and animals, in the streets and shops, and in every
person, then you discover the Lord dancing in the world
and in every human heart—
(Bede Griffiths, The Cosmic Revelation*)*

In the course of his research, the psychologist Abraham Maslow, founder of transpersonal psychology, gave the following instructions to his students:

"I would like you to think of the most wonderful experience or experiences of your life; happiest moments, ecstatic moments, moments of rapture, perhaps from being in love, or from listening to music, or suddenly being hit by a book or a painting, or from some great creative moment. And then try to tell me how you feel in such acute moments, how you feel differently from the way you feel at other times, how you are at the moment a different person in some ways, and in what ways the world looks different to you."[174]

This is a simplified way of describing these moments of revelation, but whatever we call these experiences—transcendent,

[174] Maslow, A. (1962), *Towards a Psychology of Being,* Princeton, N.J.: Van Nostrand

peak, mystical, spiritual, religious, cosmic, or simply exceptional human experiences—most people will recognize what
Maslow is talking about. Of all the manifestations of non-ordinary consciousness, the peak experience, to give it the most
neutral term, is the most common. When this happens—and it
happens spontaneously—we are taken out of our everyday
selves and move into a state of expanded awareness, sometimes blending or melding with everything we see or visual-
ize—the houses, the trees, the hills and rivers, other people
(whether we know them or not), perhaps the planets, the sun,
and the stars. The experience may or may not have an enduring effect; it may be no more than a passing moment of wonder, a memory reawakened now and then, recalled and then
dismissed, or it may bring about a change in your view of yourself or of the world around you. It may release some creative
impulse, loosen inhibitions, free you from self or socially,
imposed limitations. It may open new windows for you,
through which you perceive new vistas of beauty, hope, or
truth. Joseph Campbell said of the peak experience that it
refers to "moments in your life when you experience your relationship to the harmony of being."

Here are some personal accounts of this kind of experience, drawn from a variety of sources:

"When I was sixteen I had an experience which I can only
describe as mystical. . . . The sheer wonder and ecstasy of it
have never left me over the years. The feeling was that I suddenly, that very moment, became aware of the answer to the
mystery of life and the knowledge of it made me want to shout
with joy. It seemed at that moment so simple—I wondered why
one didn't see it and feel it and be bursting with joy! As if I had
been dead before that moment, and suddenly I was alive. Of
course the actual experience did not last long: I could not
have borne to live at that intensity for too long, I imagine, but
the memory of it has never faded, and it completely changed
my life. From time to time I have again experienced these wonderful ecstasies, always at completely unexpected times,
sometimes while washing up and doing daily chores about
the house. Always this same feeling, leaving me weeping with

a great joy and feeling of deep reverence and feeling of worship and love, I think best described as a sort of homesickness, a nostalgia for some-other-where, almost as if I had known an existence of such great beauty and indescribable happiness and am yearning and homesick for it again."[175]

Claire Myers Owens, a housewife, was writing at her desk in her house in Connecticut, when suddenly everything within her sight vanished. She could no longer see her body, the furniture in the room, or the white rain slating across the windows. She was unaware of where she was, of the day or the hour. For Claire, time and space ceased to exist. She continues: "Suddenly the entire room was filled with a great golden light, the whole world was filled with nothing but light. There was nothing anywhere except this effulgent light and my own kernel of self. The ordinary 'I' ceased to exist. Nothing of me remained but a mere nugget of consciousness. It felt as if some vast force was invading me without my volition, as if all the immanent good latent within me began to pour forth in a stream, to form a moving circle with the universal principle. Myself began to dissolve into the light that was like a great golden all-pervasive fog. It was a mystical moment of union with the mysterious infinite, with all things, all people.

"It was the grand purgation. I was washed clean and pure like a sea shell by the mighty tides of the sea. All my personal problems fell away out of sight. My ego had drowned in boundless being. Irrefutable intimations of immortality came welling up. I felt myself becoming an indestructible part of indestructible eternity. All fear vanished—especially fear of death. I felt that death would be the beginning of a new, more beautiful life...."[176]

The physicist Fritjof Capra describes the experience that inspired him to write his well-known book *The Tao of Physics:*

---

[175] Cohen, J. M. & Phipps, J. F. (1979), *The Common Experience*, London: Rider, p. 158. (Religious Experience Research Center, archive no. 975).
[176] Quoted in May (1993), from Coxhead, N., *The Relevance of Bliss.*

"I was sitting by the ocean one late summer afternoon, watching the waves rolling in and feeling the rhythm of my breathing, when I suddenly became aware of my whole environment as being engaged in a gigantic cosmic dance. Being a physicist, I knew that the sand, water, and air around me were made of vibrating molecules and atoms, and that these consisted of particles which interacted with one another by creating and destroying other particles. I knew also that the earth's atmosphere was continually bombarded by showers of 'cosmic rays,' particles of high energy undergoing multiple collisions as they penetrated the air. All this was familiar to me from my research in high-energy physics, but until that moment I had only experienced it through graphs, diagrams, and mathematical theories. As I sat on that beach my former experiences came to life; I 'saw' cascades of energy coming down from outer space, in which particles were created and destroyed in rhythmic pulses; I 'saw' the atoms of the elements and those of my body participating in this cosmic dance of energy; I felt its rhythm and I 'heard' its sound, and at that moment I knew that this was the Dance of Shiva, the Lord of Dancers worshipped by the Hindus."

In contrast, the next experience, described as "the major incident in my life" is recalled fifty years later. The writer, then aged 14, was at school.

"One hot Sunday afternoon in June 1949, lying on my back on a knoll under a lime tree, aware of the scents and sounds of summer and watching the flickering sunlight through the leaves of the lime tree, my mind went blank—I suddenly found myself surrounded, embraced by a white light, which seemed both to come from within me and from without, a very bright light but quite unlike any ordinary physical light. I was filled with an overwhelming sense of Love, of warmth, peace, and joy—a Love far, far greater than any human love could be—utterly accepting, giving, compassionate—total Love. I seemed to sense a presence, but did not see anybody. I had the feeling of being 'one' with everything, and 'knowing' all things—whatever I wanted to know, I 'knew' instantly and directly. I had the sense of this being utter Reality, the 'real,'

Real, far more 'real' and vivid than the ordinary everyday 'reality' of the physical world."

Lastly, here is an experience recalled by the late Indian philosopher Krishnamurti:

"That morning, especially so early, the valley was extraordinarily quiet. The owl had stopped hooting and there was no reply from its mate over in the distant hills. No dog was barking and the village was not yet awake. In the east there was a glow, a promise, and the Southern Cross had not yet faded. There was not even a whisper among the leaves, and the earth itself seemed to have stopped in its rotation. You could feel the silence, touch it, smell it, and it had that quality of penetration. It wasn't the silence outside in those hills, among the trees, that was still; you were of it. You and it were not two separate things. The division between noise and silence had no meaning. And those hills, dark, without a movement, were of it, as you were.

"This silence was very active. It was not the negation of noise, and strangely that morning it had come through the window like some perfume, and with it came a sense, a feeling, of the absolute. As you looked out of the window, the distance between all things disappeared, and your eyes opened with the dawn and saw all things anew."

Perhaps all of us have had one or more experiences such as these at some time in our lives. We may have dismissed them, pushed them into the back of our memory; or we may have taken them into ourselves, made them part of our vision or approach to life. They do not depend on our religion, or lack of it, on our state of health or wealth, education, or cultural background, although their content may be relevant to our interests or beliefs as is Capra's experience. These experiences are entirely personal; there is no way to corroborate them, no evidence, no proof. You cannot test them in a laboratory, measure them, or examine them through a microscope. Yet to many people they are among the most significant events of their lives.

Robert Graves, in *Poetic Craft and Principle*, recalls an experience he had one summer evening at the age of twelve:

"I was sitting on an iron roller behind the school pavilion, with nothing much in my head, when I received a sudden celestial illumination: it occurred to me that *I knew everything.* I remember letting my mind range rapidly over all its familiar subjects of knowledge; only to find that this was no foolish fancy. I *did* know everything. To be plain—though conscious of having come less than a third of the way along the path of formal education, and being weak in mathematics, shaky in French grammar, and hazy about English history—I nevertheless held the key of truth in my hand and could use it to open any lock of any door. . . ."

The next day after morning lessons, Graves locked himself into the privy and tried to record his formula on the back of an old exercise book, but his mind went too fast for his pen, and he began to cross out—a fatal mistake—and presently crumpled up the page and pulled the chain on it. That night he tried again, but the magic had evaporated.

"My vision of truth did not recur, though I went back a couple of times to sit hopefully on the roller; and before long doubts tormented me—gloomy thoughts about a great many hitherto stable concepts, such as the authenticity of the Gospels, the perfectibility of man, and the absoluteness of the Protestant moral code. All that survived was an after-glow of the bright light in my head, and the certainty that it had been no delusion. This is still with me, for I now realize that what overcame me was a sudden awareness of the power of intuition, the supra-logic that cuts out all routine processes of thought and leaps straight from problem to answer. I did not in fact know everything, but became aware that in moments of real emergency the mind can weigh an infinite mass of imponderables and make immediate sense of them. This is how poems get written."

Graves describes this as a "mystic experience" although in his retelling it does not conform to what would customarily be thought of in this way. But in this area, as with near-death and out-of-body experiences, we are dealing with recollections expressed in words; the experience itself is ineffable. This is the term that the astronaut Edgar Mitchell used in attempting to describe his own experience when returning to Earth from the moon. He was looking out of the capsule window, at first aware of the "strife and discord beneath the blue-and-white atmosphere." Mitchell continues:

"Then as I looked beyond the earth itself to the magnificence of the larger scene, there was a startling recognition that the nature of the universe was not as I had been taught. My understanding of the separate distinctness and the relative independence of movement of those cosmic bodies was shattered. There was an upwelling of fresh insight coupled with a feeling of ubiquitous harmony—a sense of interconnectedness with the celestial bodies surrounding our spacecraft."

For Mitchell this was neither a religious or otherwordly experience nor a new scientific understanding. He saw it as "a pointer, a signpost showing the direction towards new viewpoints and greater understanding." Mitchell develops this idea:

"Billions of years ago the molecules of my body, of Stu's and Alan's bodies, of this spacecraft, of the world I had come from and was now returning to, were manufactured in the furnace of an ancient generation of stars like those surrounding us. This suddenly meant something. It was now poignant, personal. Our presence here, outside the domain of the home planet, was not rooted in an accident of nature or in the capricious political whim of a technological civilization. It was rather an extension of the same universal process that evolved our molecules. And what I felt was an extraordinary personal connectedness with it. I experienced what has been described as an ecstasy of unity. I not only *saw* the connectedness, I *felt* it and experienced it sentiently. I was overwhelmed with the sensation of physically and mentally extending out into the cosmos. The restraints and boundaries of flesh and bone fell away. I realized that this was a biological response of my brain attempting to reorganize and give meaning to information about the wonderful and awesome processes that I was privileged to view from this vantage point. Although I am now more capable of articulating what I felt then, words somehow always fall short. I am convinced that it always has been and always will be an ineffable experience."[177]

---

[177] Mitchell, E. (1996), *The Way of the Explorer,* New York: Putnam, pp. 58-59. Dr. Edgar Mitchell is the founder of the Institute of Noetic Sciences. He was the sixth man to set foot on the Moon.

The experiences of Graves and Mitchell are very different in content. What they have in common is their spontaneity and their recognition that the experience *mattered*. They give quite different explanations. Graves talks about a "mystic experience" and the "sudden awareness of the power of intuition," and Mitchell believes his experience was "a biological response of my brain." Yet, considering these explanations, they might be equally applicable—if indeed they are applicable—if they were reversed. This demonstrates a major problem in discussing peak or transcendent experiences: the difficulty of defining what precisely they are. What causes them and what do they mean?

In a brilliant essay on these "astonishing moments of insight," the philosopher Alan Watts points out how the descriptions of the experience may take forms that seem to be completely different:

"One person may say that he has found the answer to the whole mystery of life, but somehow cannot put it into words. Another will say there never was a mystery and thus no answer to it, for what the experience made clear to him was the irrelevance and artificiality of all our questions. One declares himself convinced that there is no death, his true self being as eternal as the universe. Another states that death has simply ceased to matter, because the present moment is so complete that it requires no future. One feels himself taken up and united with a life infinitely other than his own. But as the beating of the heart may be regarded as something that *happens* to you or something that you *do*, depending on the point of view, so another will feel that he has experienced, not a transcendent God, but his own inmost nature. One will get the sense that his ego or self has expanded to become the entire universe, whereas another will feel that he has lost himself altogether and that what he called his ego was never anything but an abstraction. One will describe himself as infinitely enriched, while another will speak of being brought to such absolute poverty that he owns not even his mind and body, and has not a care in the world."[178]

---

[178] Watts, A. (1958/78), *This Is It*, London: Rider, pp. 20-21

Watts remarks that the experience is usually described with the use of metaphors that can mislead if taken literally. Edgar Mitchell, struggling for accuracy of description, said that it "would have been quite easy to have fallen back upon some explanation such as having touched the face of God. But as a metaphor it did not appeal to me, and it certainly wasn't literally true." Our cultural, social, and religious conditioning readily provide metaphors, which tend to obfuscate rather than clarify. In contrast, Watts quotes a passage from Bernard Berenson's *Sketch for a Self-Portrait*, which he says is one of the "simplest and 'cleanest' accounts" he has seen.

"It was a morning in early summer. A silver haze shimmered and trembled over the lime trees. The air was laden with their fragrance. The temperature was like a caress. I remember—I need not recall—that I climbed up a tree stump and felt suddenly immersed in Itness. I did not call it by that name. I had no need for words. It and I were one."

Watts comments: "Just 'It'—as when we use the word to denote the superlative, or the exact point, or intense reality, or what we were always looking for. Not the neuter sense of the mere object, but something still more alive and far wider than the personal, and for which we use this simplest of words because we have no word for it."

Berenson, like most of those whose experiences have been quoted above, does not try to interpret or explain. But man is, by nature, an enquiring soul; he wants to know the answers; he needs to understand. Viktor Frankl, founder of the Viennese school of analysis known as logotherapy, survived several years in Nazi concentration camps, learning from his experiences and observation the vital importance of searching for, and finding, meaning. Finding meaning even in the direst suffering enabled men to survive. Frankl quoted Nietzsche: "He who has a *why* to live can bear with almost any *how*." Finding meaning in these most "astonishing moments of insight" may be equally vital, although not so much for survival as for fulfillment.

What are the consequences, then, if we pay little attention to such experiences or tend to discredit or repress them? Ken

Wilber suggests that in the West this is what has been happening over the past few centuries. He defines this type of experience as touching "an awareness that transcends the individual and discloses to a person something that passes far beyond himself." We have, he believes, tended to repress the transcendent and he sees this repression as being a major cause of the discontent of our unhappy civilization. He says, "because the repressed is never really banished, but merely lies dormant gathering strength or seeps to the surface in disguised forms, we see today an increasing eruption of repressed transcendence. . . . This urge to transcendence occasionally takes on bizarre or exaggerated forms, such as black magic, occultism, misuse of psychedelic drugs, and cultic guru worship."

This is an interesting proposition. From the 1960s onwards, there has been an extraordinary outbreak of activity in these "bizarre or exaggerated forms." Essentially this activity appears to be a symptom of a search for meaning, in Frankl's phrase, an endeavour, sometimes frantic, to find a meaning and purpose to life in an age when it appears to many that old institutions are in decay, moral standards are irrelevant, traditions are seen as pointless, and when, in Yeats's words,

> *The best lack all conviction, while the worst*
> *Are full of passionate intensity.*

Except that it is sometimes hard to tell who are the best and who are the worst.

Some would ascribe this unhappy state to the failure of orthodox religion to provide what Western man needs. Yet alongside these bizarre forms, fundamentalism is flourishing. The word has ousted the spirit, except in hysterical manifestations. It sometimes seems as if only a hairsbreadth separates some forms of fundamentalism, especially when presented by televangelists, from the cultic guru worship that Wilber refers to.

With all this, there is still a strong desire for the transcendental. Many have claimed that it is not difficult to bring about such an experience through various means, including alcohol, mood-altering drugs, strobe lights, over-breathing, prolonged fasting, and various other exercises and intakes. Some of these methods have a long and dignified history. Many of the early Christian fathers who chose to lead solitary lives in the desert achieved their transcendent experiences through prolonged fasting. Mood-altering drugs, derived directly from natural substances rather than created in the laboratory, have been essential components of various religious and spiritual traditions. In this regard, how crass was the attempt to deny the use of peyote in the Native American religious ceremonies while at the same time failing to acknowledge that alcohol in the form of communion wine is a vital component of Christian worship.

However, the use of these and similar methods seems to produce not so much transcendent experiences as hallucinations. Derived from the Latin *alucinari,* this word literally means "wandering in mind." A peak experience, however, is the reverse of mind-wandering; it is a state of heightened perception in which the mind is focused on and absorbed by the experience. In a spontaneous peak experience you may feel that you are flying, but you do not translate this feeling into the action of standing on the window-sill, flapping your arms, and jumping into space.

Nevertheless, induced experiences may also produce valuable insights. Stanislav Grof researched the clinical use of psychedelic drugs for more than thirty years, finding that subjects were able to contact "sources of information that are clearly outside of the conventionally-defined range of the individual." Consciousness appeared to expand beyond the normal ego-restricted boundaries to transcend "the limitations of time and space." Some subjects seemed to return to the moment of their conception, or to recollections of the lives of their ancestors, both human and, in some instances, animal. Out-of-body experiences, space travel, communication with spirits of the dead, telepathy, and other phenomena were also frequent.

Grof added: "LSD subjects also report numerous visions of archetypal forms, individual deities and demons, and complex mythological sequences. In the extreme form, individual consciousness seems to encompass the totality of existence and identify with the Universal mind or with the Absolute. The ultimate of all experiences appears to be that of the Supracosmic and Metacosmic Void, the mysterious primordial emptiness and nothingness that is conscious of itself and contains all existence in germinal form."[179]

The use of substances to alter states of consciousness is a component of human history from the earliest times. In the words of Aldous Huxley, in *The Doors of Perception*, "All the vegetable sedatives and narcotics, all the euphorics that grow on trees, the hallucinogens that ripen in berries or can be squeezed from roots—all, without exception, have been known and systematically used by human beings from time immemorial. And to these natural modifiers of consciousness modern science has added its quota of synthetics." But in these days, he points out, in the West only alcohol and tobacco are permitted. "All the other chemical Doors in the Wall are labelled Dope, and their unauthorized takers are Fiends."

The path that Grof and others followed has now, for clinical and therapeutic purposes, been closed. Grof himself, together with his wife Christina, developed an alternative method which he calls "holotropic breathwork." This principally involves rapid over-breathing, similar to hyperventilation, undertaken in controlled conditions and accompanied by evocative music and bodywork. By affecting the oxygen intake to the brain this process takes the subject into a state of consciousness in which the early years of life may be relived, back to infancy, birth, and sometimes earlier still.

Altering the normal patterns of breathing has been a method of changing consciousness states since early times, along with drumming, dancing, chanting, and physical isolation. As Dr. Ervin Laszlo, science advisor to UNESCO and author of more than fifty books, points out: "Until the advent of Western industrial civilization, almost all cultures held such states in high esteem, for the remarkable experiences they could convey and their powers of personal healing and interpersonal contact and communication."[180] In recent

---

[179] Grof, S. (1985), *Beyond the Brain*, New York: SUNY.
[180] Laszlo, E. (1996), *The Whispering Pond*, Rockport, PA: Element.

decades, as far as the personal aspects are concerned, there has been something of a revival. Now businessmen in the industrialized countries may pop into the local "mind gymnasium" for half an hour in their lunch break to have their consciousness massaged by flashing lights and weird harmonies, or may take time out to enjoy a spell in a flotation tank or practice "yogic flying" in a converted country mansion.

The Monroe Institute's hemispheric synchronization technology, which enables individuals to move into different states of consciousness, also enables them to achieve significant experiences. A research project found that out of 156 subjects, 121 reported "peak and other powerful or significant experiences" happening to them during a week-long course. The research director concluded that the Monroe method "helps to facilitate a huge opening or expansion of consciousness," adding: "A useful metaphor to conceptualize the types of experience reported is that of 'turning up the volume on life.' One becomes more physically, mentally, emotionally, and spiritually awake."

This may be no more than entertainment unless these experiences are integrated into the subjects' daily lives. Among the aftereffects reported six months later were: a greater commitment to one's psycho-spiritual growth; a sense of being more self-determined and responsible for one's own life; living more fully in the present; a greater self-acceptance; an increased willingness to take risks; an increased desire to help others; increased feeling of inner-directedness (less willing to please others at the expense of self); increased spontaneity; and a greater love for humanity. If one or more of these effects become permanently integrated into the personality, that is good evidence of the value of the experience. [181]

One individual whose life was strongly influenced through her experience with the Monroe process was Dr. Elisabeth Kübler-Ross who has been referred to earlier. After enjoying a

---

[181] Masluk, T. J. (1996), Ph.D. Dissertation, Institute of Transpersonal Psychology, reprinted in *Hemi-Sync Journal*, XIV. 2. spring 1996.

spontaneous out-of-body experience, she became interested in following it up. She visited Monroe's laboratory and was placed in a soundproof booth to listen to the sound signals through headphones. "Suddenly I felt as if I were swept up by a tornado," Kübler-Ross writes in her autobiography *The Wheel of Life*. "At that point I was taken out of my body and I just blasted away." She continued:

"To where? Where did I go? That is the question that every one asks. Although my body was motionless, my brain took me to another dimension of existence, like another universe. The physical part of being was no longer relevant. Like the spirit that leaves the body after death, similar to the butterfly leaving its cocoon, my awareness was defined by psychic energy, not my physical body. I was simply *out there*."

Kübler-Ross uses the phrase "cosmic consciousness" to describe her experience, which she explains as "an awareness of life in every living thing." This expression was first employed by Dr. R. M. Bucke. Visiting England in 1872, Bucke had spent an evening reading poetry with friends. Journeying home alone, without any warning he found himself "wrapped around, as it were, by a flame-colored cloud." After a moment he realized that the light was within himself. Then came "a sense of exultation, of immense joyousness, accompanied or immediately followed by an intellectual illumination impossible to describe. Into his brain streamed one momentary lightning-flash of Brahmic splendor which has ever lightened his life; upon his heart fell one drop of Brahmic bliss, leaving thenceforward for always an aftertaste of heaven." This was followed by a revelation, described by Bucke in the third person:

" …he saw and knew that the Cosmos is not dead matter, but a living Presence, that the soul of man is immortal, that the universe is also built and ordered. That without any peradventure all things work together for the good of each and all, that the foundation principle of the world is what we call love, and that the happiness of everyone is in the long run absolutely certain."[182]

---

[182] May, (1993).

Bucke lived in Canada where he was first a medical doctor and later a leading psychiatrist (or medico-psychologist as it was then known). His book, *Cosmic Consciousness,* was published in 1901, twenty-nine years after his own illuminating experience and only one year before his death. Bucke sees cosmic consciousness as the final stage of human development. Everyone is born with simple consciousness, he says, and almost everyone proceeds to self-consciousness, on which the systems, cultures, and ways of thought of the world are based. From this state, a very few proceed to cosmic consciousness, which equates to the revelations of the major religions. It is this level which, in the future, mankind might attain. Bucke gives ten examples of exemplars of cosmic consciousness: the Buddha, Siddhartha Gautama; Jesus; Paul; Moses ("an imperfect and doubtful instance" because of the uncertainty of his actual existence); Dante; St. John of the Cross; Jacob Boehme; William Blake; Thoreau; and Walt Whitman (a close friend of his whom he much admired). In each case Bucke comments on quotations from each of these exemplars to demonstrate their possessions of this supreme gift.

For Bucke certain criteria are necessary to attain cosmic consciousness. These include what he calls "moral and intellectual elevation" (the latter involving "a clear conception of the meaning of the universe"), a good character, and having attained "the age of illumination," which he said seldom occurs before the age of thirty-five. He found very few instances of individuals who possessed all the criteria but he believed that the number was slowly increasing and that in time "the race at large will possess this faculty." Bucke continued:

"The same race and not the same; for a Cosmic Conscious race will not be the race that exists today....The simple truth is, that there has lived on earth, 'appearing at intervals,' for thousands of years among ordinary men, the first faint beginnings of another race; walking the earth and breathing the same air with us, but at the same time walking another earth and breathing another air of which we know little or nothing, but which is, all the same, our spiritual life, as its absence would be our spiritual death. This new race is in [the] act of being born from us ..."

The expression "cosmic consciousness" is now seldom used. Instead we might speak of a unitive experience, perhaps with the adjective "mystical" attached, or a transcendent or transpersonal experience. For Bucke, however, such terms would be inadequate. He maintained that cosmic consciousness was "the Savior of man . . . in Paul's language—the Christ."

Although some of Bucke's ideas may not have stood the test of time, and a world of Blakes and Whitmans may have its disadvantages, his work is notable for its originality and thoughtfulness. For several decades, however, it was to a large extent overlooked in favor of the new "science" of psychiatry and the work of the behaviorists J. B. Watson, Ivan Pavlov, and B.F. Skinner, for whom anything to do with consciousness was an irrelevance. In a lecture at Columbia University in 1913, Watson declared: "I believe we can write a psychology . . . and never go back upon our definition, never use the terms consciousness, mental states, mind. . . . It can be done in terms of stimulus and response, in terms of habit formation, habit integration, and the like." Later in life Watson moved into advertising, a profession then more suited to his way of thinking.

Gradually the pendulum began to swing back. In 1969, the biologist Sir Alister Hardy began his study of religious experiences, amassing a large number of personal accounts which formed the basis of the collection in the archives of what is now the Religious Experience Research Center located in Lampeter, Wales. Then in 1993, Robert May published *Cosmic Consciousness Revisited*, subtitled "the modern origins and development of a Western spiritual psychology." This surveyed the work of Bucke and included a critical review of the thinking and attitudes of Watson, Freud, Jung, Gurdjieff, Ouspensky, and Maslow, together with a chapter on "sacred psychology" and accounts of ten contemporary examples of what May considered to be cosmic consciousness, otherwise expressed as religious-mystical experiences. These are just two of several instances of a revival of interest in this phenomenon.

Before we become involved in the tangle of nomenclature it may be helpful to look at how the doctor and priest Martin

Israel replied to the question, "What exactly is a religious experience?"

"I would say that [a] religious experience is an experience of that which transcends the individual and makes him a fuller individual, which makes the personality more integrated in terms of understanding his place in the world; an experience that there is something outside of him, of which he has been made aware, that broadens his view of life, something that gives him a widened awareness, and brings him thoughts of deity. It comes spontaneously; it is not intellectually induced."

Israel uses the word "transcends," and indicates that what is usually thought of as religious is not necessarily the hallmark of such experience. There is a tendency, possibly borrowed from science, to feel it necessary to place each experience in a particular category and put a label on it. But this sort of material resists having a pattern imposed upon it. Indeed when the editors of an anthology drawn from the archives of the Religious Experience Research Center were examining what they had selected, the difficulty was revealed. "We devised guidelines, only to discard them; theories, and found they couldn't apply; categories, and had to abandon them. It was not until we came to look at the accounts very closely that we realized that we could not label what the writers hadn't labeled. These are accounts of *experiences*, and therefore each is totally unique, personal, and completely subjective."[183]

What is most significant is not the category into which an experience may be pigeonholed but the effect it has upon the individual. Is it life-changing? Does it have an enduring effect on one's outlook, values, attitudes? Or is it regarded as just a sort of hiccup on the way, something silly or embarrassing, to be pushed aside as of no importance? When this happens the experience is unlikely to be recorded. However, it is worth quoting one example, from the Religious Experience Research Center records, in illustration. This happened in St.

---

[183] Maxwell & Tschudin (1990).

Peter's, Rome, when the individual concerned suddenly felt as if he was taken by some spell:

"Couldn't move. From far away, something happening; whisper of wind, strange sensation, apprehension—what's going to happen? Wonder, beauty, body rooted, brain quite coldly commenting to me on experience like BBC sports commentator. . . . Then like tremendous wind tearing through me, powerful, overwhelming, like Aladdin's genie escaping from bottle, tearing up into that dome in ecstasy, brain saying, 'Don't kid yourself, this is art, aesthetic, not religious, it's all geared to make you feel this, human genius, not God,' etc. But great expansion from inside fills dome, out of body and at height, yes, orgasm of experience, this escaped exultant 'soul' (what better?) says to my brain, 'I don't care what you say, I am *immortal;* I have come home!' My brain replied, 'Alright, you think so now, but this will pass, you will go out the door you came in by, take up the burden of your mortality again, for that is the human reality, this is a marvelous, beautiful illusion, effect of great art,' etc.

"That is what happened. Gradually the storm subsided, I came back down to myself, my cynical brain took over again, not unkindly but sympathetically, as with a child that's lost its toys or has to live with the fact that mummy or daddy is dead. . . . The experience made no difference to my behavior."

And yet one wonders. So vivid is this account, so deeply felt and so strongly expressed, that it is hard to accept that it made no difference. The writer uses the word "behavior" but there are other aspects of the personality that the experience might have affected. Who knows? Perhaps not even the writer himself. The "meddling intellect" has intervened or, as it might have been put a few years ago, the left brain has interfered in a right brain construct. For comparison, here is an experience quoted by Robert May in *Cosmic Consciousness Revisited* sent to him by a woman after hearing him give a talk. She was with a group doing a Zen meditation walk when she looked up:

"Everything stopped. The view shifted. It is like space has cracked open and shifted. The light changes—brilliant silver flashes. Colors change. Perspective changes. There is no time.

Instantly I 'know' and see the illusion of the material world. I know that everything at every level, microcosm to macrocosm, is perfect elegant order. I feel perfect—enough—totally loved and know I always have been. I am expanding in that love to bursting. I feel beautiful inside and out, loved and cared for. I am laughing and crying. People come down the street and I see they have no substance and I hear 'they are the walking dead.' I weep with compassion for us. Everything I see around me is filled with wonder and newness—such joy and sadness. I feel loose in the universe with no boundaries. I am in bliss and despair—filled with energy and light. I am filled with gratitude and a sweetness as I gaze at the wonder of the orange I have in my hand. Little happenings are hilariously funny and bring me to tears. Such beauty—such love—such sadness and joy and life! It is overwhelming—no words describe this—no one can know the feelings, the experience."

Here the intellect has switched off and emotion and sensation have taken over. The words seem to tumble over each other as she strives to recall and record what happened. The experience is deeply personal and no attempt to categorize it seems necessary.

Not all such experiences, however, are joyful or uplifting. An investigation, published in 1999 by the Danish researcher and university teacher Dr. Merete Jakobsen, of the thousands of personal experiences in the archives of the Religious Experience Research Center, revealed that about 4 percent of the reports involved experiences that were negative or, to use the term that most of the respondents themselves used, evil. She points out that all of these drew on "a Christian understanding of spirituality," with many of the respondents using "the symbols of the Christian God as protection, the cross, the Bible, and prayer when faced with evil."[184]

Some of these experiences occurred in a dream or when waking from a dream, some were connected with a particular place, and in a few instances the evil seemed to manifest in

---

[184] Jakobsen (1999).

another person or a group of people. Especially terrifying were cases where evil in some form seemed to impose on or possess the individual. There were also instances where evil appears seemingly at random. Jakobsen quotes the experience of a woman who was travelling in the compartment of a train, empty except for a man snoozing in a corner and a "pleasant-looking girl." Suddenly she felt herself "assaulted by a sense of evil." The woman continues:

"I was filled with an indescribable feeling of mental revulsion and horror, but my mind seemed to work like that of a threatened animal as I tried to sense from where the threat came. I felt as if my mind was being threatened by some destructive force and thought it might be associated with the people or the compartment and determined to leave the train some three stations before I should normally leave.... I left the train and was aware that the evil was with me. I felt I couldn't combat it, then argued that I couldn't recoil so completely if it were part of me and that I must pray for help."

At first she feared she might be "mentally deranged" but after three days "this horror had departed and the memory gradually became less vivid, but it was one of the moving factors in my life. I have no way of describing this evil force and never thought there was a similar force till I read of the German concentration camps and thought that this was the force that planned them." She felt that "there was a tremendous conflict between what I perhaps could call elemental, unhuman forces, and that some part of me—not my reasoning mind—was engaged."

Jakobsen comments: "It is not remarkable that these experiences happen to religious people. The Bible has many references to evil in the form of the devil or evil spirits." The devil in person appeared to a few of the respondents, although most felt evil as a force or atmosphere rather than a personification. Some believed themselves involved, as one man put it, "in the eternal struggle between Good and Evil." One young man, sitting with friends, "suddenly felt totally alone, an awareness that every human being lives in his or her own concept of reality." Then he became increasingly aware of the two forces, positive and negative, good and evil on which the universe is based. "The feeling climaxed until for one split second I was aware of the meaning of the universe with its many horrors and that I, as a human being, was totally at the mercy of the two universal powers."

These negative experiences are seen by Jakobsen as struggles for the soul. She adds: "the battle is a fight against soul loss." Here is a parallel with the experience of hearing negative or destructive voices, and we are reminded of the shamanic interpretation of such phenomena. But Jakobsen maintains that these negative experiences should be treated in the same way as those of a "fulfilling and positive kind." She adds: "Both are transforming, both are recognizing the existence of a spiritual realm, and both show the vulnerability of the human condition." It is possible that such experiences are underrepresented in the archives as people may be more reluctant to reveal them for fear of being regarded as mentally ill.

The most comprehensive collection of transcendent or peak experiences is that assembled by the parapsychological researcher Rhea White in the "Exceptional Human Experience Network." She understands all these different experiences as "moments of grace that life gives us gratuitously," and asserts that they come in a multitude of forms, including near-death and out-of-body experiences, mystical experiences of oneness, strange coincidences or synchronicities, communication with animals, déjà vu, telepathy, UFO encounters, and abductions. What makes these experiences exceptional, she says, "is that for a moment or brief period of time each in its own way provides an awareness of a reality that is unlike that of our ordinary experience and transcends it in some way: the usual barriers of time, space, personality, species, and even death, vanish."

White, unlike the authors of *Seeing the Invisible*, felt the necessity to categorize these exceptional experiences and now has a list of more than 150 varieties. She invites those interested to compile their own exceptional human experience (EHE) autobiography and submit a copy to her Network. Her list aims to be comprehensive and non-judgmental; hence you are not out of order if your experience involved being abducted and taken by space ship to Sirius where you were medically examined before being returned, no more than if you witnessed the sun dancing at Medjugorje or in the moment felt yourself at one with all creation. White sees these experiences as beginnings. "In a world in which people lack meaning, a sense of connection, and contact with the sacred, these experiences can serve as seeds of new growth which can, if honored and attended to, lead to a sense of connection with others and with life, to a sense of meaning, wonder, and delight," she says.

Clearly we could go through White's list and question some of its inclusions. But our questions would differ, depending on our own beliefs and prejudices. White herself insists that a distinction is made between "real experiencing" and "delusions or illusions of some kind, especially the psychic and encounter types of anomalies." She adds: "People need to know about subliminal perception, rational inference, cryptomnesia, perceptual illusions, and other ordinary explanations of what appear to be exceptional experiences so that they don't fool themselves or are duped by others." But how are people to know? Education ignores this area, including the education and training of professionals, medical and theological, to whom others might turn for support, help, or advice. We have seen that if you have had, say, an out-of-body or precognitive experience you may be reluctant to discuss it lest you be regarded as crazy or sick. Those who can help you are those who have themselves had some similar experience. Rhea White's Network and organizations such as the Religious Experience Research Center are important in this respect.

Such experiences as near-death, out-of-body, or transcendent often have a life-changing effect. White extends this to all exceptional experiences, which she sees as initiating a process that continues through life. She quotes a phrase, "the immanent experience within ourselves of the transcendent which lies beyond ourselves" as an excellent definition of the EHE. She seeks to abolish the distinction between secular and divine, maintaining that the secular is also the divine. In this she challenges both materialists and fundamental believers as well as those who are ready to use value judgements on others' experiences or seek to relate them to some belief system of their own.

Nevertheless when we study other people's experiences it is important to bear in mind that what we are studying are stories told by individuals for whom the stories are true and who grapple with language as best they can in order to convey them to others. Often these stories are recollections going back many years. It is hard, perhaps impossible, not to consider that each recounted experience contains some element of conscious creativity. In some instances these elements become obvious. In *The Last Laugh*, Dr. Ray Moody refers to "folks who go on tour to recount their own, personal near-death experiences before live audiences." He calls them "NDEntertainers" and mentions two in particular who "borrow heavily from the techniques of the performing arts to get their message across." Shelves in bookshops are weighted down with personal accounts of all manner of exceptional experiences and it is difficult to dismiss the thought that the authors carried tape recorders with them, so detailed are their recollections of their conversations with the non-physical beings they encountered.

As we have seen from the examples at the beginning of this chapter, the transcendent experience itself is usually described—insofar as it can be described—in comparatively simple terms. In the West, generally speaking, this kind of experience happens spontaneously, although it may be inspired or sparked off by listening to music, by the beauty of natural surroundings, by a line of poetry, or the scent of a flower. In the East, however, such experiences are an integral part of spiritual life.

It may be that the search for transcendence was responsible for the appeal of Eastern spirituality piloted in the U.S. by Swami Vivekananda at the beginning of the twentieth century. In subsequent years came a succession of gurus, some of whom, including Muktananda, Maharishi Mahesh Yogi, and Rajneesh, attracted enormous followings. The realization of being able purposefully to achieve different states of consciousness led some of those followers to resort to psychedelic or so-called recreational drugs such as LSD and MDMA (Ecstasy) as short-cuts to the goal. Ill-digested spirituality is more damaging than no spirituality at all.

The happy days of the "westernized" Eastern gurus now seem to be over. Once the excesses—the ninety-three Rolls Royce cars of Rajneesh, the gilded thrones—are disregarded, we can see that in general the Eastern impact has had a beneficial effect on Western thoughts and attitudes. To take just a few examples: Inter-faith movements have gained strength; Buddhist philosophy has found many adherents in North America and several European countries; the wisdom of the Bhagavad-Gita and the Tao has influenced many thinking people; and some alternative health practitioners often talk of chakras and kundalini and find these concepts helpful.

The major world religions are drawing closer together. In Virginia in the late 1960s Sri Swami Satchidananda founded an ashram and, as it flourished and grew, he built a temple with twelve altars dedicated to the major religions with the inscription "Paths are Many, Truth is One" where people of all faiths and none come to meditate daily. Nor has the traffic been all one way. The Benedictine Abbot, Father Bede Griffiths, moved to India where he settled at Saccidananda Ashram, a Christian community in Shantivanam. Here he sought to integrate the traditions of Hinduism into Christian practice. The influence of his work spread far beyond the confines of the ashram and he became a leader in inter-faith dialogue. We may have inched just a little closer to the idea of one world united in a spiritual dimension instead of being divided by hide-bound dogmatic orthodoxy. As Bede Griffiths himself said: "The religions of the world are meeting today in a way they have never done before."[185]

The longing for transcendence is at the center of this activity. One way of achieving this is through meditation, which

---

[185] Griffiths, B. (1994) *Universal Wisdom*, London: Fount.

may be regarded as a gift from the East to the West. Essentially meditation is a means of moving into a non-ordinary state of consciousness, changing your focus from outward observation to inner attention. The English poet and scholar William Anderson, in his richly-textured study, *The Face of Glory*, published in 1996 shortly before he died, has this to say about meditation:

"Through the practice of meditation more and more people are having experience of states of awareness and unveilings of consciousness that are affecting their lives and the lives of those connected with them or influenced by them. One of the effects of this is that in religion they are beginning to trust experience rather than the magisterium or the traditional dogmas of their inherited faiths. They do not need authority in the way their fathers did. Another effect is upon the new subjects science is having to take into account, especially the nature of consciousness. . . .

"In meditation, the meditator is the audience of one in relation to the universal consciousness of God. The ideal is that he or she in meditating becomes the perfect and absorbed listener of the ultimate silence and the perfect enjoyer of the bliss of the present moment, taking the experience of calm and happiness into whatever are the activities of the daily life of that meditator. It is an ideal that goes beyond the limitations of our current religious and social boundaries and, if it seems to mean a withdrawal from what is called real life, it is a temporary withdrawal towards the source of life, the momentary experience of the ever-present rust of the golden age, the fountain of renewal in the forest glade of the mind, the peace of the mountaintop which is the place of propitiation, only in order that life should be engaged and lived more fully."

Anderson suggests that from our experience in meditation we may discover how to find our way through "the mass of information, images, and memories from the past with which we are overwhelmed today." He adds that "implicit in the practice of meditation is the premise that the consciousness to which it aspires is universal consciousness." In this he echoes a line from Traherne's poem *Silence*, "The World was more in me, than I in it."

To put this into a more conventional religious context, consider the observation of St Augustine: "I, Lord, went wandering like a strayed sheep, seeking Thee with anxious reasoning without, whilst Thou wast within me. I went round the streets and squares of the city seeking Thee; and I found Thee not, because in vain I sought for Him who was within me." Meister Eckhart, the medieval mystic who in recent decades has attracted much attention, expressed this similarly: "When a man goes out of himself to find or fetch God, he is wrong. I do not find God outside myself nor conceive him excepting as my own and in me." And, in the Gospel of Thomas, a text much studied in the later twentieth century, Jesus says, with picturesque imagery:

"If those who guide your being say to you 'behold the Kingdom is in the heaven,' then the birds of the sky will precede you. If they say to you, 'It is in the sea,' then the fish will precede you. But the kingdom is in your centers and is about you. When you know yourselves then you will be known, and you will be aware that you are the sons of the Living Father."

That state of being, "when you know yourself then you will be known" is a definable state of consciousness. It is the same as that described by Brother Laurence Freeman, leader of the World Community of the Christian Meditation as "the egoless depth in which experience of God is possible beyond all self-conscious desire." For some it may prove the ultimate experience.

Transcendent experiences may occur anywhere, in any state of health, and regardless of any belief system. They are spontaneous forays into the further reaches of consciousness where contact is made, however fleetingly, with other levels of reality, where our concepts of time and space no longer prevail and where we sense a connectedness with all there is. Such an experience must have inspired Thomas Traherne during the composition of his *Centuries of Meditation*:

"You never enjoy the world aright, till the Sea itself floweth in your veins, till you are clothed with the heavens and crowned with the stars: and perceive yourself to be the sole heir of the whole world, and more than so, because men are in it who are every one sole heirs as well as you."

And such an experience came to a man who was sitting on a low wall on the outskirts of Chittagong across the road from a tea shop stall whose proprietor was serving two customers. The sun was shining and a breeze stirred the branches of two small trees beside the stall. He could hear music coming from an upper window. A group of fishermen with baskets of fish on their heads approached along the dusty road. As they came up to him, one fish, still alive, flapped up and seemed to stand on its tail and bow. He felt great compassion for that fish.

"Suddenly everything was transformed, transfigured, translated, transcended. All was fused into one. I was the fish. The sun sang and the road sang. The music shone. The hands of the stall-keeper danced. All in time with the same music. They were the music and I was the music and I was the fish, the fishermen, the hands of the stall-keeper, the trees, the branches, the road, the sun, the music; all one and nothing separate. Not parts of the one but the one itself. [186]

Or change the viewpoint, as the astronaut Rusty Schweickart did on the *Apollo 9* mission when testing out the lunar module for future landings:

"When you go around the earth in an hour and a half, you begin to recognize that your identity is with the whole thing. ... From where you are the planet is a whole and is so beautiful and you wish you could take each individual by the hand and say, 'Look at it from this perspective. Look at what is important.' You look down and you see the surface of the globe you have lived on all this time and you know all those people down there. They are like you, they are you, and you represent them. You recognize that you are a piece of this total life, and you are out in the forefront and you have to bring that back."

---

[186] Quoted in Cohen & Phipps (1979), Religious Experience Research Center, Archive, no. 1284.

This, if you like, is truth revealed by experience. We can find corroboration of that truth coming from a quite different direction. In his study of the human genome, the science writer Dr. Matt Ridley points out that "No lifeform exists without DNA or RNA, and no DNA exists except in living creatures and their recently dead bodies. . . . Wherever you go, whatever animal, plant, bug, or blob you look at, if it is alive it will use the same dictionary and know the same code."[187]

Science is at last able to acknowledge what the mystics have always known.

In those moments when we transcend everyday reality, when our social conditioning falls away, we become aware of who and what we are. As we pursue our exploration of consciousness it is as if sunlight suddenly strikes through the canopy and illuminates everything around us. Transcendent experiences are moments of revelation when we see the truth of ourselves and of the universe to which we belong.

---

[187] Ridley (1999).

CHAPTER 8

THE VAST ENQUIRING SOUL

It is the Soul that desires to know.

(Plotinus)

Our consciousness creates our picture of the material world. What we see and hear is part of our subjective experience. Our cultural background, our beliefs, our experience of life all contribute to our interpretation of what lies around us.

This can be demonstrated by considering a description of the "New World" of North America before the great explorers arrived from Europe. But we should bear in mind that this world was new only to the explorers. It was in reality the old world, the world that Europe itself had once been. It was neither empty nor terrifying. It was a world that Columbus and his fellows never suspected and could never understand.

In his study of the Western spirit against the wilderness, *Beyond Geography* (1983), Frederick Turner describes the so-called New World as follows:

"It existed in its own light and colors, its own tides, seasons, flocks, and flowers. Circumambient, beautiful, violent, and pacific, even as nature is all of these, the New World teemed with its native life. It teemed also with the nature-inspired speculations of its humankind, the spectacular petals of myth. Here were those still captivated by the phenomena of nature, still the celebrants of it. Here those strange and strangely familiar fictions yet lived and beat in blood-pulse drums, chants, and rituals, and wholly informed the lives of the dark millions. Fragments of their myths have survived destruction to tell us what they can of a world our invading ancestors could not accept."

The material world of the Americas, the world structured by native consciousness, had a spiritual quality that depended on myth rather than on history. The world of the invaders from the maritime nations of Western Europe was quite different. A document called the *Requerimiento*, drawn up to justify the invasion led by Cortes, states that God established St. Peter as Lord and King of the universe and called on the natives to "recognize the Church and its highest priest, the Pope, as rulers of the universe, and in their name the King and Queen of Spain as rulers of this land, allowing the religious fathers to preach our holy Faith to you." Should the natives refuse to convert, or delay in so doing, "we assure you that with the help of God we shall use force against you, declaring war upon you from all sides and with all possible means, and we shall bind you to the yoke of the Church and of Their Highnesses; we shall enslave your persons, wives, and sons, sell you or dispose of you as the King sees fit; we shall harm you as much as we can as disobedient and resisting vassals." Written as it was in Latin there was little chance that the native population would make much of this, even if they were so minded as to comply.[188]

The worldview structured by the consciousness of those who composed this document and acted accordingly depended on an interpretation of history recorded in books that were believed to be divinely inspired and literally true. Hence the conquest of the Americas involved far more than territorial aggrandizement, greed, and plunder; it demanded also the destruction of the beliefs, customs, the whole way of life, the whole world structure that the consciousness of its native inhabitants had created and lived by for many, many centuries. As the neuropsychiatrist Dr. Peter Fenwick says: "The

---

[188] Turner, F. (1983), *Beyond Geography*, New Jersey: Rutgers UP.

material world takes on the form that it does only because this is the way in which it is structured in our consciousness."[189]

Today we have visible evidence of the clash of consciousnesses in, for example, Taos Pueblo in New Mexico, where the sacred Blue Lake Mountain, prohibited to visitors, looks down upon a Christian church.

If we accept that the material world is structured in our consciousness—in the consciousness of each one of us—then the orthodox scientific view of consciousness as no more than a product of the neuronal activity of the brain collapses. We experience the world subjectively and science has found it impossible to relate subjective experience to the working of the brain. As Dr. Fenwick says: "The whole scientific enterprise can take place only in the consciousness of the human mind. Without consciousness, there would be no theories and no science."[190]

Consciousness, therefore, has primacy over science, art, music, theology—over all the creations of the human mind. Without consciousness we can have no knowledge, no awareness, of the world or of ourselves. Perhaps there is a divine consciousness that created the universe and perhaps a divine consciousness will be there when the universe finally destructs. Perhaps. But the world as humanity experiences it has meaning only through the perceptions of human consciousness. In that sense consciousness is primary; all else derives from it. It permeates our lives and the universe to which we belong. As we have seen, it has no location; it is independent of space and time.

Consciousness, then, appears to operate in its own dimension, a dimension we have access to through our minds but by no other means. If this is so, then the best that our current sciences can do is to work on what are known as the correlates of consciousness—those faculties such as one's senses that are related to consciousness. In this they have achieved much success. But as the philosopher David Chalmers of the

---

[189] Fenwick & Fenwick (1999), p. 291.
[190] Ibid.

University of California, Santa Cruz, says, "Subjective experiences are arguably the central data that we want a science of consciousness to explain."[191]

What I am suggesting is that access to the dimension in which consciousness may be said to operate can be achieved through some or all of the subjective experiences we have been discussing. Investigation and research show that they are far more common than once thought so there is no need to classify them as paranormal. We have come to accept that they can no longer be dismissed as aberrations, hallucinations, delusions, fantasies, and so on. This applies not only to those phenomena usually put into the "paranormal" bracket— extrasensory perception, telepathy, precognition, and premonition—but also to near-death and out-of-body experiences, remote viewing and distant healing and, most importantly, transcendent experiences. It is especially those last experiences that bring us into contact, if only fleetingly, with an order of reality inaccessible by other means.

The theologian Huston Smith suggests that modernity is characterized by the loss of this sense of transcendence in daily life. If this is so, then this may be a reason why investigation and research have so far not succeeded in revealing the whole picture of consciousness studies. In recent years much of the research into subjective experience has taken place under the heading of "parapsychology." This means something like the study of phenomena beyond the scope of "ordinary" psychology so this would include many of the experiences described in earlier chapters. Professor Robert Morris, of the Koestler Parapsychology Unit at Edinburgh University, Scotland, draws attention to some of the problems that have gathered around this topic. He points out the connection that is often made between parapsychology and metaphysical and occult traditions, namely, that charlatans are known to exploit some who accept the reality of psychic phenomena and that this acceptance can lead to delusional systems. He contin-

---

[191]"University of Arizona Consciousness Bulletin," fall 1999.

ues:"Parapsychology threatens the precision and tidiness of traditional scientific methodology. It forces us to reexamine concepts such as consciousness and volition that have been largely ignored within science. It challenges fixed ideas, both materialist and non-materialist, about how the world works."[192]

Research in parapsychology has mostly focused on the area of extrasensory perception, the one area where experiments take place in laboratories or tightly controlled conditions and can be evaluated statistically in a way that might interest and even impress scientists from other disciplines. Elsewhere in the field, however, the shadows of metaphysical and occult traditions, the activities of charlatans, the danger of delusional systems, seem to be enough to deter most serious researchers from even opening the gate. This is not a healthy situation. The histories of the mainstream sciences, such as physics, chemistry, and biology, have their share of similar traditions, charlatanism, and delusion, but that has never prevented serious enquiry and investigation. Without such enquiry, the charlatans and the deluded will have their way.

This enquiry, however, needs to be conducted by appropriate methods. While cognitive science, psychology, physics and the biological sciences all have important and interesting things to say about the correlates of consciousness, their methods of enquiry are limited to their own disciplines. As Dr. Beverly Rubik says in *Life at the Edge of Science* (1996), "Conventional science has only explored certain aspects of consciousness such as cognition and perception, and in doing so has asked only limited questions. Science is bounded by the present dominant paradigm, which maintains that consciousness is a localized epiphenomenon of complex physical brain processes that manifests only passively in the physical world. Thus the research questions posed by the scientific community typically reflect this view."

-----

[192] See University of Edinburgh Parapsychology Unit website. Edinburgh is the only university in the U. K. to have a Chair of Parapsychology, thanks to a bequest by Arthur Koestler.

In the central study of consciousness, however, consciousness is doing its best to study itself; the observer is part of the observation, thereby becoming a participant, the experimenter is part of the experiment. This is far removed from the concept of the detached, objective observer, who is presumed to leave all subjectivity outside the laboratory door.

Ken Wilber believes that we should "continue to grope our way to a genuinely integral theory of consciousness itself." We should aim, he says, for an integral approach that "integrates the hard-headed with the soft-hearted, the natural sciences with the noetic sciences, objective realities with subjective realities, the empirical with the transcendent."[193] But we need to ask if this is really the way forward. Is it possible to incorporate the various examples that we have been considering into an integral approach? What do they have to contribute to the future of consciousness studies?

Let us begin with extrasensory perception. This involves telepathic communication, precognition, premonition, and clairvoyance, and add to those psychokinesis and remote viewing. All these phenomena demonstrate that minds are able to communicate with other minds, and that space, and in some instances time, is no barrier to perception, or the transmission and receipt of information. Thousands upon thousands of hours have been spent in experiments on the various kinds of extrasensory perception in the attempt to prove its existence by the use of recognized scientific methods. Statistically encouraging results have been obtained, but have made little impression on the attitude of orthodox science. It may be that there is a limit as to what may be discovered by examining the interaction between human beings and random effect generators or by attempting to predict the symbol on the next card to be displayed. This is not to decry the value of these experiments, but it may be that it is time to find other ways of testing and assessing the evidence for telepathy, precognition, and psychokinesis. Or perhaps enough has

---

[193] Scientific & Medical Network (1999), op. cit., pp. 183-4.

already been done to establish that these abilities really do exist and that what we need to do now is to test them in situations in the world outside the laboratory to see what they have to tell us about the range, ability, and nature of human consciousness.

Remote viewing, as we saw earlier, can be validated by accepted scientific criteria when it is performed according to a recognized protocol. The ability of the remote viewer to perceive through both space and time, and to have the accuracy of that perception verified, indicates a particular faculty of consciousness. Here intention and perception combine in bringing back information without affecting the object of the viewing. A third party is usually involved—the military, the police, a commercial organization—whichever it is that needs the information. Such bodies are very unlikely to be interested in a method lacking in credibility, especially where lives or large amounts of money are concerned. Yet of all the phenomena we have been discussing, remote viewing is probably the most obscure and has the fewest practitioners. Its reputation has suffered through the publication of sensational and unverifiable accounts and also because so much of the military information discovered during the U. S. Army's remote viewing project "Stargate" is still classified. At this time the most important contribution that remote viewing makes to our understanding of consciousness is providing evidence that it is possible to obtain practical information by the ability of the viewer to transcend space and time.

In distant healing, intention, sometimes enfolded in prayer, appears to be able to affect the well-being of another person although no physical connection with that person takes place. Space and time provide no obstacle to this type of healing. If the medical profession had not been impressed by the findings so far, the large number of trials currently in progress would not be taking place. Now that doctors in major hospitals have agreed to participate in experiments it may not be many years before distant healing becomes a recognized healing modality.

With this type of healing it does not seem to matter whether prayer, in the usual sense of the term, is involved. What is important is the focused intention of the healer. For some practitioners healing within a religious framework helps to concentrate the mind and perhaps to give a semblance of authority to the process. Essentially, however, what matters in the particular state of consciousness the healer enters into is "the unity that the healer feels with the patient [which] is infused and transformed by love and caring."[194] In distant healing, and this applies also to remote viewing, the demonstration by the physicist Alain Aspect that information can be transferred without the application of energy from one location to another, no matter how distant from each other they are, becomes relevant. Evidence is accumulating that intention and information can be passed from one consciousness to another and shared irrespective of distance and linear time.

The near-death experience, recorded by so many people in so many different circumstances and not simply confined to patients in intensive care, cannot be explained, or explained away, by the arguments of orthodox science. It is interesting to note that Mark Seelig, in his review of Kenneth Ring's *Lessons from the Light* in the *Journal of Consciousness Studies,* (October 1999), declares: "For the consciousness researcher, specifically, the book is worth reading because it is another account advancing hard evidence that consciousness is non-local, non-linear, not 'produced' by the brain, in fact non-causal altogether." He continues, "Denying the scientific validity of Ring's findings in general, and denying them significance within consciousness studies in particular, would not only mean questioning Ring's sincerity as a scientist, but would also pronounce millions of people from all walks of life as having fallen prey to mere hallucination, if not worse. And this is only people alive today in a Western society, not the overwhelming number of human beings down the history of this species, whose experiences would in one fit be pathologized, including their scriptures, philosophies, and religious beliefs."

We now understand that the near-death experience has nothing to do with response to medication, with oxygen

---

[194] Dossey (1989), pp. 69-70.

deprivation, or the effects of an anesthetic. It has everything to do with the consciousness of the experiencer responding to particular stress and opening the door to a realm inaccessible in normal circumstances. If we want to understand the near-death experience, we need to approach it through an understanding, even a partial understanding, of consciousness—what it is, where it is, and how it operates.

In the near-death and out-of-body experiences, while the physical body is out of action, consciousness, awake and alert, makes its journey and brings back its story. It may enter other realities, travel at will within this reality, or enter into a unitive state with all that is. By what it brings back, the personality may be transformed and the soul enriched. In these experiences, only the individual is involved. Science has nothing of value to tell us about these experiences. As Schrödinger said, science is ghastly silent about what really matters to us.

From studying the OBE, a frequent component of the NDE as well as an experience in its own right, we can appreciate again that consciousness is not confined to the physical brain but can float free. During an OBE your consciousness, your center of awareness, is positioned outside your body. You can view your body as if you were a spectator and return to it either by an act of will or involuntarily. At the same time, you can think and respond much as you do in ordinary circumstances. Your senses continue to operate. What is most significant about the OBE is the information it provides about the freedom of human consciousness from the confines of time and space.

But there are more controversial matters. The 1980s saw an upsurge of interest in the channeling of information from discarnate entities. It is often argued that channeling episodes tell us nothing other than the capacity of human beings to be deluded, defrauded, over-imaginative, or subject to wishful thinking. If our world is purely material then such an argument is unanswerable. But channeling has a long history and some of the information conveyed has proved of value to its recipients. It is possible that some aspect of the consciousness of the channeler, operating in an altered state, is capable of tapping into a source of information that is otherwise inaccessible. If this is so, our understanding of consciousness is thereby increased. At the same time there is no guarantee that this information is necessarily any more valuable or accurate than information obtained by more conventional means.

If the physically dead are able to communicate with the living, either directly or through a medium, then it would appear that some element of consciousness—perhaps what the Dalai Lama describes as "the continuity of innermost subtle consciousness"—survives the death of the body and retains sufficient interest, for a time at least, in earthly matters pertaining to those relatives and friends who remain alive. Some element of consciousness would also have survived in those who are convinced that they have lived before, once or many times. This element might be characterized as the "astral body," or the "dream body," or even "the soul." But whatever you believe—whether you have to keep coming back until you "get it right" or become enlightened, when you can leave this cycle and head for the Source, Nirvana, Heaven or wherever—or whether you come back only when you want to, to learn and experience more—or whether you are part of a grand design or simply a plaything of Fate—it is, until further notice, simply a matter of belief. This belief may derive from a religion or a philosophy, or it may be a conviction obtained from a dream, a déjà vu experience, or under hypnosis, but essentially—and again, until further notice—it is a belief. Therefore while such beliefs may suggest something about consciousness, they cannot provide the evidence upon which a theory can be built. But who knows? When the Human Genome Project is completed it may throw light upon this problem. As the science writer Matt Ridley says, "Being able to read the genome will tell us more about our origins, our evolution, our nature, and our minds than all the efforts of science to date."[195]

The Human Genome Project, however, may not tell us much about the soul. While the terms "spirit" and "spiritual" are

---

[195] Ridley (1999)

expressions commonly used nowadays, "soul" seems comparatively out of favor and "soulful" is used mainly in connection with a special look in the eyes of dogs. In an age whose science is largely dominated by materialism, the soul seems more of an onlooker than a participant. In his *Principles of Psychology,* 1885, William James had this to say: "The reader who finds any comfort in the idea of the Soul is, however, perfectly free to continue to believe in it; for our reasonings have not established the non-existence of the Soul; they have only proved its superfluity for scientific purposes."

James does not mean that scientists do not possess souls. Nor do we have to agree that "reasonings" are the only approach, although for scientists they are certainly the preferred method. As so often Meister Eckhart takes us into the heart of the problem: "God has made the soul so cunningly and so secretly that no one knows truly what she is." Contemporary lexicographers would appreciate this, finding it difficult, if not impossible, to define soul without using the word "spirit," or spirit without the word "soul." Yet in everyday conversation we seem to know the difference instinctively. We would say, "the ship sank with the loss of forty souls," not "forty spirits." The writer Thomas Moore talks of the "deep, earthbound soul" and the "loftier spirit". To change the metaphor, in this context you might say that the soul is the candle and the spirit the light it gives out.

In these times while we hear plenty about the study of consciousness we hear little about the consciousness of those who are doing the studying. It is other people's consciousnesses that are being studied, not one's own. For philosophers and scientists this study is likely to be part of their professional interest. At the end of the day, or more likely when a particular hour strikes, there may be a Nobel Prize waiting. But for the rest of us it is more of a personal matter. If it takes consciousness to explore consciousness, then what is it in us that has the need for this exploration? What is it that asks the question? The Neoplatonist philosopher Plotinus knew the answer. "It is the soul that desires to know." This reminds us of Traherne's "busy, vast enquiring Soul," that brooks no control, endures no limits and will see all.

The seventeenth-century English poets were experts on the soul. Edmund Waller has a wonderful verse on the relationship between soul and body in old age:

> *The soul's dark cottage, batter'd and decay'd,*
> *Lets in new light through chinks that time has made;*
> *Stronger by weakness, wiser men become,*
> *As they draw near to their eternal home.*
> *Leaving the old, both worlds at once they view,*
> *That stand upon the threshold of the new.*

Andrew Marvell, in his ecstatic poem "The Garden," visualizes his soul gliding into the branches and sitting there like a bird, singing and combing its wings. George Herbert writes of "a sweet and virtuous soul" that "Like season'd timber, never gives." Donne, like Herbert, one of the leading metaphysical poets of his time, sees his soul merging with his lover's, and then plays with the idea that if they are two, they are like a pair of compasses:

> *My soul the fix'd foot makes no show*
> *To move, but doth if th'other do....*

Thomas Carew, another lyricist, writes of the Lady Mary Villiers as,

> *The purest soul that e'er was sent*
> *Into a clayey tenement.*

To these poets, and hence by extension to their readers, the soul was the essence of man and woman, so much so that you could hardly write about anyone without referring to their soul. Then with the scientific revolution in the West, encapsulated by the work of Isaac Newton and the founding of the Royal Society, came the dawn of the so-called Age of Enlightenment. Souls for the most part retreated to Sunday worship. However, in the late eighteenth century, souls returned with Romanticism in the work of Rousseau, Schiller, and Goethe, the English Romantic poets (Blake,Wordsworth, Coleridge, Byron, Shelley, and Keats), the great Russian novelists, and the Americans Thoreau and Whitman. Professor Richard Tarnas, of the California Institute of Integral Studies, in San Francisco, California, expresses in *The Passion of the Western Mind*, the contrast between the enlightenment-scientific mind and the Romantic:

"While the scientist sought truth that was testable and concretely effective, the Romantic sought truth that was inwardly transfiguring and sublime. Thus Wordsworth saw nature as ensouled with spiritual meaning and beauty, while Schiller considered the impersonal mechanisms of science a poor substitute for the Greek deities who had animated nature for the scientists. Both modern temperaments, scientific and Romantic, looked to present human experience and the natural world for fulfillment, but what the Romantics sought and found in those domains reflected a radically different universe from that of the scientist."

Tarnas continues by demonstrating the difference between the contrasting attitudes towards human awareness:

"The Enlightenment-scientific examination of the mind was empirical and epistemological, gradually becoming focused on sense perception, cognitive development, and quantitative behavioral studies. By contrast . . . the Romantics' interest in human consciousness was fuelled by a newly-intense sense of self-awareness and a focus on the complex nature of the human self, and was comparatively unconstrained by the limits of the scientific perspective. Emotion and imagination, rather than reason and perception, were of prime importance. . . . To explore the mysteries of interiority, of moods and motives, love and desire, fear and angst, inner conflicts and contradictions, memories and dreams; to experience extreme and incommunicable states of consciousness; to be inwardly grasped in epiphanic ecstasy; to plumb the depths of the human soul; to bring the unconscious into consciousness; to know the infinite—such were the imperatives of Romantic introspection."

With regard to religion, both attitudes rejected the old dogmas and institutionalized forms and traditions. The Romantics, however, maintained the centrality of the sacred, which science no longer had time for. Tarnas declares: "God was rediscovered in Romanticism—not the God of orthodoxy or deism but of mysticism, pantheism, and immanent cosmic process; not the juridical, monotheistic patriarch but a divinity more ineffably mysterious, pluralistic, all-embracing, neutral or even feminine in gender; not an absentee creator but a numinous creative force within nature and within the human spirit."

So when we talk about the soul in the context of consciousness we are in a sense lining up with our inheritance of the Romantic attitude. Perhaps revival would be a better term than inheritance, as Romanticism became largely submerged between the late Victorian period and the last decades of the twentieth century. The soul itself, however, still struggles for recognition. In the opening paragraphs of an essay "Soul and Self in Ancient Philosophy," published in 1999, professor of Ancient Philosophy at King's College, London, Richard Sorabji, asks the question "Do we have a soul?" He continues:

"How many of us now believe we have souls? There are at least two reasons why we hesitate. First, we tend to think of the soul as something immortal, and in the English-speaking countries doubt has spread about immortality. Second, Descartes revised the Aristotelian concept of soul and marked the revision by switching to the word 'mind.' As a result all of us, I believe, would think we had minds, but many would doubt if we had souls."[196]

We believe what we choose to believe, influenced to some extent by our education, religion (if any), parents (for or against), our emotions, and our experience. I am not sure that Descartes, for most of us, figures largely among these influences that we are aware of, but there are signs that the concept of soul is coming back into fashion. Larry Dossey suggests that "If there is an aspect of the mind that is indeed non-local, then

---

[196] Crabbe, M. (ed) (1999), *From Soul to Self*, London: Routledge. Seven distinguished contributors write on different aspects of soul and self from Aristotle to the present day.

this entity comes to resemble the soul—something that is timeless, spaceless, and immortal."[197] However, he finds it impossible to separate the concepts of mind, soul, and consciousness "in a universally acceptable way." Many of us will have a feeling for the difference between these three but expressing that difference verbally may be beyond us. We might associate mind mostly with mental activity, emotional and physical response—a sort of extension of our idea of the brain. We might see imagination as a function of mind, and see memory as a function of brain. Consciousness we might associate with our awareness, both of self and of the world without. Our consciousness, we might think, is what distinguishes us from everyone else and at the same time it is a quality or process that we can share with others. That leaves us with soul. . . .

Have we travelled too far from our attempt to add just a fraction or two to our understanding of consciousness? I hope not. Research into consciousness that treats consciousness in isolation from whatever else goes to make up man can go so far and no further. It comes to a full stop, as do attempts to study consciousness from within one discipline only—cognitive science, physics, psychology, and so on. Similarly it does not help if we discuss consciousness using the vocabulary of the hard sciences. We can measure the brain, but we cannot measure mind or consciousness. We have talked about the nonlocality of consciousness, meaning that it is not localized, or situated, in the brain—or, for that matter, anywhere else. Soul, on the other hand, would seem to be localized within the body during the lifetime of the individual. So how do soul and consciousness relate?

Before attempting this question, let us put the soul itself into an historical context, but doing this by looking at a few snapshots rather than by a lengthy discourse. Consider first one of the most thorough studies of the soul, that of Aristotle. He saw the soul as mortal, conferring form and substance on the body, while the mind, the seat of reason, had the potential

---

[197] Dossey (1989).

for immortality. Aristotle maintained that plants and animals also possessed souls that controlled their specific functions, nutritive for plants and sensory for animals, but that humans were distinguished by possessing in addition an intellectual or rational soul. This view persisted, with variations, for several centuries. Rupert Sheldrake, in *The Rebirth of Nature*, gives a tidy summary of the popular medieval view of the soul that owes a clear debt to Aristotle.

"The orthodox philosophy of nature, taught in the cathedral schools and medieval universities, was animistic: all living creatures had souls. The soul was not in the body, rather the body was in the soul, which permeated all parts of the body. Through its formative powers, it caused the embryo to grow and develop so that the organism assumed the form of its species. For example an acorn sprouted into a seedling and grew into an oak tree because it was drawn or attracted towards the mature form of the tree by its soul, the soul of the oak.

"In animals, a further kind of soul underlay sensory perception and behavior, and gave rise to the instincts: the animal or sensitive soul. Our English word 'animal' comes, obviously enough, from *anima,* the Latin word for soul. In human beings, in addition to the animal instincts, there was the rational aspect of the soul: the mind or intellect. This added the qualities of thinking and free choice to those aspects of the soul that were shared with animals and plants. The human intellect was not separate from the animal and vegetative souls; rather, the rational mind was linked to animal and bodily aspects of the same soul, which were generally unconscious. In other words, the human soul included both a person's conscious mind or spiritual essence, and the life of the body—senses, bodily activities, and animal instincts."[198]

In contrast, Plotinus regarded individual souls as descending from the World Soul, which is responsible for the creation of the material world, remaining above it and illuminating it while having no physical contact with it. The individual soul

---

[198] Sheldrake, R. (1990) *The Rebirth of Nature*, London: Century.

has free choice between good and evil. If it remains pure its greatest delight will be to return to its source, the World Soul. But if it becomes involved with material pursuits and becomes subject to sin, if it "falls in love with itself and its products and forgets its source," it is condemned to transmigrating from body to body until it has completed its expiation. Early Christianity tended to follow the Neoplatonist view until Aquinas rejected the plurality of souls but adopted the intellectual or thinking soul as the hallmark of the human being. For Aquinas there is no sense of the soul having to transmigrate until it achieves perfection.

Later, with the influence of Descartes and the rise of materialist science, the Western philosophical concept of soul disappeared entirely from the world of nature, from trees, plants, and animals. Christianity still talked of the soul but no longer related it to the natural world. It became the immortal part of man, although subject to sin, and its purpose was, through repentance and faith, to be saved along with the resurrected body.

The great religions of the East have their own traditional teachings. Islam regards the soul as being breathed into the first human beings by God. At death, if the soul is sufficiently worthy, it ascends to the presence of God. In Hinduism, the *Atman* is considered to be both divine and eternal, but because it is so involved with matter it is compelled to reincarnate until it is so purified as to merge again with the divine. Buddhism in contrast teaches that there is no such thing as an individual soul. It is no more than an illusion created by the processes of the human mind. It is an element of consciousness that reincarnates, not soul. Shamanic cultures, on the other hand, place the highest priority on the soul. As we have already noted, in shamanism the soul is not tied to the body but is able to travel free. It can be stolen or captured by evil spirits and its loss is a cause of sickness, mental and physical.

A contemporary Christian view is expressed by Canon Michael Perry of Durham Cathedral, England, president of the Church's Fellowship for Psychical and Spiritual Studies. Seeking to answer the questions as to whether the soul can be said to exist and, assuming it does, if it survives the death of the physical body, he replied as follows:

"Yes. It exists in the same way that the personality exists, and it will continue to exist after the physical body has gone to dust." He added: "It is a shorthand term for the value in God's sight of a pattern of matter and energy, genes and experiences. . . . The soul is not an entity. It is a word we use when we are talking about the 'superior controlling center which accompanies, expresses, and directs the existence of that totality [which is a human person] and one which, especially, provides the life to the whole. ' And that controlling center, or pattern, which is me will continue after the physical body has ceased to be the method by which control is exercised. How that will be is a mystery. *That* it will be is a religious certainty."[199]

Normandi Ellis, a student of Egyptian language and myth, and translator of *The Egyptian Book of the Dead*, takes a different view in making a brave attempt to clarify the meaning of soul. She writes: "Soul, like the body, is a process. Though we are born with a soul, soul continues to develop, secretly adding to its luster like a pearl hidden inside an oyster. . . . All our experience—our sorrows, passions, thoughts, and deeds—develop soul. Without incarnation, soul could not develop. It is tied to its body during life, imprisoned in form—as the god Osiris was imprisoned in the Tree of Life at Byblos—because soul cannot have meaning without the accretion of experience in the world. 'If the soul could have known God without the world,' Meister Eckhart said, 'the world would never have been created.' . . . Whatever catches your consciousness and holds it is making soul abundantly." Ellis adds: "If we wish to know where soul exists, look to where one puts one's energy."[200]

It might help to regard both soul and consciousness as processes. It is debatable as to exactly when individual consciousness begins to function but we do know that it

---

[199] *The Christian Parapsychologist*, vol. 12, no. 3. Sept. 1996.
[200] *Parabola*, vol. XXI. 2. summer 1996.

develops as the physical body itself develops from the fetal stage through childhood. Dr. Susan Greenfield, professor of pharmacology at Oxford University, puts it like this: "As the brain gets more complex in the womb, then, like a dimmer switch, consciousness gradually grows and burgeons until, of course, in adulthood it reaches its particular pinnacles or depths."[201] Our experience demonstrates that consciousness is variable, moving from one state to another as our perceptions shift and change. Throughout one's life soul and consciousness inform each other. When consciousness sleeps, soul remains awake. As the poet A.E. Housman expresses it, soul is:

My kind and foolish comrade
That breathes all night for me.

In his discussion of the soul and immortality, Canon Perry does not use the term "consciousness" at all. Similarly, scientists tend to avoid the word "soul." As Greenfield says, "Scientists are concerned with the individual, a 'mortal soul,' which could be more accurately equated with mind or consciousness."[202] But some of the great pioneers of science were well aware that soul, mortal or immortal, cannot be left out of the picture even if it is not their task to put it there. Nobel Prize-winning physicist Louis De Broglie, writing a few years after the second World War, expressed it like this:

"Confronted by the dangers with which the advances of science can, if employed for evil, face him, man has need of a 'supplement of soul' and he must force himself to acquire it promptly before it is too late. It is the duty of those who have the mission of being the spiritual or intellectual guides of humanity to labor to awaken in it this supplement of soul."[203]

Taking this further, here is an extract from a conversation between Wolfgang Pauli and Werner Heisenberg, two of the

---

[201] Crabbe (1999), p. 111.
[202] Ibid. p. 108.
[203] Wilber (1985), p. 125

greatest scientists of the twentieth century, both Nobel Prizewinners in physics. Pauli asked Heisenberg if he believed in a personal God. Heisenberg asked if he could rephrase the question as follows:

"Can you, or anyone else, reach the central order of things and events, whose existence seems beyond doubt, as directly as you can reach the soul of another human being? I am using the term 'soul' quite deliberately so as not to be misunderstood. If you put your question like that, I would say 'yes' ...."

"In other words, you think that you can become aware of the central order with the same intensity as of the soul of another person?" Pauli rejoined.

"Perhaps."

"Why did you use the word 'soul' and not simply speak of another person?" asked Pauli.

"Precisely because the word 'soul' refers to the central order, to the inner core of a being whose outer manifestations may be highly diverse and pass our understanding." Heisenberg replied.[204]

Not mind, not consciousness, but soul. No, you cannot leave it out.

Now, leaving aside the debate as to whether the soul is mortal or immortal, we should be able to accept that the soul in some sense exists. So we can return to consider its relation to consciousness and see where our exploration has taken us. If "soul" does refer to "the central order, the inner core of a being," in Heisenberg's words, or "the superior controlling center . . . which directs the existence of that totality," as Canon Perry says, then within the context of a human being it is soul that is supreme. Hence it is soul that directs that share of universal consciousness that is within the compass of the individual. Neither soul nor consciousness is static, which is why they are better regarded as processes than entities. In simple terms, it is soul, the inner core or controlling center, that asks the question and consciousness, our subjective awareness

---

[204] Ibid p. 38.

that establishes our perception and relationship with the world around us, that looks for the answer.

Our exploration of consciousness, then, is soul-inspired. To evaluate the answer, the information that consciousness provides, our soul, our inner core, seeks to understand how that answer is arrived at, and for that it needs to understand not only what consciousness is, but how it works. But so far, to take up a metaphor used earlier, what we have are pieces of a jigsaw puzzle, but we don't know what the complete puzzle, assuming eventually we can find all the pieces and fit them together, will reveal.

This exploration has been conducted almost entirely by scientists, each studying, as it were, his own collection of pieces of the puzzle, with the aim of eventually contributing to the construction of an integral or inter-disciplinary science of consciousness that will reveal the whole picture. So far, as Dean Radin says: "While consciousness is still a complete mystery, each approach to understanding it has offered a glimpse at what might be going on."[205] Recalling Ken Wilber's twelve different approaches outlined in chapter 1, we can assume we have at least twelve glimpses. It is as if twelve individuals, each with a pocket torch, are trying to illuminate the interior of a vast cathedral. If only someone could find the switch to turn on the overhead lights!

There are some scientists, however, who seek to attain an overview of the problem of consciousness and who are aware of particular difficulties with the conventional approach. We need to pay attention to what they say.

One of these scientists was Willis Harman, late president of the Institute of Noetic Sciences. In a brief but brilliant survey, he outlines two sciences that he calls Separateness Science and Wholeness Science. In the first, the basic ontological assumption is that "the universe is made up, ultimately, of fundamental particles and quanta which are separate from one another except insofar as there are specifiable connections

---

[205] Scientific & Medical Network (1999), p. 216.

(such as fields)." In Wholeness Science, the assumption differs: "The universe is basically a single whole within which every part is connected to every other part. The wholeness includes every aspect accessible to human awareness—the physical world as discerned through our physical senses, and all the contents of consciousness."[206] Wholeness Science would include "the entire spectrum of states of consciousness," including all the phenomena we have been considering. And the validity of Wholeness Science is witnessed by the most recent major biological discovery. As Matt Ridley expresses it: "Until the genetic code was cracked in the 1960s, we did not know what we now know; that all life is one; seaweed is your distant cousin and anthrax one of your advanced relatives. The unity of life is an empirical fact."[207]

In Wholeness Science, consciousness would permeate the entire field of study. A round table conference of fifteen scientists convened by Willis Harman in 1992 agreed on a number of proposed characteristics "for science that accommodates consciousness and also regards it as a fundamental that cannot be ignored." One of the conclusions of the conference was that the scientist's persona is critical in the observation process, as each scientist brings a unique genetic profile, experience and way of seeing. Hence creative discovery in science is not just an accident but results from a unique process of exploration. In addition, the scientist himself may be transformed in the exploration process through a shift in consciousness, especially in the personal exploration of it.

This is important. In talking so much of "science" the role of the individual scientist can often be overlooked. Beverly Rubik declares: "Contemporary science largely ignores the psychological aspects of both experimenters and participants, assuming that its validity depends only on operations for gathering evidence." She adds: "We need to transcend our attachment to 'objectivity' and our perceptual split between observer and

---

[206] Ibid pp. 254-5.
[207] Ridley (1999), p. 22.

the observed, between mind and matter, between self and u-
verse." Rubik also draws attention to the language of conventional science, which she describes as "the language of
patriarchy—of boys' games elevated to war games," illustrating
this by quoting expressions such as "the war on cancer," "the
master blueprint of life," "the Big Bang theory," "building
blocks," and "physical laws obeyed by nature." "Both the language of science and its methodology of taking apart and
analyzing reflects a simple mechanical order reflective of the
man-made world of machines."[208]

While Rubik sees the need for what she describes as a "gender balance in the sciences" the mathematician Alwyn Scott
finds a "troubling aspect of current research" in the intense com-
petitiveness which, he maintains, "has risen to pathological pro-
portions during the century now drawing to a close, especially
in the United States. . . . Competition, with all its wars, is firmly
established in the collective mind of late twentieth-century
America and our mainstream science vividly reflects this cultural configuration." He continues: "For a truly integrated theory
of consciousness to emerge, we must transform ourselves into a
culture where people typically listen to each other and give
intuition a seat above the salt, a culture in which the immense-
ly multifaceted nature of consciousness can be imagined."[209]

A scientist whose career illustrates the points raised by
Rubik and Scott is the biochemist Candace Pert. Disillusioned
by the methods and approaches of her colleagues when she
worked in the Natural Institutes of Health and deprived of
public recognition for her discovery of the brain's opiate
receptor (owing to male dominance in her department), she
found herself some time later moved to consider what science
essentially is:

"In its essence, science has very little to do with competition, control, separation—all qualities that have come to be

---

[208] Rubik, B. (1996), *Life at the Edge of Science*, Philadelphia: Institute
for Frontier Science.
[209] Noetic Sciences Review, winter 1996.

associated with science in its male-dominated, twentieth-century form. The science I have come to know and love is unifying, spontaneous, intuitive, caring—a process more akin to surrender than to domination. I have come to believe that science, at its very core, is a spiritual endeavour. Some of my best insights have come to me through what I can only call a mystical process. It's like having God whisper in your ear. . . ."[210]

All those referred to or quoted above are serious scientists from different disciplines. What they have in common are the imagination, based on experience, to see the way ahead for science and the ability to express their thoughts with clarity and precision. They are aware that science by itself is not enough. In this they sympathize with the oft-quoted view of Albert Einstein: "Science without religion is lame, religion without science is blind." What Einstein is referring to here is not any orthodox belief system but what he calls "cosmic religious feeling," a kind of religious feeling "which knows no dogma and no God conceived in man's image; so that there can be no church whose central teachings are based on it." He sees the heretics of every age, who were often regarded as atheists—or sometimes as saints—as those who exemplified this kind of feeling. He adds: "Cosmic religious feeling is the strongest and noblest motive for scientific research."[211]

Willis Harman's group of scientists agreed that what is needed is "a science that accommodates consciousness." Yet there is another approach—one that turns the situation around. The mathematical physicist C. J. S. Clarke, using the term "mind" rather than "consciousness," believes that the way ahead "is to place mind first as *the* key aspect of the universe."[212] Following this route, no further justification would be needed for working towards an understanding of consciousness that accommodates science. Such an understanding—or

---

[210] Pert (1997), pp. 314-5.
[211] Wilber (1985), pp. 102-3.
[212] Clarke C. J. S., "The Nonlocality of Mind," *Journal of Consciousness Studies* vol. 2 no. 3, 1995.

science, if you prefer—would depend more on synthesis than analysis and on expansion rather than reduction. Subjective experience would move into the center of the enquiry and man—man's mind—would again be established as the measure of all things.

There have been glimpses of Einstein's "cosmic religious feeling" in some of the transcendent experiences recorded earlier. Of all the experiences we have described (and without experience there is not much of worth to say about consciousness), it is the transcendent (or sometimes mystical) experience, the common experience, that brings us closest to the relationship between soul and consciousness, and perhaps also to a fragment of understanding of the universe itself. The glory of the transcendent experience is that you don't have to be in any special physical or mental state to be able to have it. You only have to be there.

In this type of experience, when you are aware only of your connectedness with all that is, your consciousness melds with the consciousness of creation and your soul reaches out to union with the One. It is in reflecting on such experiences that we can understand what the Sufi teacher Pir Vilayat Khan means when he says, "The assumption of being an individual is our greatest limitation," and appreciate the truth of Plotinus's words, "When man ceases to be an individual he raises himself again and penetrates the whole world."

A personal expression of the experience of transcendence is that of the American poet and dramatist Robinson Jeffers: "I believe that the Universe is one being, all its parts are different expressions of the same energy, and they are all in communication with each other. This whole is so beautiful and is felt by me to be so intensely in earnest, that I am compelled to love it, and to think of it as divine. It seems to me that this whole alone is worthy of the deeper sort of love; and that there is peace, freedom—I might say a kind of salvation."

To me this says what thousands of others have sought to express following a transcendent experience. The individual is at one with the universe and is irradiated by the love and compassion that this realization brings.

Towards the end of his moving and influential book, *Man's Search for Meaning*, Victor Frankl tells a story which in a quite different way establishes a similar truth to that revealed to Jeffers. Frankl came across a young woman in Auschwitz concentration camp who knew that she would die in the next few days but was cheerful despite this knowledge. "It is a simple story," he says. "There is little to tell and it may sound as if I invented it; but to me it seems like a poem."

"I am grateful that fate has hit me so hard," the young woman said to Frankl. "In my former life I was spoiled and did not take spiritual accomplishments seriously." Pointing through the window of the hut, she said; "This tree here is the only friend I have in my loneliness." Through that window she could see just one branch of a chestnut tree, and on the branch were two blossoms.

"I often talk to that tree," she continued. Frankl was startled and didn't quite know how to take her words. He wondered if she was delirious or had occasional hallucinations. Anxiously he asked her if the tree replied. "Yes," she said. "What did it say to you?" he asked.

She answered: "It said to me, 'I am here—I am here—I am life, eternal life.'"

It is this "deeper sort of love" that the nameless young woman felt for her only friend that binds us together with the universe, with all that is. This takes us a very long way from the assertion that the individual is no more than Crick's "pack of neurones" and consciousness no more than a consequence of the neuronal activity of the brain. It is like moving from a dingy cul-de-sac to a broad highway, heading towards the threshold of the new.

This brings us to the end of our present exploration. There are huge areas in the study of consciousness into which we have not ventured. I have beside me a copy of the first book I have bought in this new millennium: *The Feeling of What Happens*, by Antonio Damasio, professor and head of the Department of Neurology at the University of Iowa College of Medicine. When it arrived my first thought was: "If only I had been able to read this before I started on chapter 1." It looks to be a brilliant analysis and I still wish it had appeared a few months sooner. From his knowledge of neurophysiology, expressed with elegance and clarity, Damasio adds much to our understanding of the relationship between consciousness and the brain. If there is to be a science of consciousness or, as I hope, an understanding of consciousness that accommodates science, Damasio's work will have an important contribution to make. But having skimmed through some of the chapters I don't think reading it would have changed what I had to say.

Damasio, like almost all scientific investigators of consciousness, does not refer to any of the phenomena I have been discussing in these chapters. His exploration takes him into a different part of the territory and our tracks nowhere coincide. Our journey has led us into the further reaches, those areas which are only accessible when consciousness moves, for whatever cause or reason, into a non-ordinary or altered state. It is what we can learn about consciousness from these experiences and abilities that I have been seeking to show.

One of these lessons, a very important one, is that most of us impose too many limitations upon ourselves. Too readily we assume that it is only other people who are able to travel out-of-body, for instance, or communicate mind-to-mind, to heal at a distance or glimpse a reality different from that we are accustomed to. Allowing that it is possible for such things to happen is at least a start to developing one or more of these abilities for ourselves. The more we can discover about the range and capacity of our own consciousness, the more fulfilled as human beings we are likely to be. We shall then be on our way to finding out what Plotinus meant when he said "Each being contains in itself the whole intelligible world."

Brain (the subtly engineered stuff in the head), mind (active and responsive, permeating brain and the whole physical and emotional body), and consciousness (the faculty of awareness and knowing, responding to the self, the world around and the realms beyond) are intimately connected and interdependent.

We do not need to look at case studies to see that disorder in any one of these affects the others. We have learned from the near-death experience, however, that the process of consciousness does not cease when the brain is, as far as medical technology can record, out of action. From the out-of-body and transcendent experiences we find that consciousness can operate independently of the physical senses. At such times, freed from the constraints of the physical brain and body, consciousness is able to venture into realms otherwise inaccessible and bring back its discoveries. So we can say that while brain, mind, and consciousness for the most part work in the closest of relationships, this interdependence is not total.

Enough evidence has accumulated to demonstrate that these experiences are genuine. The same is true of the various abilities we have examined: distant healing, extrasensory perception, psychokinesis, and remote viewing. Taken together, all these abilities point in the same direction. For them to occur, consciousness has to be independent of time and space. To complicate the issue, it is through our consciousness that we experience time and space. It is as if in order to function in the everyday world we are not able to cope with reality without giving it a specific location and relating it to the calendar and the hands of the clock. Yet the out-of-body experience defies space, and precognition and second-sight defy time. Telepathic communication, distant healing, and remote viewing defy both space and time. In the transcendent experience, space and time both fall away and we find ourselves united with all that is. The transcendent experience reminds us of our immortality. At such moments we do not need to be told that we are immortal; we know that we are.

I do not think that this perception has anything to do with past life or reincarnation theories, with transmigration of souls or with ideas of heaven or hell. "I am a part of all that I have met," said Tennyson's Ulysses, but I think it goes further than that. I am a part of all that ever was, created from the dust out of which the first stars took shape. My consciousness is a part of the universal consciousness that began to emerge when life itself began to emerge and that developed as life itself developed. That is how my consciousness is able to communicate with the consciousness of others, wherever they may be. Whatever happens to my physical body when it ceases to function, whether it is burnt, buried, or blasted away in some explosion, the ash or dust that remains is ultimately indestructible. My immortality is in that element of my consciousness that endures in the consciousness of others—those I love, those I have in some way affected—and has its permanence in the universal consciousness that enfolds us all.

Mind, brain, consciousness, emotions, the physical body—what is it that holds all these together within the individual? I believe that it is, as I have suggested, that essential part of us to which we give the name "soul." While ancient Indian philosophy identified soul and self in the concept of *Atman,* modern psychology has focused on "self" and left "soul" aside. To me this seems to tear the psychic equivalent of the heart out of the human being. A materialist would say there is no such thing as the psychic equivalent of the heart; there is no such thing as "soul." But I am not a materialist. To me, the soul is the essential "I." Recall Bernard Berenson's experience, when for a moment he was aware of the unity of his total self with all that is, summed up in the simplest of words: "It and I were one."

The soul both encompasses and encapsulates all that I am—all that each and every individual is. Hence as the poet Traherne says, it is "vast." It endures no limits; it wants to know all, even Eternity. It is indeed "the vast enquiring soul."

BIBLIOGRAPHY

Anderson, William (1996) *The Face of Glory*. London: Bloomsbury.

Atwater, Phyllis (1988) *Coming Back to Life*. New York: Ballantine Books.

Bailey, Lee & Yates, Jenny (1996) *The Near-Death Experience: A Reader*. New York & London: Routledge.

Blackmore, Susan. (1993) *Dying to Live*. London: Harper Collins.

Brown, Mick (1998) *The Spiritual Tourist*. London: Bloomsbury.

Brown, Michael F. (1997) *The Channeling Zone*. Cambridge, Mass.: Harvard University Press.

Campbell, Joseph (1988) *The Power of Myth*. New York: Doubleday.

Capra, Fritjof (1988) *Uncommon Wisdom*. London: Hutchinson.

Chimes, Julie (1995) *A Stranger in Paradise*. London: Bloomsbury.

Cohen, J. M. & Phipps, John-Francis (1979) *The Common Experience*. London: Rider.

Crabbe, M. James C. (ed) (1999) *From Soul to Self*. London: Routledge.

Crookall, Robert (1961) *The Study and Practice of Astral Projection*. London: Aquarian Press.

———. (1961) *The Supreme Adventure*. Cambridge, Mass.: James Clarke.

———. (1965) *Intimations of Immortality*. Cambridge, Mass.: James Clarke.

Damasio, Antonio (2000) *The Feeling of What Happens*. London: William Heinemann.

Dawkins, Richard (1998) *Unweaving the Rainbow*. London: Penguin.

Dennett, Daniel C. (1992) *Consciousness Explained*. London: Allen Lane

Dossey, Larry (1989) *Recovering the Soul*. New York: Bantam Books.

————. (1993) *Healing Words*. San Francisco: Harper.

————. (1996) *Prayer is Good Medicine*. San Francisco: Harper.

————. (1997) *Be Careful What You Pray For . . .* San Francisco: Harper.

Eadie, Betty J. (1994) *Embraced by the Light*. London: Aquarian Press.

Edelman, Gerald (1992) *Bright Air, Brilliant Fire*. London: Allen Lane.

Eliade, Mircea (1972) *Shamanism*. Princeton University Press (Bollingen Series 76).

Fenwick, Peter & Fenwick, Elizabeth (1995). *The Truth in the Light*. London: Headline.

————. (1999). *Past Lives*. London: Headline.

Fox, Oliver. (1962) *Astral Projection*. Secaucus New Jersey: Citadel Press.

Frankl, Viktor E. (1964) *Man's Search for Meaning*. London: Hodder & Stoughton.

Goswami, Amit (1995) *The Self-Aware Universe*. New York: Putnam.

Greaves, Helen (1989) *Testimony of Light*. Marina DelRey, Calif.; Devorss & Co.

Greenfield, Susan (1997) *The Human Brain*. London: Weidenfeld & Nicholson.

Grof, Stanislav (1990) *The Holotropic Mind*. San Francisco: Harper.

————. (1998) *The Cosmic Game*. New York: State University of New York.

Harner, Michael (1980) *The Way of the Shaman*. New York: Harper Collins.

Huxley, Aldous (ed) (1946) *The Perennial Philosophy*. London: Chatto & Windus.

————. (1956) *The Doors of Perception, and Heaven and Hell*. New York: Harper & Row.

Ingerman, Sandra (1991) *Soul Retrieval*. San Francisco: Harper.

Jahn, Robert G. & Dunne, Brenda J. (1987) *Margins of Reality*. New York: Harcourt Brace.

James, William (1902) *The Varieties of Religious Experience*. New York: Longmans Green.

————. (1995) *Selected Writings*. London: Dent.

Jovanovic, Pierre (1995) *An Inquiry into the Existence of Guardian Angels*. New York: Evans.

Jung, Carl G. (1963) *Memories, Dreams, Reflections*. London: Collins.

Klimo, Jon (1987) *Channeling*. Los Angeles: Tarcher.

Krippner, Stanley (1980) *Human Possibilities*. New York: Anchor Press, Doubleday.

Krippner, Stanley (ed) *Advances in Parapsychological Research*, Vols 7 & 8. Jefferson, N.C.: McFarland.

Kübler-Ross, Elisabeth (1997) *The Wheel of Life*. New York: Scribner.

Laszlo, Ervin (1996) *The Whispering Pond*. Shaftesbury: Element.

Laszlo, Ervin (ed) (1999) *The Consciousness Revolution*. Shaftesbury: Element.

Le Shan, Lawrence (1987) *The Science of the Paranormal*. Wellingborough: The Aquarian Press.

———. (1974) *Clairvoyant Reality*. Wellingborough: Turnstone Press.

Lorimer, David (1984) *Survival?* London: Routledge.

———. (1990) *Whole in One*. London: Arkana.

Lorimer, David (ed) (1999) *Wider Horizons*. Fife: Scientific & Medical Network.

Ma'sumian, Farnaz. (1995) *Life after Death*. Oxford: Oneworld.

Mallasz, Gita (1988) *Talking with Angels*. Einsielden: Daimon Verlag.

Maslow, Abraham H. (1962) *Towards a Psychology of Being*. Princeton: Van Nostrand.

Maxwell, Meg & Tschudin, Verena (1990) *Seeing the Invisible*. London: Arkana.

May, Robert M. (1991) *Cosmic Consciousness Revisited*. Shaftesbury: Element.

McMoneagle, Joseph (1993, 1997) *Mind Trek*. Charlottesville, Virginia: Hampton Roads.

———. (1998) *The Ultimate Time Machine*. Charlottesville, Virginia: Hampton Roads.

Mehl-Madrona, Lewis (1997) *Coyote Medicine*. London: Rider.

Metzinger, Thomas (ed) (1995) *Conscious Experience*. Schoningh: Imprint Academic.

Mishlove, Jeremy (1993) *The Roots of Consciousness*. Tulsa: Council Oak Books.

Mitchell, Edgar (1996) *The Way of the Explorer*. New York: Putnam.

Monroe, Robert A. (1971) *Journeys out of the Body*. New York: Doubleday.

———. (1985) *Far Journeys*. New York: Doubleday.

————. (1994) *Ultimate Journey.* New York: Doubleday.

Moody, Raymond (1975) *Life after Life.* Atlanta: Mockingbird Books.

————. (1977) *Reflections on Life after Life.* Atlanta: Mockingbird Books.

————. (1999) *The Last Laugh.* Charlottesville, Va.: Hampton Roads.

Muldoon, Sylvan & Carrington, Hereward (1929) *The Projection of the Astral Body.* London: Rider.

Myss, Caroline (1996) *Anatomy of the Spirit.* New York: Harmony Books.

————. (1997) *Why People Don't Heal and How They Can.* New York: Harmony Books.

O'Brien, Elmer (1964) *The Essential Plotinus.* N.p.: New American Library.

Ornstein, Robert (1986) *The Psychology of Consciousness.* London: Penguin.

Pearsall, Paul (1998) *The Heart's Code.* New York: Broadway Books.

Pert, Candace (1997) *Molecules of Emotion.* New York: Simon & Schuster.

Peterson, Robert (1997) *Out-of-Body Experiences.* Charlottesville, Va.: Hampton Roads.

Pinker, Steven (1997) *How the Mind Works.* London: Penguin.

Radin, Dean (1997) *The Conscious Universe.* San Francisco: Harper.

Read, Jim & Reynolds, Jill (ed) (1996) *Speaking Our Minds.* Open University. London: Macmillan.

Ridley, Matt (1999) *Genome: the Autobiography of a Species in 23 Chapters.* London: Fourth Estate.

Ring, Kenneth (1980) *Life at Death.* New York: Quill.

————. (1984) *Heading Towards Omega.* New York: Quill.

————. (1998) *Lessons from the Light.* New York: Plenum Press.

Rinpoche, Sogyal (1992) *The Tibetan Book of Living & Dying.* London: Rider

Rist, J.M. (1967) *Plotinus: The Road to Reality.* Cambridge: Cambridge University Press.

Romme, Marius & Escher, Sandra (1993) *Accepting Voices.* London: Mind Publications.

Rubik, Beverly (1996) *Life at the Edge of Science.* Philadelphia: Institute for Frontier Science.

Russell, Peter (1988) *The Awakening Earth.* London: Arkana.

————. (1992) *The White Hole in Time.* London: Aquarian.

Russell, Ronald (ed) (1993) *Using the Whole Brain*. Charlottesville, Virginia: Hampton Roads.

Sabom, Michael (1981) *Recollections of Death*. New York: Harper & Row.

Schnabel, Jim (1997) *Remote Viewers*. New York: Dell.

Searle, John R (1997) *The Mystery of Consciousness*. London: Granta.

Sheldrake, Rupert (1988) *The Presence of the Past*. London: Collins.

Swimme, Brian & Berry, Thomas (1992) *The Universe Story*. San Francisco: Harper.

Talbot, Michael (1991) *The Holographic Universe*. New York: Harper Collins.

Targ, Russell & Harary, Keith (1984) *The Mind Race*. New York: Villard Books.

Targ, Russell & Katra, Jane (1998) *Miracles of Mind*. Novato, Calif.: New World Library.

Targ, Russell & Puthoff, Hal (1977) *Mind-Reach*. New York: Dell.

Tarnas, Richard (1991, 1996) *The Passion of the Western Mind*. London: Pimlico.

Tart, Charles (1989) *Open Mind, Discriminating Mind*. San Francisco: Harper & Row.

Tart, Charles (ed) (1997) *Body Mind Spirit*. Charlottesville, Virginia: Hampton Roads.

Thompson, Francis (1976) *The Supernatural Highlands*. London: Robert Hale.

Turner, Frederick (1983) *Beyond Geography*. New Brunswick, New Jersey: Rutgers University Press.

Valarino, Evelyn Elsaesser (1997) *On the Other Side of Life*. New York: Plenum Press.

Watts, Alan (1958, 1978) *This Is It*. London: Rider.

Whiteman, J. Michael (1986) *The Meaning of Life (Vol 1) An Introduction to Scientific Mysticism*. Gerrards Cross: Colin Smythe.

Wilber, Kenneth (1981) *No Boundary*. Boston, Mass: Shambhala.

Wilber, Kenneth (ed) (1985) *Quantum Questions*. Boston, Mass: Shambhala.

Wilson, Ian (1987) *The After Death Experience*. London: Sidgwick & Jackson.

Wolman, Benjamin & Ullman, Montagu (ed) (1986) *Handbook of States of Consciousness*. New York: Van Nostrand Reinhold.

Zaleski, Carol (1987) *Otherworld Journeys*. Oxford: Oxford University Press.

INDEX

A

activity, in OBEs, 134, 154-55
afterlife, belief in, 172, 185, 200, 240
   See also near-death experience
   (NDE)
After the Light, 102
Age of Enlightenment, 242
alam almithal, 194
alcohol
   and peak experience, 212-13
   "spirits" of, 81
"Altered States and the Survival of
   Death" (Tart), 201
alucinari, 213
American Institutes for Research, 41
American Society of Psychical
   Research, 15
Americas, spiritual quality of, 231-32
Anderson, William, 227
Andreasen, Tony, 1, 4n1
anesthesia, and NDEs, 113, 122-23, 239
angels, 178
   Talking with Angels (Mallasz), 179-82
Anguttara Nikaya (Buddha), 136
anima, 246
animals
   communication with, 33, 223
   consciousness of, 14
   in shamanism, 79-81
   souls of, 246
"An Integral Theory of
   Consciousness" (Wilber), 17-18
anomalous cognition. *See* remote
   viewing (RV)
Aquinas, Thomas, Saint, 247
Aristotle, 25, 88, 245-46
Ascent into the Empyrean (Bosch), 95
Aspect, Alain, 21n15, 238
assistance, after death, 186, 194-95
*Astonishing Hypothesis—the
   Scientific Search for the Soul, The*
   (Crick), 10
astral body, 135, 144, 240
   definition of, 138-39
astral projection, 132, 135
astral travel, 132, 135

astrology, 11
Atman (soul), 247, 259
Atwater, Phyllis, 106-7, 118, 126
Augustine, Saint, 228
auras, in healing, 60, 87
Avicenna, 57
Awakening Earth, The (Russell), 5
awareness
   and consciousness, 13-14, 245, 258
   in healing, 62-63
   need for, 26-27
   in OBEs, 134
   of other planes, 169-70
   transcendental, 111
   See also consciousness; transcendent experience
Ayer, A.J., 104-5, 112

B

Babylon, 14
Bailey, Alice, 174
Banks, Frances, 182-84, 185-86
Bartholomew (channeled entity), 173
Bede, the Venerable, 128, 137
being of light, in NDE, 102-3, 106
belief
   in afterlife, 172, 185, 200, 240
   effect of in healing, 69-70, 89
   in paranormal, 196
Bell's theorem, 21n15, 83
Benedict, Mellen-Thomas, 106, 118
Benor, Daniel, 59, 75
Benson, Herbert, 68
Berenson, Bernard, 211, 259
Bergson, Henry, 82
Berry, Thomas, 14, 26
Beyond Geography (Turner), 231-32
Beyond the Light, 102
Bhagavad-Gita, 226
Bible
   prophecy, and "hearing voices," 163
   reference to OBE, 135-36
Black Elk (medicine man), 106
Blackmore, Susan, 12n6, 122, 123, 127
Blake, William, 3, 217, 243
Blaker, George, 16
Blavatsky, H.P., 172-73

Hampton Roads Publishing Company

. . . for the evolving human spirit

Hampton Roads Publishing Company
publishes books on a variety of subjects,
including metaphysics, health, integrative medicine,
visionary fiction, and other related topics.

For a copy of our latest catalog, call toll-free
(800) 766-8009, or send your name and address to:

Hampton Roads Publishing Company, Inc.
1125 Stoney Ridge Road
Charlottesville, VA 22902

e-mail: hrpc@hrpub.com
Website: www.hrpub.com